Big Sur

Big Sur

THE MAKING OF A PRIZED CALIFORNIA LANDSCAPE

Shelley Alden Brooks

UNIVERSITY OF CALIFORNIA PRESS

University of California Press, one of the most distinguished university presses in the United States, enriches lives around the world by advancing scholarship in the humanities, social sciences, and natural sciences. Its activities are supported by the UC Press Foundation and by philanthropic contributions from individuals and institutions. For more information, visit www.ucpress.edu.

University of California Press
Oakland, California

Library of Congress Cataloging-in-Publication Data

Names: Brooks, Shelley Alden, author.
Title: Big Sur : the making of a prized California landscape / Shelley Alden Brooks.
Description: Oakland, California : University of California Press, [2017] | Includes bibliographical references and index.
Identifiers: LCCN 2017015969| ISBN 9780520294417 (cloth : alk. paper) | ISBN 9780520294424 (pbk. : alk. paper)
Subjects: LCSH: Big Sur (Calif—Environmental conditions—21st century. | Landscapes—California—Big Sur—21st century. | Economic development—California—Big Sur—21st century. | Big Sur (Calif.)
Classification: LCC GE155.C2 B76 2017 | DDC 979.4/7—dc23
LC record available at https://lccn.loc.gov/2017015969

Manufactured in the United States of America
24 23 22 21 20 19 18 17
10 9 8 7 6 5 4 3 2 1

For Alden, a bright spirit

CONTENTS

ILLUSTRATIONS

MAPS

FIGURES

ACKNOWLEDGMENTS

I have had the good fortune of being surrounded by inspiring and supportive people as I worked on this project, though my gratitude extends to people who set me on this path well before any research and writing began. My first exposure to California history happened when I moved from northern Virginia to California's central coast. While working for the Monterey History and Art Association, I began to learn about the rich history of this region. I have Marilyn Erickson to thank for that opportunity. Two of my colleagues there, Tim Thomas and Dennis Copeland, who are steeped in Monterey history, inspired me to follow my love of this subject into graduate school. I respect the work that they, and others, do to preserve and interpret the history of Monterey County.

Research trips brought me deep into Big Sur and its environs, where several excellent archivists and others helped me locate sources and refine my project. Jeff Norman, the most knowledgeable person I know regarding Big Sur history, kindly took the time to sit down with me at Deetjen's Inn to share some of his wonderful stories of the people and places of this coastline. An early-morning breakfast meeting lasted well into the lunch hour, and I am thankful that I had this time with him before he passed away. He is greatly missed, but his many excellent writings about the region continue to inform discussions about Big Sur's past. Further up the road, from his utterly charming Big Sur River Inn, Alan Perlmutter provided insight into the challenges facing Big Sur and its community, and the ways that he and some of his neighbors have sought to address the issues over the past many years. Martha Diehl, a particularly involved member of this community, generously shared many thoughts with me about Big Sur's past, present, and possible future. I admire the time and effort that these residents and many others have put in over the years to protect and build the best features of this small community.

Tony Miller, to my delight, shared with me memories and insights into the life of his father, Henry, in Big Sur. State Park Ranger Kathy Wilson spent time reflecting on the issues relating to land use, preservation, and community in Big Sur. Staff at the Big Sur Library, the Harrison Memorial Library, the Henry Miller Library, and the Central Coast office of the California Coastal Commission have all been helpful in providing me access to documents. The Leon and Sylvia Panetta Institute also generously opened their archive to me, as did the Monterey County Historical Society. I have always found the Monterey County offices in Salinas to be staffed with professional and helpful people. Morgan Yates and Matthew Roth of the Auto Club Archives in Los Angeles have helped me track down information about the early history of the highway through Big Sur while providing good cheer and collegiality.

Two editors at the University of California Press, Kate Marshall and Bradley Depew, have been nothing but professional and delightful. Paul Psoinos provided copyediting as well as numerous thoughtful and helpful suggestions. I am grateful to Kate Marshall for her keen sense of California and its stories, and for steering me toward the final shape of this project. Her suggestions led me to reach out to Coastal Commissioner Mary Shallenberger, who took her valuable time to discuss matters of conservation and habitation along the California coast. I am grateful for the work that she and others do to preserve what is best about our beloved coastline. I also thank scholars Eric Boime, David Rich Lewis, and Dan Selmi for sharing valuable insights on California and the West. In the end, the interpretations found in this book are my own, and I hope will prove satisfactory to the many people who helped me form them.

I worked with wonderful historians at UC Davis, one of whom is Louis Warren, my dissertation advisor. I continue to benefit from his compelling ideas about the West and its environments. I also thank Kathy Olmsted, who I have long admired for her superb teaching, scholarship, and mentorship. Fellow graduate students—Lizzie Grennan Browning, Katharine Cortes, Jessie Hewitt, Chau Johnsen Kelly, Bob Reinhardt, and Alison Steiner—helped make my studies more meaningful and enjoyable. For the past six years I have had the good fortune to work with an exceptional team of historians and educators at the California History–Social Science Project, including Shennan Hutton, Nancy McTygue, Beth Slutsky, and Tuyen Tran. I am continually impressed by their dedication to enhancing K–12 history education. Their work inspires me, and their friendship is a gift.

I have been blessed with a wonderful network of friends outside the university as well. The Armstrongs, Elizabeth Cellinese-Dickinson, Yvonne

Hunter, Leah McMillan, and other friends and neighbors in Davis have all made life here quite rich indeed. I am grateful for the many years of friendship with the Darwish-Pochapin and Rosenberg-Burbank families, who have opened their hearts and doors to me as if I were family. Farther afield, my lifelong friends Melissa Mason and Katie Hodgdon have consistently buoyed my spirits, and it is not a stretch to say that their friendship over the past many decades has helped me see the world as brightly as I do.

If ever there were angels in my life, they have been Vino and Nava Roy. These amazing friends have provided guidance, encouragement, and love over the past fifteen years, in addition to room and board during numerous research trips to the Monterey area. No trip to Big Sur was complete without a many-hours-long conversation around their dinner table, where we delved into matters both large and small. I could not ask for truer friends or more admirable mentors.

I thank my mother, Ann Brooks, not only for taking the time to read and edit this manuscript, but for the much larger gift of her constant encouragement and love. Long ago she set me on the path of a good education, and for this I will be forever grateful. I thank my brother Adam for introducing me to California on that cross-country adventure so many years ago, my sister, Rachel, for enjoying the wildflowers with me, and my brother Josh for sharing his enormous heart and his priceless wit.

With deep appreciation I thank Edward Ross Dickinson for his part in this project. His close reading of this manuscript, insightful questions, and deep interest in his beloved home state have all helped me to sharpen my focus and improve my interpretation of this story. Meanwhile, our other shared adventures, both simple and grand, have made life immeasurably sweeter.

My heart is full of gratitude for my son, Alden, who was born around the same time as I began this project. He has accompanied me on many camping and hiking trips in Big Sur and throughout California, where his keen enthusiasm and his bright spirit have served as reminders to me of just how important it is that we maintain places of wonder, as well as viable human communities, in this remarkable state. What a joy it has been to share these experiences with him and to wake each day to learn and explore together. To Alden I affectionately dedicate this endeavor.

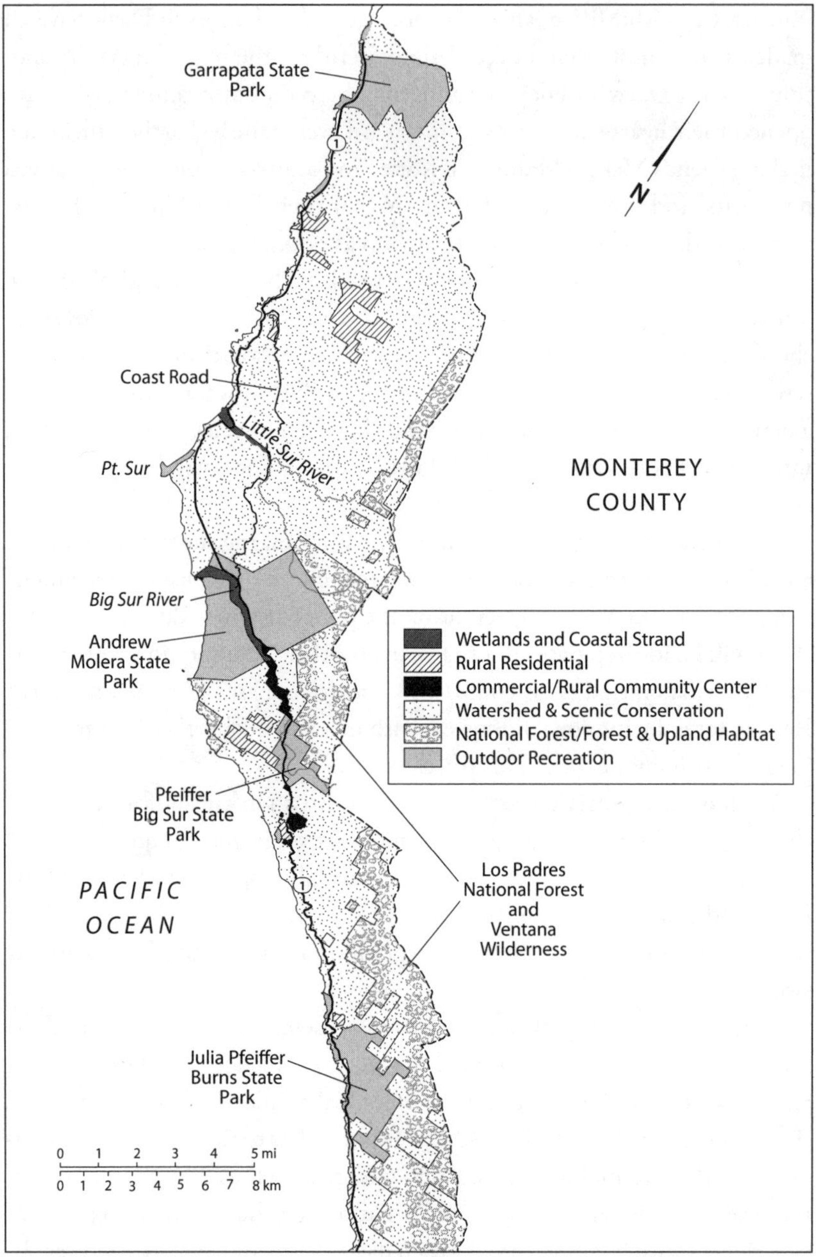

Garrapata State Park
1
N
Coast Road
Little Sur River
Pt. Sur
MONTEREY COUNTY
Big Sur River
Andrew Molera State Park
Wetlands and Coastal Strand
Rural Residential
Commercial/Rural Community Center
Watershed & Scenic Conservation
National Forest/Forest & Upland Habitat
Outdoor Recreation
Pfeiffer Big Sur State Park
Los Padres National Forest and Ventana Wilderness
PACIFIC OCEAN
1
Julia Pfeiffer Burns State Park
0 1 2 3 4 5 mi
0 1 2 3 4 5 6 7 8 km

Land Use in Big Sur, from the Big Sur Land Use Plan, Monterey County. (Maps: Bill Nelson.)

MAP 1. Big Sur, North.

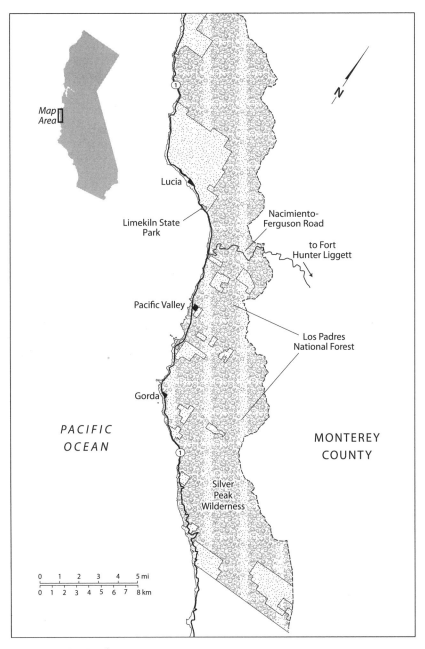

Map Area

Lucia

Limekiln State Park

Nacimiento-Ferguson Road

to Fort Hunter Liggett

Pacific Valley

Los Padres National Forest

Gorda

PACIFIC OCEAN

MONTEREY COUNTY

Silver Peak Wilderness

| 0 | 1 | 2 | 3 | 4 | 5 mi |
| 0 | 1 | 2 | 3 | 4 | 5 | 6 | 7 | 8 km |

MAP 2. Big Sur, South.

Introduction

Surely no more beautiful and spiritually uplifting coastline exists
on this earth.

ANSEL ADAMS

FOR SEVENTY-FIVE MILES along California's central coast stretches an
exceptional landscape known as Big Sur. The steep Santa Lucia Mountains
of Big Sur contain some of California's most complex geology, including vol-
canic rock, sandstone, and the high-grade limestone of the prominent Pico
Blanco. The mountains rise over five thousand feet from the Pacific Ocean in
just three miles—a grade greater than that of any other coastline in the con-
tiguous United States, and eclipsing even the eastern escarpment of the Sierra
Nevada range. The mountains bring cool temperatures and thick fog in the
summer. Big Sur is a place where disparate worlds meet. Two ecological ocean
provinces bring not only flora and fauna specific to the areas to the north and
south, but also those that exist only in the transition zone between the two.

Lush ferns, newts, salamanders, and the southernmost stretch of redwoods all thrive in the wet ravines. Chaparral and coastal scrub cover more
than half of the Santa Lucia Mountains, with yucca plants from southern
deserts, lupine, sagebrush, and manzanita growing on the drier slopes.
Together, these two zones provide habitat for mountain lions, bobcats, coyotes, deer, squirrels, and numerous other animals. For over a century these
animals have been free of the competition and predation of grizzly bears and
wolves, large carnivores that also once roamed these mountains before ranchers and homesteaders eliminated them.

Young vegetation is common in these stretches, where fire is a regular
ecological force and plants have adapted to fire-induced regeneration. The

FIGURE I. A redwood grove and creek in Big Sur. The redwood is endemic to a narrow strip of land stretching from Big Sur to just north of the California-Oregon border. (Photo: author.)

redwood, with its natural resistance to fire, can continue to increase in girth despite charred bark. Other flora survives in less fire-prone stretches. The endemic Santa Lucia Fir stands in the high, rocky ravines, where little other vegetation grows, while maples, sycamores and alders do well in the riparian corridors. The steep hillsides pose a challenge to fire containment, and evidence of bulldozer cuts attests to the history of firefighting efforts along the ridge tops. A season of heavy rain following a fire brings mudslides where new roots have failed to take hold in the steep hillside soil—a reminder that the angle of repose in Big Sur is, quite simply, steep.

Some of the more recognizable flora in Big Sur is not native to California's central coast but arrived intentionally or otherwise with settlers and their domesticated animals. Nonnative plants can spread rapidly in burned-over stretches; in this way, pampas grass, native to Argentina, and the South African ice plant have proliferated. In particular the feathery, golden pampas grass does so partly because of the so-called honeymoon effect, spreading seeds from reeds that visitors attach to their car antennas. Nearly half of Big Sur's grasses have been transplanted by local residents, often with the intention to create cattle pasture. Nonnative wild oats and ripgut brome are now common to the area.

For all the splendor of the mountains, the Pacific Ocean is the commanding feature of Big Sur. It defines the look, the feel, and the life of this region. Big Sur's flora, fauna, industry, and reputation all take their shape from the great expanse of cool Pacific water and its weather patterns. Throughout the summer, steady winds of the North Pacific high-pressure system keep storms at bay, and the dry months coincide with the prime summer tourist season. Rain returns in the late fall, when the pressure system moves south. This same system triggers effects that bring an upwelling of deep, cold Pacific water to the surface from March to July, producing coastal fog that enables certain species—like the redwood—to survive the dry period. This upwelling also brings deep-water nutrients to Big Sur's coastal waters that nourish a rich marine life. Gray whales, harbor seals, sea lions, abalone, sea urchins, numerous kelps, pelicans, and herons all thrive in this environment; so does the southern sea otter, a creature that was once thought to have been driven to extinction by overhunting but that had survived by taking refuge along Big Sur's rocky and isolated coast.[1]

Countless humans also came to Big Sur seeking distance from society. Big Sur's timeless landscape compelled California legislators to cater to the growing automobile-based tourism of the 1920s by penetrating the isolated Big Sur with the Carmel–San Simeon Highway, later known as Highway 1. For over seventy-five years this ribbon of road, carved into the Santa Lucia Mountains, has delivered millions of admirers to the dramatic Big Sur coastline. Except when the mountainsides cease to be tamed by this road, and landslides, including the largest in state history, temporarily close the highway and remind an admiring public of nature's power along this stretch of coast.[2] These vivid examples of a dynamic landscape prompt further fascination with Big Sur, but visitors also flock here because this coastal community

FIGURE 2. The view looking southwest from Garrapata State Park. The park spans both sides of Highway 1 (California State Route 1). Within the park, a mortar ground into a creekside boulder and an old barn near the highway attest to the area's shifting land use. In the summer of 2016, an illegal campfire set in this park spread to more than 130,000 acres. The Soberanes Fire became the costliest fire in U.S. history. (Photo: author.)

has long been a cultural symbol of California and the West, a place rife with meaning in contemporary society.

Some of Big Sur's most ardent admirers have been iconic writers and artists who created an enduring mystique for this coastline. Through their interpretation of its charm and the allure of their very presence, the poet Robinson Jeffers, the authors Henry Miller and Jack Kerouac, and the photographer Ansel Adams have helped ensure that Big Sur would receive international attention.[3] With the reputation built by these artists and a host of other creative and unconventional residents, the popular media started in the middle of the twentieth century to present Big Sur as a spot unique to California. Its impressive natural features represented the best of the West, while its avant-garde reputation beckoned to those who saw in Big Sur's way of life the opportunity to nourish or recreate themselves far from mainstream society.

The renowned poet Robinson Jeffers, considered by many to be California's finest, left an indelible mark upon Big Sur.[4] As a young but well-traveled artist, Jeffers settled in California's central coast in 1914. Big Sur, situated to the south of his Carmel home, became Jeffers's place of inspiration and escape from a larger civilization that he perceived as "dying at the core."[5] He used Big Sur's formidable backdrop as the setting for his popular works, many of which challenged the dominant American attitude regarding progress, material gain, and the seemingly indiscriminate transformation and destruction of the natural world. In his succinct verse Jeffers explained Big Sur's worth, what he characterized as an aesthetic or spiritual quality that was superior to any monetary value: "No better gift for men but one supreme, / Your beauty without price."[6]

In the mid-1940s, Henry Miller, author of the controversial *Tropic of Cancer*, settled in Big Sur and began to echo much of Jeffers's social criticism and, like the poet, heaped praise upon this remote coastline. Miller, like Jeffers, respected the longtime residents who adapted to the constraints posed by Big Sur's topography and chose to live at a pace that was out of step with much of bustling California. Miller's 1957 memoir, *Big Sur and the Oranges of Hieronymus Bosch*, cast Big Sur as an earthly paradise: "the California that men dreamed of years ago . . . this is the face of the earth as the Creator intended it to look." Miller's representation of Big Sur, and his belief that its culture and landscape embodied "something truly American, something simple, primitive, and as yet unspoiled," juxtaposed this coastline with California as a whole. The state's growth was breaking all records as its jobs, its beauty, and its western life style attracted millions of new residents. As California's metropolitan areas exploded in this era, people looked to Big Sur as a place apart.

Big Sur held considerable appeal for those searching for meaning in the midst of a rapidly evolving society. Here along this stretch of coast was a place to reconnect with the landscapes of the old West; a place to find oneself, as so many adherents of the counterculture—following Jack Kerouac's steps— attempted to do in Big Sur's forests and beaches; or a place to experiment with the New Age spiritual and psychological developments of the Esalen Institute. The apparent freedom and looseness offered by Big Sur's open spaces and unconventional community beckoned to Jeffers, Miller, and Kerouac (all of whom hailed from the eastern seaboard), and to countless others. For all it came to represent, Big Sur was integral to California's status as a cultural trendsetter in twentieth-century America. Significantly, despite its popularity, Big Sur never lost its natural allure. By the time of Robinson Jeffers's death, in the early 1960s, the *San Francisco Chronicle* labeled the Big Sur coast a "Timeless Eden."[7] Big Sur became a place as well as an idea worth preserving.

Notably, Jeffers's, Miller's, and later Ansel Adams's work all reinforced the idea of special preservation for Big Sur and complicated the issue besides by increasing the number of its admirers. But Monterey County officials, cognizant of the potential for tourism, had already begun to grapple with how to preserve Big Sur's particularly scenic stretch of coastline. Beginning with aesthetic zoning during the interwar period, Monterey County, often at the behest of Big Sur residents, continued throughout the course of the century to develop low-density and environmentally sensitive planning measures for the coast. At midcentury, as the burgeoning California population transformed large swaths of the valuable coastline, Big Sur diverged from contemporary developments. Its residents and local government officials crafted land-management tools, including open-space measures, a land trust, and transfer-development credits, while also co-opting the state's resources and environmental guidelines, in order to protect the land and the place of the fortunate few who lived there. They worked to retain, and even cultivate, a look of timelessness for this region that ultimately corresponded with the reputation fostered by its rural residents. This coordinated effort became the basis for securing a local voice in state and federal debates regarding Big Sur's land management.

Big Sur's beauty and reputation inspired many different approaches to preservation, including Ansel Adams's plan in 1980 to incorporate Big Sur as a national seashore. His vision for this coastal region ran against the social and political realities of this era. The 1960s and 1970s had seen a national surge of support for environmental legislation, but Adams's proposal came during a backlash against government regulation of natural resources. Conservative western voters were beginning to employ rights-based arguments to successfully oppose government ownership of land and resources. Concurrently, diminishing state funds in the wake of Proposition 13 and a national economic recession both circumscribed preservation efforts. The discussion that ensued over whether to establish a public seashore in Big Sur ultimately rested on questions of individual rights, the reach of the federal government, and the importance of environmental protection.

The tensions in this debate reflected some of the paradoxes that characterized Big Sur during the late twentieth century. Though Big Sur attracted more visitors than Yosemite National Park, private ownership accounted for close to one-quarter of the land area, situated within and alongside Los Padres National Forest and numerous state parks.[8] Residents, deemed rural by the quality of their environment, lived in homes that cost nearly four times the national average and nearly three times the state's.[9] Aware of the power that their wealth commanded, residents boldly asserted their right to steward the land without a federal landlord. These residents, the majority of whom were Democrats, tapped into the growing movement for private-property rights and disenchantment with the federal government to argue for greater autonomy in land management. Yet to secure a voice in the regulatory framework, they worked with county and state officials to protect and promote a "semi-wilderness" in Big Sur by banning all new development within view of Highway 1 as well as other restrictive zoning and open-space measures.[10] Paradoxically, then, even though Big Sur had long been synonymous with individualism, locals worked collectively in the name of the common good: they accepted unusual property restrictions that would preserve the remarkable scenery for themselves as well as for visitors.

In an era of increasing federal reach and authority, the independent-minded residents of Big Sur found that a measure of autonomy came not from trying to buck the government but from envisioning and helping craft a role for the individual community member to support federally and state-mandated preservation. That Big Sur could be both wild and inhabited is directly related to this ability on the part of the residents and the government to compromise some priorities in search of securing the larger goals of a viable community and a world-class scenic destination. To varying degrees this compromise has been sought in multiple locations along the California coast where communities wish to retain coherence and the government seeks to preserve natural habitats and public access. The creative coastal protection methods applied early on in Big Sur, including open-space planning, conservation easements, intergovernmental collaboration, citizen activism, land trusts, and to a limited extent transfer-development credits, became tools employed along California's coast during an era of increasingly high land values, unpredictable government funding, and erratic voter support for preservation ballot propositions. Big Sur's particular success lay in the fact that these conservation measures served the residents, the tourists, and, to a large extent, the land itself, which continued to at least appear wild despite (and because of) the government's increasing management of the nature within. Henry Miller was right, Big Sur was indeed quintessentially American, but deceptively so.

MONTEREY COUNTY'S EARLY HISTORY

Much of Big Sur's history reads like that of other western landscapes that passed from an undeveloped state to a highly governed space. The imposing natural elements that inspire so many admirers in Big Sur long served as an obstacle to settlement. Millennia ago, the Penutian peoples migrated south until they reached the steep Santa Lucia Mountains. Though the Penutians absorbed earlier inhabitants of the central coast, the Esselen remained autonomous in the Big Sur region.[11] In the nineteenth century, few of the Esselen survived the Spanish missions to return to their mountainous coastal home. Nonnative settlers were slow to inhabit this coastal stretch, arriving only after other prime lands were no longer available. Under the Mexican government, Big Sur saw only two land grants established along its seventy-five-mile coastline. In the years after California statehood, homesteaders sought to make ranching and farming lucrative in a place lacking easy access to markets and where "any piece of flat-land big as a blanket has a name to itself."[12] Last-chance gold miners and timber companies flourished briefly at the turn of the twentieth century but folded when the most accessible resources had been harvested. Transportation costs out of this rugged coastline rendered more extensive development uneconomical. Even the National Forest Service came late to Big Sur, during the third round of forest reserves created by the federal government in California. Established in 1906, the Monterey Forest Reserve encompassed the majority of the inland mountainsides. This forest, now called Los Padres, includes a small stretch of the remote Big Sur coastline, making it the only national forest in California to extend to the Pacific Ocean.[13]

Perhaps the most famous of Monterey County's landscapes, Big Sur is but one area within this historic region. Monterey, once the capital of Alta California under Spain and Mexico, is an old and significant California city. The gold rush shifted economic dominance and political authority to San Francisco and Sacramento, but it was in Monterey that California delegates gathered to write the state constitution. In the 1880s Monterey turned to tourism, most notably with the world-famous Hotel Del Monte, and by the turn of the twentieth century its tourist economy was developing in tandem with industrial agriculture and the canning industry. Monterey Bay's prolific sardine run gave rise to Cannery Row in the 1920s, with the fish renderings going to local farmers for chicken feed and the smell remaining for everyone along the city's shoreline.[14] The inland part of Monterey County—Salinas Valley—grew a large share of the nation's lettuce and sugar beets. Within the Monterey Peninsula itself, the Methodist Church in 1875 founded the town of Pacific Grove as a restful and inspiring retreat, and Carmel-by-the-Sea became a quaint storybook-like village popular among artists. The peninsula's demographic and economic diversity inspired a popular saying: "Carmel by the Sea, Monterey by the smell, and Pacific Grove by God."

Unlike these towns, Big Sur was largely inaccessible at the turn of the century and provided neither significant property taxes nor other types of revenue for Monterey County. But as the construction of Highway 1 portended further tourism, leaders in Monterey County came to understand the economic importance of maintaining a scenic environment and the challenges of balancing this with other economic enterprises. In this way, Monterey County fit into a particular category of western locales that sought to incorporate tourism as an essential part of a diversified economy rather than allow it to dominate or be overshadowed by other economic endeavors.[15] Tourism—whether along the county's spectacular southern coast or in historic Monterey—was one element in the county's larger economic equation, which also included large-scale agriculture and military installations. And though today tourism drives Big Sur's economy, this stretch of coastline also encompasses private lands and community resources that add depth to Big Sur's scenic qualities.

BIG SUR AND IDEAS OF WILDERNESS

To many of its admirers Big Sur is a wild place; but this coastline is also a storied landscape with a rich human history. This complexity is why Big Sur departs from dominant concepts of land use. The Wilderness Act of 1964 codified the idea of wilderness as a place "where man himself is but a visitor who does not remain." As a result of both prevailing opinion and government policy, Americans tend to preserve wilderness for recreation and study while treating areas of habitation and work as largely separate from nature. The historian William Cronon critiques this illogical, sentimental relationship to the land and its resources in his influential and controversial essay "The Trouble with Wilderness." Cronon argues that Americans have constructed and then preserved wildernesses to suit our ideas of sublime nature while disregarding the well-being of less striking landscapes. Americans most often view only the former as a true representation of nature and therefore worthy of preservation. The result, Cronon laments, is that Americans have subverted most efforts at sustainable, ethical relationships for people with nature.[16] This dichotomy between places of nature and places of people does not explain Big Sur. Instead, the story of Big Sur reveals the complex processes by which residents and authorities have combined in at least one place to create a wild but inhabited land.

At the turn of the twenty-first century, a *Nature*/PBS film labeled Big Sur's well-preserved coastline a "Living Eden" for its remarkable beauty and powerful natural elements. Big Sur's reputation derives primarily from its physical landscape, but its cultural significance is closely intertwined with its popularity. Around the same time as this PBS film aired, *National Geographic Traveler* recognized Big Sur as one of the world's fifty greatest destinations— a fine example of "civilization and nature in harmony," opined the magazine. More than a place of remarkable beauty situated between Los Angeles and San Francisco, Big Sur occupies a hybrid space somewhere between American ideals of development and wilderness. It is a space that challenges the way that most Americans think of nature, its relationship to people, and what in fact makes a place wild. Big Sur's preservation model may portend other creative responses to the priorities of tourism, private-property rights, and conservation, but its specific combination of social privilege and striking natural features may be the key to its success. What is clear, however, is that wilderness is a fluid concept—one that may benefit from greater flexibility in scholarship and within the American landscape.

CHAPTER OUTLINE

The book opens with Robinson Jeffers's introduction to the Big Sur landscape in 1914. Jeffers's impressions of the coast led him to view it as a world apart—a place that shared few similarities with the landscapes and cultures he knew from Europe, the eastern United States, and southern California. Big Sur's rugged setting had long served as an obstacle to settlement or exploration, so that early in the century this coastline was sparsely populated and without modern technologies. Human endeavors had produced few permanent edifices, despite centuries of habitation and decades of small-scale extractive industries. The Spanish name for this coastline, *el sur* ("the south") represented how most people viewed the area in the eighteenth and nineteenth centuries, and even into the twentieth: as a rather inconsequential place that existed to the south of the more manageable, and profitable, Monterey Peninsula and its surrounding valley. Not until the 1920s, when highways and commercial tourism proceeded at a rapid pace throughout the country and Jeffers's published verse on Big Sur gained popularity, did Big Sur's isolation and underdevelopment become recast as a great asset. Chapter 1 examines how Jeffers's approbation of locals' archaic mode of life helped to establish the sense that nature's elemental forces and Big Sur's inhabitants could together produce the most appealing landscape.

Despite Big Sur's apparent immutability, Jeffers's haven was a shifting landscape, and he came to know it on the eve of its greatest transformation. Chapter

2 examines the transformative effect of the opening of Highway 1 in 1937 and Big Sur's incorporation into California tourism. This chapter argues that planning foresight positioned Big Sur to become one of the state's best-preserved coastlines while popular representations of its dramatic natural elements provided the justification for such preservation. As the highway slowly advanced along the coastline during the 1920s, Monterey County established some of the first ordinances in the nation to prohibit billboards and require well-designed construction along the highway. Tourists responded with enthusiasm. They were drawn by Jeffers's powerful verse and countless national newspaper stories extolling Big Sur's beauty, all of which depicted this coast as a vestige of early California. In 1944 the avant-garde writer Henry Miller stumbled upon an unexpected treasure when he arrived in Big Sur. Demoralized and disgusted by international politics and modern American society in particular, Miller saw in Big Sur the perfect meeting of people and nature, and he chose to make it his home for nearly twenty years. Like Jeffers's work, Miller's representation of Big Sur left the impression that people belonged in and to this landscape. The highway set Big Sur on an irrevocable course toward participation in contemporary society, but aesthetic zoning, praise from the national media, and laudatory accounts from residents like Miller worked to blur the modern aspects of this coastal destination. Visitors to Big Sur sought a glimpse of the frontier that had supposedly closed four decades earlier, but ironically the frontier that they encountered derived at least in part from government regulations that responded to California's phenomenal growth.

The West that emerged from World War II—a rapidly growing, suburban, industrialized, consumer-oriented region—shaped American culture, and this culture became the foil against which Miller and many others imagined Big Sur. Big Sur sat perched at the literal, and increasingly at the figurative, edge of the United States, and its cultural significance grew as the state continued to flourish. Chapter 3 examines the efforts from within and without to paint Big Sur as a place apart, but also as a hyperrepresentation of California, complete with an exceptional landscape, a relatively young and flexible culture, a compelling life style, and a place of perceived personal freedom. Notably, this freedom and flexibility thrived within the zoning parameters established by Monterey County. A growing number of the diverse inhabitants of Big Sur, including the beatniks, the artists, the professionals, and the upper-class residents, all shared at least one quality: they possessed social privilege and could use this capital to work with county officials to protect their haven from becoming one more commercialized coastal strip.

Chapter 4 revolves around the pivotal year 1962, when Monterey County planners and Big Sur residents crafted a pioneering open-space master plan that foreshadowed the state's commitment to coastal conservation in the following decades. At a time when even the National Park Service fell into line with the national pro-growth sentiment, Big Sur residents and county officials sustained a critique of this resource-dependent relationship to nature. But this did not place them in the same camp as the wilderness advocates who gained traction in the early 1960s. Residents of Big Sur did not want to create a wilderness; they wanted to retain control of their home environment, and their strongest ally was their local government. Some residents balked at the idea of submitting to increased regulation, but the majority of residents understood that the government was going to have growing influence over the shape of landscapes and acknowledged the paradox that in order to retain a sense of the wild residents would have to work alongside the government to determine viable residential and tourist features. Their combined efforts helped to secure in Big Sur a landscape quite distinct from two other notable California destinations: the rapidly commercializing Tahoe region and the newly established Point Reyes National Seashore. By accommodating a spectrum of visitors while restricting the numbers who could settle here, Big Sur locals and county officials secured the appearance of a democratic landscape long associated with the West while in fact creating an increasingly exclusive landscape more representative of contemporary California.

By the late 1960s Big Sur retained its alternative image despite accommodating an increasingly wealthy population and registering as a top tourist destination in the state. During the counterculture era of the 1960s and early 1970s, Big Sur became a magnet for hippies, back-to-the-land activists, and New Age visitors exploring the mind-expanding retreats at the Esalen Institute. Added to these arrivals was the steady stream of families flocking to the state parks and beaches. Chapter 5 examines the arrival of these various admirers, including the new residents, and their influence on Big Sur's image and land management. This chapter also broadens the picture to examine the impact of the increasingly affluent California population that solidified environmental legislation to protect such places as Big Sur. The 1969 Santa Barbara oil spill was a wake-up call to the state and the nation, reinforcing the linkage between the quality of the environment and Americans' quality of life. It spurred the passage of Proposition 20 in 1972, which led to the creation of the California Coastal Commission to protect California's prized coastline. New state regulations required environmentally sensitive land-management plans from all coastal counties. This chapter argues that Big Sur residents understood the importance of coalescing into a vibrant community as they began to draft one of the most stringent antidevelopment plans in the state. Their sophisticated knowledge of land management helped retain this coastline's distinction and their prized place within it.

By the late 1970s residents and county officials were operating against the grain as they sought to limit residential, commercial, and resource development. The nation's faltering economy challenged bipartisan support for environmental protection and helped prompt western property-rights advocates to call for deregulating the use of the nation's natural resources. In response, Ansel Adams turned his considerable influence toward securing federal protection for this increasingly popular coastline. Adams endeavored to secure the designation of a Big Sur National Seashore while Democrats still controlled Congress and the White House, but he had an uphill battle during the conservative ascendancy in 1980. Adams also misread the vehemence with which locals guarded their right to steward the land and live without a federal landlord. Chapter 6 examines the battle over Big Sur as Adams, U.S. congressmen and senators, the Wilderness Society, Monterey County officials, and Big Sur residents debated the cultural, political, and environmental borders of this prized landscape. The chapter argues that like other debates of the era, the question of management authority for Big Sur became value-laden as issues of constitutional rights, personal freedom, and spirituality played key roles in shaping opinions on the appropriate relationship between people and nature. A place as popular as Yosemite could not escape such national attention, but remarkably Big Sur's small number of residents could harness the conservative turn to argue successfully for local management of a national treasure.

Chapter 7 argues that in the 1980s, while California dealt with the financial impact of Proposition 13, and while the federal government called for reduced-cost preservation as a growing number of Americans rejected federal land acquisition, Big Sur became a successful test case for an emerging preservation model that relied upon private and public partnerships and novel conservation methods. The impetus behind the Coastal Act represented the growing sense among Californians that their coastline was a public commons. This 1,072-mile band of prized California landscape therefore became a flash point for hashing out shifting ideas about the role and responsibility of the government and private citizens to protect the coast, public access, and property rights. This chapter examines the work of the California Coastal Commission, the California State Coastal Conservancy, Monterey County officials, and Big Sur residents to protect the region's natural and cultural resources. Embedded in Big Sur's state-mandated Local Coastal Program was a form of preservation wrought by the political and economic possibilities of the late twentieth century, premised upon the cultural significance of this coastline as a last best place.

Big Sur is compelling not only for its exceptional beauty but for what it reveals about Californians' relationship to their coastline. The epilogue examines several key people and places that illustrate contemporary economic and social realities along the Big Sur and California coast, including Peter Douglas, the late, influential executive director of the California Coastal Commission; Bill Post, a fourth-generation Big Sur resident who helped design the luxury resort Post Ranch Inn; and the idiosyncrasies of the Big Sur softball league. Today Big Sur epitomizes the contradictions and paradoxes of coastal preservation in a society simultaneously committed to a developmental ideology of property rights and material opportunity, as well as to the idea that a profound relationship to the land has shaped the nation's character.

Finally, a note about the terms: while the term "Sur" long applied to the coastal area south of Monterey and north of the San Luis Obispo County line, this label often came from the outside. The early inhabitants of this region more often oriented themselves to some smaller, more specific location, such as Little Sur along the river of the same name, or any number of creeks, such as Rocky, Mill, or Granite. Companies lent their names to certain areas, such as the shipping spots Bixby's, Anderson's, and Notley's landings. As certain settlers became established figures, their names and homesteads defined an area, like Partington Ridge or Gamboa Point. In 1915, the local post office took on the name Big Sur, thereby providing a label for this long stretch of coastline.[17] The less densely settled southern portion of this region has old names of its own—Pacific Valley, Gorda, and Lucia—and though these places are encompassed within the area regarded as Big Sur, local residents may feel less connected to the region as a whole than to their nearby community. I use the term "Big Sur" throughout to connote the region included within Monterey County's Big Sur Planning Area, from Mal Paso Creek in the north to the Monterey–San Luis Obispo County line in the south. In all, this is a 234-square-mile area stretching for seventy-five miles along the Pacific coast and reaching about three miles inland.

ONE

Jeffers's Country

A horseman high alone as an eagle on the spur of the mountain
over Mirmas Canyon draws rein, looks down
At the bridge-builders, men, trucks, the power-shovels, the
   teeming
end of the new coast-road at the mountain's base.
He sees the loops of the road go northward, headland beyond
headland, into gray mist over Eraser's Point,
He shakes his fist and makes the gesture of wringing a chicken's
neck, scowls and rides higher.
I too
Believe that the life of men who ride horses, herders of cattle on
the mountain pasture, plowers of remote
Rock-narrowed farms in poverty and freedom, is a good life. At
the far end of those loops of road
Is what will come and destroy it, a rich and vulgar and bewildered
civilization dying at the core.

ROBINSON JEFFERS, *"The Coast-Road" (1937)*

AS A CHRISTMAS GIFT to each other in 1914, a husband and wife paid six dollars for a return-trip mail-coach ride down the rugged Coast Road from their Carmel home. As they traversed the stormy, somber day, their driver regaled them with Big Sur lore. The couple learned of the man who killed his father with rat poison and married his stepmother; the man who had taken a trip to San Francisco, where he was shanghaied, eventually managing to escape and return home to Big Sur only to die shortly thereafter; the hermit who ordered pilot biscuit through the mail but had no teeth with which to chew; and the old man who lay alone dying and could not care for the forty beehives outside his house. As they navigated the narrow lane carved into the hillside, the driver pointed out the precipice from which a wagonload of bodies from a shipwreck had toppled down the mountainside, never to be fully recovered. In all, the couple passed but a handful of homes during their thirty-mile trek into Sur country.[1] These stories were set against a dramatic backdrop that made a deep impression on the visitors, who noted that the coast had displayed "all its winter magic for us: drifts of silver rain through great gorges, clouds dragging on the summits, storm on the rock shore, sacred calm under the redwoods."[2]

It was this meeting—of an artist and a powerful landscape—that set in motion a relationship destined to shape the way the outside world perceived the Big Sur country. This was the introduction to Big Sur for the poet Robinson Jeffers, whose name would soon become synonymous with this coastal region. His narrative and epic poetry, set within this awe-inspiring landscape, won great popularity throughout the country and abroad beginning in the 1920s, bringing a familiarity with "Jeffers Country" to a population that had never traveled to this rugged coast.[3] In the following decade, Jeffers's work earned him distinction as one of the few poets ever featured on the cover of *TIME Magazine*.[4] By the close of the century, nearly forty years after his death, Jeffers was still considered California's greatest poet.[5]

Significantly, Jeffers's verse began with the assumption that people belonged in this place. He portrayed Big Sur inhabitants not as interlopers but as individuals whose lives were etched out of the formidable landscape. Jeffers's characters ranged from incestuous to noble and their stories unfolded in relationship to scenery that had commanded Jeffers's attention during his visits. As he later remarked: "Each of my stories has grown up like a plant from some particular canyon or promontory, some particular relationship of rock and water, wood, grass and mountain."[6] In these poems the land did not suffer at the hand of its people but remained a constant, powerful force that dictated the options available to its inhabitants. Jeffers extracted what he considered the essence of the coast to craft his poetry and in so doing unintentionally helped transform the landscape he loved.[7] Countless readers felt compelled to visit this storied landscape. But Jeffers did more than call attention to a remarkable region; his work helped define a distinctive conservation ethic for the Big Sur country.

A PLACE IN TRANSITION

When Jeffers made his first venture into Big Sur in 1914 he encountered what would have passed as a western scene from a bygone era. Residents relied on animal-powered transportation and lived without electricity, telephones, or indoor plumbing. The area still retained its ranching character, with a smattering of active and abandoned lumber, limestone, and gold-mining operations tucked into the mountainsides and canyons. But a closer look at the landscape revealed several perceptible changes that situated the Big Sur country in the modern era. In 1906 the Monterey Forest Reserve introduced a new level of bureaucracy into this backcountry, where locals had had to instigate the postal service and build their own schoolhouses. In tandem with the designation of the forest, this region gained favor with tourists as well as those who could relocate their work and home to an appealing location. The 1910 census revealed that for the first time a full quarter of the coast's residents were professionals and artists.[8] As its popularity grew, Big Sur's connection to agriculture and industry would diminish. A Monterey newspaper reported as early as 1906 that extractive industries were giving way to tourist priorities along the Big Sur coast.[9] National Forest records later revealed that beginning in 1915 the agency issued a steadily declining number of grazing permits and a steady increase in residential use permits.[10] No longer solely an agrarian outpost by the early twentieth century, Big Sur was becoming increasingly prominent in Monterey County and beyond.

Like many other transplants to California in the early twentieth century, Jeffers felt drawn to the West's young culture and dramatic scenery. Though born in Pennsylvania, Jeffers had spent a portion of his childhood in European schools and attended college in Southern California before moving to the central coast. He established himself in the artist's community of Carmel-by-the-Sea, where he and his wife, Una, built Tor House and raised their twin sons. From here, Jeffers could entertain the many visitors who sought contact with the bard, but his introverted nature compelled him to plant a small forest around his home, into which he could retreat from admirers and focus on his work. Situated in the southern part of the Monterey Peninsula, Jeffers's Carmel home was an ideal launching point for his work and recreational trips into the Big Sur country. He found his poetic inspiration most readily on the days of winter rain and summer fog, when Big Sur's natural elements appeared even more imposing.[11] Jeffers's powerful verse left the impression of a landscape of unrivaled grandeur, of natural forces that dwarfed human activity.

Unlike his many contemporaries who extolled progress in the early twentieth century, Jeffers recoiled at the advance of modernity and set up a dichotomy between what he saw as free and noble within Big Sur and the morally bankrupt society that he perceived at its periphery. As an area without potential for successful farms or urban development (in a state where large-scale agriculture dominated the inland valleys and cities expanded along the coast), Big Sur could be seen as either hostile to success or blessedly removed. Jeffers's view on this point was clear: he felt horror at the approach of the outside world and upheld the good life to be lived far from modern society. Three-quarters of Big Sur's inhabitants, however, derived an income from their property or some nearby natural resource and harbored a much more accommodating attitude toward engagement with the larger economy.[12] When Jeffers first encountered the coast, he observed the second generation of homesteaders and laborers seeking to make Big Sur productive and profitable. Like all rational homesteaders, they looked for ways to capitalize on nature and establish connections to outside markets. They had little hope of competing with the more efficient inland ranches and farms, however, and had learned by the early twentieth century that their most valuable resource might very well be the abundant scenery. Big Sur's economic and social transition coincided with Jeffers's arrival. His acclaimed poems idealized the pastoral tradition, and though it was far from his intention, his work also secured attention from the outside world that helped to transform the region from a working landscape into a revered scenic destination.

EARLY TOURISM IN BIG SUR

Well before Jeffers settled in nearby Carmel and began his treks into Big Sur, a few locals tried their hands at the business of catering to visitors. They took a gamble that was no more risky than investing in the local extractive industries. Tapping into the image of the West as good for the health, Thomas Slate established the earliest tourist destination along the coast, Slate's Hot Springs, in the 1880s. Situated forty-five miles from Monterey, Slate's featured spring-fed baths perched just above the bracing Pacific waters. Slate believed that the sulfur springs had eased his arthritis and wanted to offer this experience to others—for a price.[13] Though Slate himself did not operate the resort for long, the springs have remained a tourist destination ever since and in 1962 were encompassed within the grounds of the spiritual retreat the Esalen Institute. A turn-of-the-century resort, the rustic Idlewild, advertised itself as a family resort and campground, catering to hunters, traveling artists, writers, botanists, and photographers. W. T. Mitchell, Idlewild's proprietor, banked on the area's beauty, claiming that the trip to Idlewild from Monterey was a stagecoach drive "that for beauty and varied interest cannot be excelled in this state of famous drives."[14] By the time of Prohibition, Idlewild also attracted travelers and locals alike for its ready supply of bootleg alcohol.[15] As

FIGURE 3. This 116-foot tunnel leads out to Partington Landing, where at the turn of the twentieth century John Partington and his partners shipped tan bark harvested from the nearby tan oak trees. Sled roads or wagon roads led down the steep canyon to reach one of the few harbors along the Big Sur coastline. (Photo: Edward Dickinson.)

Jeffers noted, a tiny harbor in Partington's Cove, tucked into the foot of a particularly steep coastal mountain and once used to ship timber, became a "favorite working ground" for rumrunners during the 1920s, while hollow, dying redwoods served as covert liquor stills.[16]

Some women of the coast appreciated the opportunity to commodify their labor by providing hospitality from their own homes. Florence Pfeiffer opened the Pfeiffer Ranch Resort in 1908 on the land she and her husband owned. She handled all related accounts and used the income to make improvements such as running water and flush toilets, and even a lumber mill that provided the building material for her resort.[17] Robinson Jeffers enjoyed his visit to the resort, noting that Florence was "agreeable and active" and supplied her guests with home-churned butter and real cream that was "the freshest tasted in a long while." The Pfeiffers' property sat along the dirt Coast Road, which brought visitors from Monterey. Jeffers was one such visitor, though he was dismayed to encounter the "multitudes" of other tourists traveling along the road just south of the inn. In one half-hour he observed "at least six horsemen, and a woman driving a buggy." Florence Pfeiffer welcomed and helped contribute to the traffic, whereas Jeffers considered it simply "too crowded."[18] It was due to Pfeiffer's business acumen, and the beautiful setting, that the Pfeiffer Ranch eventually became Pfeiffer Big Sur State Park—one of the crown jewels in the California State Park system. Indeed, Pfeiffer and her inn can be credited with helping develop tourism in Big Sur.[19]

These early resorts, and other economic pursuits along this coast, were severely limited by the impermanence of the dirt Coast Road during the winter and spring rains. In anticipation of the 1916 summer tourist season, Pfeiffer wrote to the owner of El Sur Ranch, Andrew Molera, to discuss the status of the road:[20]

> I am so troubled over those river crossing at your place; because an Auto can't cross them. . . . And I have been told the men at the ranch refuse to let people go through the yard (and I can't blame you for that either). But what am I to do? Here I have a nice business started that I am interested in. About 25 people have engaged room and board for the first of May alone. And I am afraid they can't get here. I am so anxious to make good this season. . . . I write you this requesting that you allow the fence set in again and until such a time as may be needful; or the county can get a better road where you most desire it to be builded [sic].

Pfeiffer explained to Molera that she and her husband had recently borrowed money in order to run their sawmill and expand the resort as well as to purchase a neighboring property. After publishing notice of her resort in five cities, Florence expected a good tourist season—if the road could hold the traffic. Her correspondence points to the tensions that developed in the Big Sur country during the first decades of the twentieth century. Ranching still dominated much of this coastline, but some residents increasingly staked their future on the potential economic rewards of tourism. The Monterey newspaper reported that "the coast section is becoming more popular yearly with summer visitors" and that in response "many of the ranchers are building additions to their houses to accommodate summer visitors."[21] These ranchers banked on the area's reputation "as one of the most famous cattle ranging areas of the state where the old time care-free cowboy life of the West exists."[22] But in order to continue drawing curious tourists, the Big Sur country would have to retain its premodern look while still accommodating tourists' modern tastes for comfort. This would require considerable innovation in local and county planning, and would become a hallmark feature of Big Sur throughout the twentieth century.

Residents and tourists alike saw the benefit of improving the road along this coast, for rains could make steep grades unpassable. Residents regularly rebuilt washed-out road but found two particular stretches of 16- and 20-percent grade too difficult to maintain on their own. Monterey County Surveyor Lou Hare reported these conditions to the Board of Supervisors in 1896, and in 1902 Big Sur residents petitioned the county for improvements to reduce these two grades.[23] The Coast Road was the only north-south thoroughfare in Big Sur, and it actually ceased to be a road in roughly thirteen different locations where a river or stream ran toward the ocean. In some areas a wooden bridge provided easier crossing, but powerful storms and heavy loads weakened these impermanent structures. Jeffers recalled that the driver of the mail stage in 1914 was "solemnly" warned about a perilous bridge crossing that had been compromised by the driving of a large number of dairy cattle across its wooden timbers.[24] At the turn of the century most roads in the United States were dirt, including the thirty miles of county road that connected Big Sur to Monterey. The first national census of roads determined in 1904 that fewer than 110,000 of the 2,151,570 miles of road were improved by pavement or gravel.[25] Residents of Big Sur knew they would have to be proactive about keeping intact their connection to town and market. Ranchers trying to haul feed to their cattle or their cattle to market, innkeepers, who anticipated visitors, and, really, anyone oriented toward development or the market appreciated the great economic potential of expanded and improved transportation.

It would require the involvement of a well-connected businessman to develop the idea that a permanent road through Big Sur was both necessary and possible. Dr. John Roberts, a young physician of Monterey County, was called to duty when a passenger vessel shipwrecked off the Big Sur coast in 1894. Concerned by the coast's inaccessibility (it had taken him several hours to travel from the peninsula to reach the victims), Roberts made an early pitch for a permanent road. In 1897 he walked from Carmel to San Simeon surveying the topography for the highway, estimating that such a road would cost fifty thousand dollars.[26] As the founder of the city of Seaside, just north of Monterey, Roberts also had a personal stake in the future growth of Monterey County. Moreover, by 1915 he had helped to determine where to commit county funds as a member of the Monterey County Board of Supervisors.[27] A permanent road promised further development, which

FIGURE 4. The windy, steep, unpaved Coast Road predates Highway 1, stretching back into the Santa Lucia Mountains and skirting the rivers, creeks, and canyons so difficult to bridge. (Photo: Edward Dickinson.)

would augment the tax base and create the potential for considerable tourism that could thrive year-round, not just in the dry months. Acknowledging this potential, Monterey business owners offered to provide aid to the state in order to create the new highway along the county's southern coastline.[28]

Highway proponents tapped into the nascent Good Roads movement to further this plan. In the opening years of the century, hundreds of groups emerged across the country to focus on the development of local highway projects. As in Monterey County, agriculturalists and business owners formed the backbone of these good-roads societies.[29] In California, the Good Roads Bureau of the California State Automobile Association (CSAA) coordinated newspaper posts extolling the economic benefits of good roads and convened town-hall meetings to encourage residents to petition their local boards of supervisors. In his history of the state's highways up to 1920, Ben Blow of the CSAA dedicated his book to the women of California, "who have helped more than any other agency in the fight for good roads."[30] Women created a wide-reaching network of phone calls and postcards to advocate for voter-approved road funding. They cited better access to schools, health care, and cultural offerings as reasons to support the new roads. A contemporary argument called for mothers "to aid in creating good roads sentiment, so that their children will as future citizens be educated to the axiomatic truth that good roads are the milestone that backs the advancement of civilization."[31] In contrast to Robinson Jeffers's negative assessment of civilization's effects on a once-isolated community, these advocates welcomed faster and more permanent connections to the broader world. Indeed, the good-roads campaign was premised upon the idea that growth and development were harbingers of opportunity as well as of social and cultural well-being.

With agricultural interests, business owners, and a significant number of women involved in the good-roads campaign, California voters showed considerable interest in promoting the construction of highways through the state.[32] In 1909, the year in which Henry Ford achieved full production of the Model T, California legislators passed the first state highway act, committing eighteen million dollars toward road building to connect county seats. In 1910 voters approved a bond measure that included the construction of two main roads running the length of the state, one near the coast and the other through the interior valleys.[33] By 1916 an even greater majority of voters approved a second highway bond to help complete these routes and their extensions to the county seats. In 1919, yet another bond passed to further the construction of good roads throughout the state, and it was with this bond that the state planned to construct the ninety-seven-mile Carmel–San Simeon Highway through Big Sur.[34] California drivers became so numerous that these bond measures failed to keep pace with the demand for new and improved roads, and so in 1923 California instituted a gasoline tax, two cents on the gallon, which helped fund additional construction. As happened with so many other infrastructure projects, the state could not shoulder all the costs on its own and relied upon federal aid for nearly 20 percent of its road budget.[35] Jeffers's rejection of this broad commitment to modernizing this coastline placed him firmly in the minority.

Highway plans for Big Sur proceeded smoothly as landowners granted rights-of-way to the state in order to obtain the convenience, new economic opportunities, and increased land values that the highway portended.[36] After William Randolph Hearst granted the right-of-way through his estate, State Senator Elmer S. Rigdon, of Cambria, sent a telegram to the head engineer urging him forward: "Engineer Gibson is considering some small change in routing of San Simeon–Carmel Highway. Delay at this late date for such a reason is unwarranted. Will you please hurry him up. Hearst has signed deeds. I am extremely anxious that bids on sections of this highway should be called for at once."[37] As a newspaper magnate and wealthy heir, Hearst was by far the most powerful and influential resident along this remote coast (though his estate sat in Cambria, to the south of the area regarded as Big Sur). Senator Rigdon, who served on California's Senate Committee on Roads and Highways, must have seen in this highway proposal a great boon to tourism for his constituents in Cambria. Rigdon no doubt understood that Hearst could make the project either much easier or much more difficult to complete depending on his opinion of the highway. Apparently Hearst, like the majority of the coast residents, appreciated the promise of the new road.

WORKING BETWEEN THE DEVIL
AND THE DEEP BLUE SEA

State construction crews moved into Big Sur in 1921, initiating a slow but powerful change to this rugged landscape. Two work crews tackled the job and worked toward each other from opposite ends of Big Sur. Concrete bridge pilings extended down into the beaches and river banks below; local redwoods became embankments supporting the highway; and highway crews blasted one hillside to fill the canyon below in order to save the state twenty thousand dollars in bridge work.[38] Dirt plummeted to the ocean, filling the shallow waters and disrupting marine life.[39] Many locals linked the construction to the disappearance of the abalone along the Big Sur coast, and the work no doubt harmed other aquatic life as well.[40]

One passionate resident of Big Sur, Jaime de Angulo, wrote of his horror at the sight of the increasing number of scars in the landscape, believing that the coast had been no less than "defiled and raped."[41] As an anthropologist and medical doctor, de Angulo was less economically dependent on the road than most residents, and more likely than the average resident to want to retain its premodern state. In all, highway construction removed thirteen million cubic yards of rock and earth from Big Sur, leading many locals to feel justifiably alarmed at such manipulation. At the same time, engineers and laborers felt that they worked between "the devil and the deep blue sea"—the devil of slides and erosion, and the ocean's fury below.[42] From any perspective, human beings were in the midst of inflicting unprecedented change upon this coastline.

The building process was anything but straightforward. Transporting supplies alone was a challenge in this terrain, as was spanning huge canyons and waterways, and carving out mountainsides. One contractor devised a system to bring equipment and supplies via ship to a landing once used to load timber.[43] One of the most difficult projects was the building of the Malpaso Creek Bridge. As the name suggests, this creek had been difficult to cross since the days of the Spanish. Though lacking similar appellations, numerous points along the seventy-five-mile-long stretch of Big Sur challenged the ability of construction crews and their machinery. More than one worker perished in the effort.[44] Winter storms with heavy rains and winds up to seventy miles per hour regularly delayed construction and at times wiped out bridge scaffolding.[45] Mudslides caused the state to close finished portions of the road until crews could clear the debris.[46] At times it must have seemed to workers that they were moving backwards in their efforts to tame Big Sur or that any progress was merely temporary. Onlookers likened the task to "an epic of conquest with elements no less heroic than those of Homer," but noted one important distinction: Homer wrote of "deeds purely fictive that are even surpassed by modern fact."[47]

Jeffers argued with the very premise of trying to conquer the land. As highway crews worked at subduing the land, he increasingly portrayed nature as the end value, something that humans cannot, and should not, hope to control.[48] The poet penned one of his stronger critiques of American society as a reaction to the transformation of Big Sur's landscape. In "The Coast-Road" Jeffers lamented the appearance of the new road, seeing something precious lost for the locals and their way of life. Jeffers created the image of a lone horseman high on the Santa Lucia Mountains looking down on the construction and feeling so disgusted that he shakes "his fist and makes the gesture of wringing a chicken's / neck" as he scowls and rides higher and away. The poem pits in opposition the "rich and vulgar and bewildered / civilization dying at the core" that lay beyond the new road and the people of Big Sur, those "men who ride horses, herders of cattle on / the mountain pasture, plowers of remote / Rock-narrowed farms in poverty and freedom." Jeffers portrayed these settlers as living "a good life," while he likened the advancing civilization to an "old drunken whore, pathetically eager to impose

/ the seduction of her fled charms / On all that through ignorance or isolation might have escaped / them."[49] Published in the late 1930s, just as the highway opened to travel, Jeffers's "The Coast-Road" challenged the notion that technological progress brought benefits to all.

In the romantic tradition, Jeffers consistently painted these early residents as partaking in a mutually beneficial relationship with the land and its resources. As in other backcountries, homesteaders in Big Sur lived slower, less materially-oriented lives when compared with those in the growing urban areas of the United States. Jeffers interpreted these homesteaders' intimate relationship to the land and its resources as therefore indicative of a more balanced way of life. Of course, this intimacy was largely driven by a dependence on these resources for food and income. Like many Americans lamenting the passing of the country's rural tradition, Jeffers looked kindly upon those still living off the land while turning his critique toward interwar politics and society.[50] And as with most Americans, Jeffers's frustration with modernity did not prevent him from taking part in it. In 1916 he purchased a Ford that he and his family used to visit relatives in Los Angeles as well to venture into Big Sur. He called the car "vulgar" yet could not help but admit that such vehicles were "hardy and economical as goats or jackasses," and in this case Jeffers opted for the machine.[51]

Though Jeffers abhorred the thought of what the road would bring, he did not take to task the residents themselves for helping instigate change. Many residents no doubt recoiled at the sight of the dynamited hillsides and polluted canyons, but they also recognized that this was the only way to create a year-round dependable road through Big Sur, a project that they themselves had set in motion decades earlier. Whereas Jeffers felt deep sorrow as the highway advanced through Big Sur, many locals had a more pragmatic response to the changes around them. Highway construction provided jobs for numerous men in Big Sur, and they became intimately involved in transforming their landscape. Members of original homesteader families worked with road surveyors, guiding them through Big Sur on horseback to map the highway route. Frank Pfeiffer joined the highway crew in the early 1930s, evidently committed to the new road after struggling to transport his mother's body for burial during a wet winter.[52] Sadly, he later perished on the job when a landslide broke at Hurricane Point.[53] In addition to employment, the construction provided residents with valuable building materials. Finished lumber was a rarity in Big Sur, and so locals quickly dismantled dynamite boxes and used discarded wood scaffolding in their homes and outbuildings.[54] The other advantage of the coming highway, locals learned, was the money they received from the state for rights-of-way. One resident's daughter remembered vividly how her father felt "exultant" at the offer of four thousand dollars for an easement across his property and anticipated further profits from tourism.[55] In an economically marginal region such as Big Sur, residents explored multiple avenues of income in order to maintain a footing in this formidable landscape. Though they likely felt anxious about the inevitable changes on the horizon, most residents needed the land and its resources to provide income and were therefore willing to pursue the most promising leads. As did so many other Americans in this era, Big Sur residents grappled with finding a balance between retaining tradition and embracing modern technologies that were destined to transform their way of life.

A MODERN FRONTIER

State legislators were cognizant of this coast's appeal and invested in the highway in order to showcase the region's stunning beauty to a public eager to consume it. Notably, the new highway route lay much closer to the coastline than the Coast Road, promising arresting views of the Pacific for nearly its entire length. Even before road construction began, a state employee acknowledged that the new highway was "intended purely for a touring road," on account of its "glorious scenic attraction."[56] It was more than beauty alone that compelled tourists to visit, however. With the dawn of the twentieth century, the frontier—a place where Americans had to negotiate space for themselves within a wild and inhospitable landscape—seemed to have vanished, and Americans were wont to look nostalgically upon this (largely imagined) past.[57] Not coincidentally, as the country became noticeably more urban, the rural tradition of the West took on a new importance in the nation's psyche. The popularity of western films and novels indicated that many Americans imagined a great contrast between the wide-open spaces of the West and the modern developments that permeated their daily urban lives.

News features on Big Sur reinforced the distinction between the old and the new, sometimes showing images of local ranchers in cowboy hats astride their horses with words of criticism for the increased land values, land speculators, and higher taxes that the new highway portended.[58] Journalists drew a stark contrast between this coastal stretch and much of the rest of the state, pointing out that while Hollywood glittered and high-rises graced the San

Francisco skyline, the majority of Big Sur residents continued to live without electricity or plumbing, and horses and mules still provided dependable transportation. Work and chores in this steep landscape were distinct from those required in the more modern inland farms and ranches. As late as 1935 a journalist traveling to Big Sur recorded a local rancher's method of sowing hillsides by throwing the seeds over his shoulder from his horse.[59] Big Sur children still attended one-room schoolhouses, and their teachers boarded with families along the coast.[60] A next-door neighbor could live miles away, and a trip for groceries or other household goods took at least a full day. Big Sur's vast undeveloped stretches, its rugged topography, and its homesteader families all evoked the look and feel of an early American landscape.

While the frontier had slipped into the nation's history, the automobile promised freedom to encounter these once-wild stretches in a new form of personal exploration. Early marketing by *Sunset,* the promotional magazine of the West, recommended the experience of driving in these landscapes to the person "who thrills in an elemental contact with the reality of nature. . . . There is more than 'scenery' to be complacently inspected; there is the life and the atmosphere of the West to be lived."[61] Advertising came of age in the 1920s, at the same time as Americans gained access to credit, which allowed them to consume on a larger scale. Increased wealth and leisure time, together with the decreasing costs of automobiles and gasoline during the interwar period, enabled a growing number of Americans to venture into nature as consumers.[62] Increasingly bounded by the tourist industry and the government, nature became a consumer good valued for its aesthetic and symbolic qualities and for its apparent separation from the realities of labor and work that defined urban, commercial, mass society.[63]

In Big Sur, the iconic California scenes of redwood canyons, coastal mountains, rolling pastures, cliffs, and bluffs, and the seemingly infinite expanse of the Pacific Ocean led many a journalist to praise this "last coastal frontier."[64] The irony of such praise was that it would help to erode the coast's prized frontier qualities. Throughout the West, automobile tourists ventured into dramatic landscapes deemed wild despite their tourist amenities. Visitors to Yosemite in the early twentieth century enjoyed a dance pavilion, a heated swimming pool, and the firefall from Yosemite Falls.[65] The federal government during the interwar period encouraged even more Americans to partake of such landscapes by building scenic highways such as the Natchez Trace and Blue Ridge parkways.[66] This period also saw the construction of the Going-to-the-Sun Road, in Glacier National Park, Generals Highway, in

FIGURE 5. Completed in 1932, Bixby Bridge is one of world's largest single-span concrete arch bridges. A protected two-lane scenic highway minimizes development possibilities along the Big Sur coast. (Photo: author.)

Sequoia National Park, and the reconstruction of the Old Wawona Road, in Yosemite. Like these other famous roads, the Carmel–San Simeon Highway was intended to showcase the remarkable landscape. The highway's most iconic feature, Bixby Bridge, is a 714-foot-long concrete-arch structure that rises 260 feet above Bixby Creek, making it the largest bridge of its kind in the West. The state designed the highway's route so that drivers could admire Bixby Bridge as they approached it.[67] In the early twentieth century, Americans' love for nature and technology merged to make many believe that they could simultaneously protect and enjoy the nation's most beautiful landscapes.[68]

There were those who criticized this belief that roads and inspirational landscapes could coexist. Bob Marshall, a forester and avid outdoorsman, and the conservationist Aldo Leopold pushed for the creation of wilderness areas that would exist without human developments, specifically roads.[69] The wilderness movement of the interwar period was a response to the popularity of the car and nature at a time when tourism in the nation's treasured landscapes was increasingly cast as a patriotic duty.[70] Wilderness areas, as their advocates intended them, were meant to provide an escape from consumer-oriented society.[71] As wilderness proponents pushed forward the idea of creating reserves in the national parks, the Regional Forester in San Francisco set aside forty-five thousand acres in Big Sur as the Ventana Wild Area in 1929. Two years later, using the new L-20 Regulation developed by the Forest Service, Chief Forester Stuart reclassified it as the Ventana Primitive Area.[72] Under this designation, the primitive forms of transportation, subsistence, habitation, and environment were to be maintained "to the fullest degree compatible with their highest public use."[73] With the construction of the highway under way, there were those who felt the urgency of protecting Big Sur's pastoral traditions from being transformed by admirers.

The Ventana Primitive Area existed within the larger boundaries of the Monterey Forest Reserve. The U.S. Forest Service, like most modern developments, came late to this stretch of California. President Roosevelt's June 1906 proclamation bounded 335,495 acres within the reserve, and within two years the president approved an additional 25,000 acres. By 1908 the Monterey Forest Reserve encompassed nearly one-half of the Big Sur landscape.[74] Government officials noted that decades of settlement, cattle grazing, timber removal, and the inevitable wildfires within the Santa Lucia Mountains all threatened the quality and quantity of the water flow to the fertile lowlands of Monterey County. As in other western landscapes, the Forest Service assumed management for areas recently worked over by industrialists and provided specific, government-directed plans for the vast rural lands. In Big Sur, protecting the watershed required providing oversight for resources subject to the dwindling industrial pursuits along this coast. Though the local gold mining ended before the turn of the century, the Monterey Lime Company extracted limestone until 1911, and the last major redwood cut happened in 1921.[75] The Monterey Forest Reserve would help administer Big Sur's transition from an industrial and agricultural landscape to an increasingly visited and inhabited coastal haven.

In numerous ways, the U.S. Forest Service shaped the landscape and its resources. Supervisor N. O. Torstenson's first project for the reserve was to lay twenty-seven miles of telephone line from the district office to rangers' head-quarters within the forest. This line would assist in firefighting and also transmit other important information between the office and the ranger station. To the delight of nearby landowners, their contribution in helping lay the telephone line would gain them free access to it. Other early projects in the reserve included stocking the streams of the Santa Lucia Mountains with non-native trout, planting pine trees within the logged-out spaces of the forest, and clearing the old path formerly used by the area's indigenous peoples to cross the ridge of the Santa Lucia Mountains. The forest service hired a bounty hunter in 1909 to reduce the population of native predators that threatened ranchers' livestock. In the end, rangers helped kill sixty-six coyotes and more than one hundred wild cats. And when a different sort of threat loomed—a disgruntled resident who threatened to burn the lands of his more prosperous neighbors—residents turned to a forest ranger for assistance.[76] The Monterey Forest Reserve, later known as the Los Padres National Forest, provided certain benefits to residents and also implemented policies that restricted traditional practices of prescribed burns and timber removal. The national forest added a layer of complexity to Big Sur's land management and instituted a number of projects that eased the logistics of living along this coast. Most important, the forest service secured a large portion of Big Sur as public land not subject to commercial and residential development, thereby dictating to a considerable extent Big Sur's future land use and preservation.

PROPERTY AND PRESERVATION

As property values increased along the highway's path, all major landowners in Big Sur faced a difficult dilemma: increased taxes did not coincide with increased productivity of the land. Many could not carry the burden of higher taxes or resist the lure of good money from wealthy developers. Even before the completion of the highway, a half-dozen investors purchased land from private owners. Several large ranches fell under the ownership of investors as far away as Chicago, or these businessmen or wealthy second-home owners would consolidate multiple homesteads to form their own gentlemen's ranches.[77] In a personal correspondence in 1928 Jeffers noted the subdivision of Malpaso Canyon and the recent purchase of the ranch at Point Sur by "some wealthy person who intends to breed polo-ponies there." Although Jeffers may have labeled high-end horse breeding effete, he considered it "certainly more decent than subdivision," which would bring even more people and their trappings.[78] Locals and journalists alike noted that this was the beginning of a new era for land ownership in Big Sur. By 1929 real-estate speculators had confidence in an investment along this coast.[79]

As the highway progressed and property values rose, the state moved quickly to secure a piece of Big Sur to meet the demand of outdoor-recreation tourism. In 1924 the California Board of Forestry conducted a survey of portions of Big Sur for a general report on the redwoods in Monterey County. In his report, R. E. Roach summarized the varied recreational opportunities in Big Sur, noting the abundant fishing and the striking and varied scenery ranging from "quiet redwood groves along the river" to "rugged mountains and cliffs." Roach predicted that with the completion of the highway, Big Sur would experience "a volume of tourist travel unsurpassed by any place in the State." This report identified John and Florence Pfeiffer's property as holding great potential for recreation because of its beautiful redwood groves, its ample water from the Big Sur River, its proximity to the road, its protection from the wind and fog, and its rich pioneer history.[80]

In the early 1930s John and Florence Pfeiffer made an important decision regarding their property. A native of Big Sur, John was born in 1862 into one of the original homesteading families. While Florence ran the resort, John kept cattle and bees. Now close to sixty and seventy years old, respectively, the couple looked to sell their inn and find a buyer for a portion of their increasingly valuable property. As the highway progressed, several developers eyed the Pfeiffers' 1,200 acres along the Big Sur River and highway. John and Florence entertained these developers' proposals until they realized that these businessmen intended to seriously alter the area with extensive subdividing and tourist amenities. The Pfeiffers resisted selling under such conditions because, as Florence explained, she and her husband wanted the "river and trees left for 'always' just *as is*."[81] Meanwhile, in 1928 California voters approved a bond measure to provide matching funds for parkland acquisition. Many Californians eagerly sought additional recreational opportunities, especially along the coastline.[82] Local governments or private sources had to provide the other half of the needed funds. William Colby, a member of the Sierra Club staff, a California State Parks commissioner, and a future resident of Big Sur, successfully encouraged the Pfeiffers to sell half of their land to the state for the creation of a park in 1933. The Pfeiffers sold a portion of their property to the state for $100,000, effectively donating the difference between this price and the assessed value, $167,500. Monterey County provided additional funds, and Pfeiffer Big Sur State Park officially opened in 1937.[83] Within the new park's boundaries several small inholdings compelled the state to define how it would operate within this new locale. The state offered to buy all these inholdings to create a unified state park, but one landowner rejected the offer. William Baker, a 95-year-old Civil War veteran "absolutely refused to sell" his land to the state, and it was not until 1960, when the state won a condemnation suit with Baker's heirs, that his land was incorporated into the park.[84] Locals would learn, if they had not already, that the government worked on a different timetable than real-estate developers and could persist in ways that a private party could not.

The State of California had now initiated a recreational highway through Big Sur and established a park to satisfy the many admirers of this redwood-studded coastline. The federal government followed suit, providing funds designated by the National Industrial Recovery Administration to complete the highway and assigning Civilian Conservation Corps (CCC) workers to projects within Pfeiffer Big Sur State Park. The CCC helped define the character of the park, including the development of multiple campsites and amenities such as recreational fields, an outdoor theater, a dance pavilion, barbecue pits, a swimming area complete with a boating channel, four sandy beaches, and a wooded island.[85] The Big Sur River was dammed and diverted to create a swimming pool, which was just one of several reasons why Pfeiffer became an overwhelmingly popular park.[86]

The story of Pfeiffer Big Sur State Park illustrates dilemmas that have continued to be central to the history of land preservation in Big Sur ever since. By selling and virtually donating part of their land to the state, the Pfeiffers became the first family of Big Sur to decide that their land should be stewarded by the government instead of sold to private individuals. The Pfeiffers, like other homesteading families who had amassed extensive properties through consolidation and purchase, had the ability to pass vast expanses of land into public ownership.[87] The parks that resulted from such donations boosted tourism and opened the beauty of Big Sur to many more people. An alternative option would have been to maximize profit by selling to a private developer who intended to build a single, private residence and keep the rest of the land in open space. Some would argue that this scenario demanded less of the land than a public park, which would accommodate thousands of visitors per year. A private owner, however, was well within his or her right to maximize development, whereas the state had an obligation to keep its parks largely undeveloped. To this day, locals grapple with the appropriate balance of private and public property in Big Sur. There never has been, and it is unlikely there ever will be, consensus on what constitutes ideal land management.

IMAGINING A DIFFERENT PATH

Speaking through his poetry and not in any official capacity, Jeffers himself made what was in some respects the strongest case for Big Sur's preservation. It would be impossible to prove that Jeffers directly influenced the preservation-oriented land-use plans written in the decades after World War II (though the introduction to a 1960 Big Sur master plan includes stanzas from Jeffers's "The Continent's End"), but through his work he created a popular and powerful argument for leaving intact Big Sur's beauty and pastoral landscape. He craved a place where one experienced nature first and foremost; and like Marshall and Leopold, Jeffers recognized the human value of such a landscape. In "Storm as Deliverer" Jeffers compared his beloved Big Sur to a more productive land and argued in favor of the aesthetic value of the former:[88]

> Dear hills and seaward-opening glens that fold
> In your strange beauty many a woodland stream
> But nothing rich of corn or wine, no gold
> Nor silver vein nor layer of stones that gleam,
> You pasture your few cattle and you hold
> No better gift for men but one supreme,
> Your beauty without price.

Jeffers's career encompassed decades in which the Western world engaged in brutal warfare, suffered through economic depression, and built up machinery to alter the earth and inflict human suffering. He could not find peace with this, and instead adopted what he called an "inhumanist" approach to world affairs. He described his philosophy as "the devaluation of human-centered illusions, the turning outward from man to what is boundlessly greater" in the quest toward human development.[89] He described his poetic treatment of such themes as incest and patricide as symbols of "human-turned inwardness, the perpetual struggle to get ahead of each other."[90] Big Sur, according to Jeffers, could remind people how to live in a nondestructive manner, how to value noninvasive interactions with the earth, and how to protect natural beauty in the face of such human-inflicted horrors.

FIGURE 6. The view looking north from atop Point Sur. The Santa Lucia Mountains meet the Pacific Ocean in dramatic fashion throughout much of Big Sur, with only an occasional meadow or glen punctuating the rugged coastline. (Photo: author.)

Jeffers, Marshall, and others juxtaposed so-called true nature and modern-day civilization, and it was their great fear that the latter would obliterate the former. It is significant that these advocates did not argue that people and nature could not coexist; instead, they advocated simpler, more archaic modes of life.[91] Jeffers and wilderness advocates watched with trepidation the development of the transportation infrastructure in the early part of the century, when businesses, consumers, and the government all converged to modernize America. In response, proponents of wilderness hoped to protect some places as representations of noncommercial landscapes. The Carmel–San Simeon Highway ensured that Big Sur would never be able to escape the influence of commercial tourism, but it did not mean that Big Sur was destined to become an overdeveloped scenic attraction.

In 1937, as the highway first opened to the motoring public, *Motorland Magazine* crowed: "Now man's genius and man's courage have brought to triumphant conclusion the titan task under way for almost 20 years."[92] At the same time, those who used the past for guidance could easily predict that the highway certainly did not tame Big Sur. Some locals claimed as early as 1938 that "there will always be landslides, that this country won't stand being tampered with by a lot of bridge builders."[93] Jeffers echoed this belief, for despite his fear of the human power to destroy, he saw it pale in comparison with the power of nature. In the closing of his poem "The Coast-Road," Jeffers reflected on one consolation: that despite the destruction caused by the creation of the highway, the Santa Lucia Mountains themselves were "Not the least hurt by this ribbon of road carved on their sea-foot."[94]

The highway in and of itself did not have the power to overwhelm the land—people would have to do that—but the road stood as a symbol of and a conduit for a shifting relationship between people and the Big Sur landscape. Had the highway arrived two decades earlier, the outcome might have been quite different, but to the benefit of the land and its admirers, Big Sur opened to the public during an era of thoughtful critique about the impact of roads and commercialism. Though locals had largely championed the highway, these residents, along with county officials and other interested outsiders, began to imagine an unconventional land-management approach for Big Sur, one that would sustain the open spaces, the great beauty, and the feeling of independence still possible along this largely undeveloped coastal stretch. In the years to come, Jeffers's beloved depictions of a dynamic land and people would compel countless Americans to want to preserve Big Sur and the way of life made possible within this remarkable terrain. Jeffers's verse therefore helped not only to protect locals' place within the landscape but also to empower residents to serve as stewards over one of the nation's great natural treasures.

TWO

Nature's Highway

An inviting land—but hard to conquer. It seeks to remain
unspoiled, uninhabited by man.

HENRY MILLER, *Big Sur and the Oranges of Hieronymus Bosch*

JUST TWO WEEKS AFTER THE official opening of the Carmel–San
Simeon Highway on 27 June 1937, state officials reported that the road carried 60 percent more traffic than predicted, at anywhere from 1,800 to 2,000
cars per day.[1] "No one in their wildest dreams had any idea it would be used
so much," remarked George Loorz, William Randolph Hearst's construction
manager in San Simeon. A "continuous line of cars" now passing the Hearst
Castle prompted Loorz to exclaim: "We are no longer isolated here in San
Simeon."[2] Given the small number of local residents, and the more efficient
Highway 101 on the inland side of the Santa Lucia Mountains, these traffic
figures indicate the considerable popularity of this new tourist destination
during the Great Depression. The state could feel confident in its investment;
by providing permanent access to this coast, legislators had dissolved the only
barrier to Big Sur's full incorporation into the burgeoning tourist industry.

Newspapers from the West and the East, and national magazines, did
their part in casting Big Sur as a place apart—yet accessible. Media heralded
the highway as a wonder, drawing Americans looking for a novel and inexpensive vacation. Situated within a day's drive of San Francisco or Los
Angeles, Big Sur became popular among those looking for a beautiful drive,
a stay at a rustic cabin or lodge, or a camping experience among the stately
redwoods. Adjectives such as "sublime," "enchanting," and "majestic" as well
as "forbidding," "grotesque," and "wild" described Big Sur's remarkable landscape. The *New York Herald Tribune* gushed over this newest link of coastal
highway, labeling the region "a hundred miles of the least known, the wildest,
the most inaccessible, the most scenic coastal reach in all our country."[3]
Americans seemed both fascinated and perhaps intimidated by this near-
wilderness suddenly open to society.

With national attention now focused on Big Sur, outside forces increasingly shaped local land-management decisions. Paradoxically, deliberate management choices increased how wild this coastline appeared. This beguiling countryside could now be accessed by the very modern automobile, bringing visitors who delighted in a landscape made even more alluring by county zoning that prioritized residential and agricultural land use and limited commercial developments.[4] And, with so much invested in the region's infrastructure, Monterey County also prohibited billboards along the highway in order to maximize tourist appeal and protect property values. In short, as Americans idealized the supposed freedom and connections with nature in a place like Big Sur, multiple layers of government—from the national forest, to the state parks and highway, to county zoning—shaped the land and the opportunities available to inhabitants and visitors alike.

Despite the highway (and indeed perhaps because of the road's setting), by the late 1930s Big Sur still had a reputation as a wild coastal landscape. One particular event confirmed the special nature of Big Sur, surprising the entire scientific community. For nearly a century the southern sea otter was thought to be extinct from fur hunting, but in 1938 a local couple noted what appeared to be otters swimming offshore from Bixby Bridge and contacted the local fish and game authorities. A scientist connected to Hopkins Marine Laboratory, on the Monterey Peninsula, confirmed this discovery and posited that in the years of the heaviest hunting, when over a thousand otters could be killed in a matter of months, these creatures had found a safe haven in the waters off the remote and dangerously rocky Sur coast.[5] The protection afforded these animals by the isolated and protected inlets of Big Sur allowed them to reproduce their average one cub every two years, and a 1909 international law forbidding the sale or possession of otter pelts protected California's rediscovered otters. The California condor, the largest North American flying bird, also survived in Big Sur when egg hunting had helped drive the bird close to extinction.[6] A 1941 federal report claimed that in Big Sur the condor "was making its last stand."[7] That Big Sur could be the home to such creatures served as further proof that this region deserved preservation-oriented management. The wildness that had been an obstacle for two generations of Big Sur homesteaders now became the area's greatest asset as tourists and new residents prioritized nondevelopment.

For generations, open land in the West had provided hope and allure, and during an era of economic depression and a second World War, Big Sur's beauty and undeveloped landscape offered an escape from the destructive forces shaping society. Even in the more prosperous times that followed, others began to echo Robinson Jeffers's praise for Big Sur's separation. The author Henry Miller, who settled in Big Sur when the highway was still new, joined Jeffers in sustaining the notion of Big Sur as a place apart, a foil to the rest of the rapidly commercializing national culture, and as a place to retreat from what they both perceived as a government-led belligerent society. The popularity of their works beckoned the mass culture to Big Sur while their writings also helped to justify aesthetic zoning for this prized landscape. County officials would become strong allies in preserving Big Sur by employing innovative government regulations. By the mid-twentieth century, Big Sur's land management and its artistic representations managed to reinforce each other, while defining new ways to treat wild and inhabited lands.

THE CONVERGENCE OF GOVERNMENT, TECHNOLOGY, AND TOURISM

Big Sur's reputation as a timeless land- and seascape was built upon government policies that were themselves on the cutting edge of land management. In 1938, one year after the completion of the highway, a resident named Bassett moved his gas station half a mile down the Carmel–San Simeon Highway, and in so doing left a commercial district and entered an area zoned for agriculture. Instead of obtaining a permit for the new building or requesting zoning reclassification, Bassett went forward without county approval. When the county sued Bassett, he called the zoning ordinance unconstitutional in its restrictions on private property.[8]

Zoning emerged in the United States around the turn of the century to address the development issues associated with rapidly growing urban populations. In 1926 the U.S. Supreme Court decided *Euclid v. Ambler Realty,* a landmark zoning case. The court upheld a zoning measure that excluded industrial and multifamily buildings from a residential zone because of the adverse impact upon public health, safety, morals, and general welfare.[9] The *Euclid* case addressed the externalities imposed on suburban residences by the introduction of high-density or industrial development, and challenged the rights of property owners to realize maximum productivity on their land without regard for the local impact caused by the subsequent pollution, traffic congestion, or other nuisances.[10] With increasing land scarcity, regulation in the form of zoning became a means to protect the quality of life to be enjoyed by those who could afford property zoned for low-density residential use. The justices acknowledged as much in *Euclid,* noting specifically the negative impact of apartment houses that, with their "height and bulk," interfere "with the free circulation of air" and monopolize "the rays of the sun which otherwise would fall upon the smaller homes," contributing to congestion while "depriving children of the privilege of quiet and open spaces for play, enjoyed by those in more favored localities." The justices reasoned that "the residential character" of a neighborhood and its "desirability as a place of detached residences" could be "utterly destroyed" by apartment houses.[11]

Around the same time as the *Euclid* ruling, Monterey County developed restrictive zoning in anticipation of the highway's completion. Though Big Sur was far from an urban area with increasing land scarcity, its sudden accessibility prompted important questions about future land use. The majority of coastal frontage property remained in private ownership and had great potential for commercial and residential development, limited only by county zoning. A scholar at the time noted that in developing zoning for the Big Sur coast, Monterey County sought "to protect adjoining property values, or the investment of public funds spent in the construction of scenic roads."[12] In 1938 Judge Maurice T. Dooling of the Superior Court of San Benito County presided over Bassett's case and issued a groundbreaking decision that upheld the county's zoning measures.[13] Arguing that "scenic attractiveness" is a public asset because it brings and maintains tourism and is pleasing to residents, Judge Dooling denied Bassett's right to relocate his gas station to an agricultural district. Aesthetics alone did not stand as a constitutional basis for disallowing the gas station, but Judge Dooling believed that in this case protecting the scenic quality of the highway in turn protected property values and stood to benefit the general economic welfare. Emerging on the cusp of changing opinion regarding the constitutionality of restricting private property rights, Judge Dooling's decision echoed *Euclid* in protecting a certain quality of life and property values for nearby property owners. But Dooling went further, taking into account the aesthetic experience to be had along the Big Sur coast. He admitted that a higher court might decide that he had attempted to "force the hands of the clock forward too rapidly," but remained confident that time would ultimately justify his judgment." He reasoned that "any person of average sensibilities who has seen so many of our highways defaced with the customary clutter of hot-dog stands and other commercially used eye-sores" would have sympathy for the purpose of the zoning ordinance.[14]

Dooling's read on national sentiment was correct. The vice president of the National Municipal League noted as early as 1931 that the "rank and file of the people are coming to look upon [zoning] as merely a matter of maintaining or increasing property values," and by the late 1930s many Americans approved of aesthetic zoning.[15] Indeed, Judge Dooling's opinion and the strict zoning ordinances that prohibited billboards along the length of the highway brought praise from around the state. An Inglewood newspaper opined: "the road is the more beautiful and unique in that no signboards were permitted through its entire length and buildings . . . must be erected under zoning ordinances."[16] Monterey County officials presided over one of the nation's most remarkable natural treasures and proactively developed protective measures for this coastline well before public sentiment, the state, or the federal government demanded it.

As Robinson Jeffers had predicted, the highway brought important aspects of the modern economy to Big Sur. Even for some who were less emotionally attached to Big Sur than Jeffers, there existed perceptible discomfort with the idea of bringing together technology and areas of such beauty. In 1937 the *San Jose Mercury-Herald* reported on the new highway and gave voice to this particular dilemma: "For some, this invasion of an almost unknown land is sacrilege, despoliation of a truly virgin wilderness in the name of high-speed transportation. But to the vast majority of the motoring public, it is but a great forward step in the realization of California's most abundant heritage, its incomparable scenery."[17] For decades, Americans had pointed with great satisfaction to their stunning landscapes, holding them up as the equal of Europe's historic landmarks. The opening of Big Sur in the 1930s, along with the Blue Ridge and Natchez Trace parkways in the East, served as further proof of America's wealth, and in the former case, of the significance of the West. If Americans looked to leisure in nature as a way to express the national character, then recreation within Big Sur's majestic mountains, thousands of forested acres, and stunning ocean vistas could be a source of great pride for Americans.[18]

The United States' entry into World War II, and subsequent gas rationing, meant that recreational travel necessarily slowed, bringing a little quiet to Big Sur after the rush of popularity in the late 1930s. The recent technological advance of the highway would now serve another national purpose. In early 1941 the federal government expanded its presence in Big Sur by establishing the Hunter Liggett Military Reservation for tank- and artillery-warfare training. High in the Santa Lucia Mountains, partially within the national forest boundaries, soldiers practiced with the most advanced warfare technology, using the tanks and antiaircraft weaponry being churned out of American factories at astounding rates.[19] The military chose this location for its diverse topography (and distance from population centers), believing that soldiers would gain experience on nearly every terrain that they were likely to encounter in the war. Despite the most modern equipment, the military found that in Big Sur mules still provided essential services for transport and rescue missions where vehicles could not handle the terrain. The political realities of World War II entered Big Sur, but as usual, the land itself helped dictate how events unfolded.

The U.S. Forest Service, too, would employ its latest technology and scientific understanding in Big Sur's backcountry. Its policies would serve to alternately protect and develop this landscape. Bounding off large expanses of land from residential and commercial development, Los Padres National Forest protected vistas and habitats in accordance with parklike preservation. And though the forest service could not determine land policy outside its boundaries, its very presence circumscribed Big Sur's residential and commercial development. At the same time, the forest service built roads and supported ranching and mineral exploration that spoiled the notion of a pristine landscape. Local ranchers, engaged in the primary agricultural pursuit that persisted in Big Sur past midcentury, relied upon the range offered within the boundaries of Los Padres National Forest. In support of this land use, the forest service provided stock-watering troughs and required no more than a small use fee from ranchers who could turn their animals out to graze on pastures that they did not have to maintain or seed.[20]

Arguably, Los Padres National Forest's largest impact on the Big Sur landscape was its fire management. Internal improvements during the war years included more telephone lines and watchtowers to improve fire communication, new roads through the forest, and better-trained firefighters with more advanced equipment (at least where terrain permitted). Because of the severe fire threat posed by military maneuvers, the Civilian Conservation Corps aided the forest service in building fire roads and firebreaks throughout the forested and chaparral-covered mountainsides.[21] Forest rangers actively suppressed fire to the extent that the interval between major fires became ever greater in the years after the founding of the national forest.[22]

This policy of fire suppression was not based upon Big Sur's natural fire ecosystem. Recent studies of mudflows in the Big Sur River Basin and other indicators of past burns have led scientists to conclude that large fires (of

FIGURE 7. Aerial view of the Santa Lucia Mountains in Big Sur, including Highway 1, Bixby Bridge, and the winding, unpaved Coast Road. (Photo: Carol M. Highsmith; Library of Congress image.)

roughly 50,000 acres or more) have occurred almost every seventy-five years over the past six centuries.[23] In the mid-twentieth century, settlers and the forest service had not occupied Big Sur long enough, nor did they have the scientific data, to be aware of this fire pattern. Deliberate fire suppression allowed for the buildup of fuel and tinder to dangerous levels, while also hindering the growth of certain native vegetation that thrives in burned-over patches or depends upon fire propagation. Inevitably, massive fires did occasionally spread through the landscape, burning thousands of acres of forest as well as some residences and businesses. Subsequent mudslides washed out portions of the highway. Fire and its aftermath challenged the notion that even the latest technology could successfully tame Big Sur.

A government publication authored by the Works Progress Administration (WPA) in 1941 suggested that Big Sur's remote, rugged terrain would not easily be bent to the purposes of an admiring public, nor, ostensibly, the designs of forest administrators. An assessment of this coastline led the author to argue that "the new highway brings every year a steadily growing number of people to the fringes of the Big Sur country—but only to the fringes. The inner mountain fastnesses—fold after fold of rugged mountains—still guard their lonely isolation."[24] By the end of World War II, Big Sur lacked a clearly defined status. In many ways, it was distinctive for what it was not: neither a national park, nor a fertile agricultural or ranching center, nor a busy population center with increasing amounts of pavement and concrete, nor a backcountry wilderness—though elements of each of these existed in this era. The powerful forces of tourism, technology, and government all exerted considerable influence on this coastline but could not entirely dictate the future of Big Sur, a place where residents were solidifying their own ideals for this landscape and would come to command considerable influence in land management.

ARTISTIC REPRESENTATIONS OF BIG SUR

Fewer than three hundred residents lived in the seventy-five-mile stretch of Big Sur after the highway opened. A local ballad asserting that "The South Coast's a wild coast, and lonely," suggested that residents appreciated their relative isolation, or at least understood that these qualities were what made Big Sur distinct.[25] Local writers were inspired by and worked to perpetuate this reputation. Like Robinson Jeffers, they interpreted Big Sur for national audiences, thereby shaping the way that outsiders imagined and experienced this exceptional landscape. Such artistic representations of life in Big Sur inevitably influenced the way that the county and business-oriented locals framed future development.

As modern conveniences such as indoor plumbing and electricity crept into Big Sur, and as the country witnessed remarkable technological feats in the name of wartime defense, the idea of a frontierlike expanse along California's popular central coast held growing allure.[26] One resident, Lillian Bos Ross, capitalized on this fascination with the homesteading period by penning two popular novels set in the late-nineteenth-century Big Sur country. *The Stranger* (1942), followed by the sequel *Blaze Allan* (1944), met with literary success in the 1940s, and in 1974 Hollywood turned the story into a feature film, *Zandy's Bride* (which enjoyed considerably less praise than the novels).[27] Ross depicted the struggles of pioneer life in Big Sur, including the manual labor along the steep mountainsides and the intense isolation, but she also expressed the joy and camaraderie that came when the scattered settlers gathered to celebrate weddings or held multiday fiestas along the beach to

FIGURE 8. Deetjen's Inn and restaurant opened not long after the completion of Highway 1. It is listed on the National Register of Historic Places. (Photo: Carol M. Highsmith; Library of Congress image.)

collect shipped-in supplies. Echoing the WPA publication from the previous year, Ross's preface to *The Stranger* suggested that the "harsh and lovely" Santa Lucia Mountains still "hold fast to their ancient loneliness."[28] Ross painted a place of untamed nature, and though she wrote about the days of old, most homes in the 1940s still lacked electricity and regular telephone service. Readers across the nation likely imagined a unique and charming countryside far from most modern-day realities.

Less quaint was John Steinbeck's treatment of this coastline, though he portrayed an equally timeless landscape. Steinbeck's 1938 short story *Flight* follows Pepe, a young man trying to hide from the law in the thick forests and steep slopes of the Santa Lucia Mountains. During a supply trip to Monterey from his native Big Sur, Pepe upholds his honor by challenging a man who speaks ill of him. Pepe knifes and kills the man, then races home in hopes of escaping retribution, where his mother and younger siblings prepare a horse and supplies for his escape into the mountains. His family recites their prayers as he rides away, considering him as good as dead as he sets out along the steep trail to the east. Pepe rather easily avoids the mountain lions and rattlesnakes, but he suffers considerably from exposure and thirst. In an act of desperation, Pepe stands tall and accepts the rifle fire of the posse that is pursuing him. As he tumbles down the mountainside, he gathers rocks and earth and ends up buried beneath the slide. Though Steinbeck wrote extensively of Monterey, this short story was his only treatment of Big Sur. His description of its landscape reveals his familiarity with the area, which came from time spent working on a highway-surveying crew in the early 1920s.[29] Steinbeck saw the area as potentially hostile to those who hoped to earn a living from its soil. His description of Pepe's family's farm is of an establishment barely surviving its harsh setting:[30]

> The farm buildings huddled like the clinging aphids on the mountain skirts, crouched low to the ground as though the wind might blow them into the sea. The little shack, the rattling, rotting barn were gray-bitten with sea salt, beaten by the damp wind until they had taken on the color of the granite hills.... A little corn was raised on the sterile slope, and it grew short and thick under the wind, and all the cobs formed on the landward sides of the stalks.

With such a story Steinbeck potentially deterred would-be residents but also bolstered the image of Big Sur as a place to experience nature's elemental forces. Published in the year after the opening of California State Highway 1, *Flight* did not depict a modern landscape tamed by technology but instead evoked the image of Old California.

Ross and Steinbeck brought heightened attention to Big Sur, and like Jeffers they emphasized the primitive qualities of life along this coast. But it would be another author—Henry Miller—who would create in Big Sur a mecca for those who not only loved its landscape but sought the freedom and artistic inspiration that it supposedly offered.[31] Miller possessed a broad cultural perspective after spending ten years as an expatriate in Paris and Greece, during which time he published the controversial *Tropic of Cancer* and *Tropic of Capricorn*. The politics of war sent him home to his native New York, where a publisher gave him $500 to tour his home country and record his impressions of the people and culture he encountered in each region. As he drifted across the United States during the war, a stranger in his homeland, he consistently noted his disappointment, if not disgust, with the dominant culture. Indeed, he titled the book *The Air-Conditioned Nightmare,* and he did not mince words within it, either: "We are a vulgar, pushing mob whose passions are easily mobilized by demagogues.... To call this a society of free peoples is blasphemous. What have we to offer the world beside the supera-bundant loot which we recklessly plunder from the earth under the maniacal delusion that this insane activity represents progress and enlightenment?"[32]

Miller was troubled by much in the American character, including its disregard for the well-being of the earth. He was therefore predisposed to like what he found in Big Sur: a community content to live within a powerful landscape. Miller's tour had ended by 1944, when he visited a friend and fellow artist in Monterey who suggested that Miller introduce himself to the artist Lynda Sargent of Big Sur. With little money and no home, Miller pre-vailed upon Sargent for a temporary landing spot along this coast, a region that he later described as his "first real home."[33] Prior to moving to Big Sur, Miller's only familiarity with the region was through his reading of Robinson Jeffers's collection "Women at Point Sur." The place was an odd choice for someone who had spent his life in cities such as New York and Paris, but perhaps the ravages of war led Miller to seek seclusion in nature. He explained the move to a close friend as good for his work and his personal well-being: "I have much work to finish and am seeking peace and isolation. I am com-pletely out of the world there."[34] It was from Big Sur that he finalized *The Air-Conditioned Nightmare,* contemplating modern American society from the vantage point of its apparent antithesis.

After years spent living abroad Miller nursed a romantic vision of his homeland that his cross-country tour had almost shattered. He had held in high regard his native land, "nourished by the dreams and visions of great Americans—the poets and seers." Disillusionment followed, however, when his assessment of the nation led him to believe that "some other breed of man has won out." Miller found much to condemn in the newly invigorated post-war culture. He felt particularly disgusted with American materialism and the moral bankruptcy of the mass media, and he characterized the ubiqui-tous suburb as horrendous. Unimpressed by the technological prowess of the United States, Miller turned this achievement on its head. He used Walt Disney as an example: "Walt Disney . . . is the master of the nightmare. . . . Disney works fast—like greased lightning. That's how we'll all operate soon. What we dream we become. We'll get the knack of it soon. We'll learn how to annihilate the whole planet in the wink of an eye—just wait and see."[35]

Miller's tour through his homeland led him to condemn American society as the civilization most disconnected from the natural world: "Nowhere else in the world is the divorce between man and nature so complete."[36] This struck him as particularly self-defeating, for as he acknowledged: "We may succeed in altering the face of the earth until it is unrecognizable even to the Creator, but if we are unaffected," or "If we ourselves remain the same restless, miserable, frustrated creatures we were before . . . wherein lies the meaning?"[37] Miller did not equate technological progress with progress as a society. He labeled America as deluded by a "false progress, a progress which stinks. It is a world cluttered with useless objects which men and women, in order to be exploited and degraded, are taught to regard as useful."[38] Miller, like Jeffers, held that modern technologies seemed to merely amplify and complicate the problems inherent in and among people.

But Big Sur became Miller's saving grace, for it was here that he believed he had finally found "a region which corresponded to my notion of something truly American, something simple, primitive, and as yet unspoiled."[39] Such ruminations led Miller to feel "suddenly quite free" in his adopted home.[40] But the landscape and community that Miller had come to love were themselves shifting entities. Half a century earlier Big Sur's population sat close to a thousand inhabitants because of the work available in multiple extractive industries. By the time Miller settled along this coast, its population sat closer to three hundred, and no industrial operations remained.[41] Big Sur's natural resources were afforded a reprieve for several decades before the completed highway brought new types of investors. Arriving in Big Sur on the heels of World War II, Miller was privy to the full impact that postwar prosperity could make along this coast. But Miller found comfort in his conviction that Big Sur's imposing landscape resisted incursions. Moreover, Miller believed that nature exerted a force upon residents that promoted preservation: "Something about the land makes one long to keep it intact."[42]

In 1952, eight years after settling in Big Sur, Miller took his first trip to Europe since the outbreak of war, only to find himself homesick for the first time in his life. He claimed that he had experienced a shift, where no longer did he find satisfaction in the "cultural, intellectual life," which he characterized as "too much talk, rehash, etc."[43] Now, far from the vibrant, cosmopolitan environment where he had spent much of his professional life (and as a child in the Bronx), Miller embraced the slow and unstructured pace of life of Big Sur. One of Big Sur's best qualities, according to Miller, was the absence of a status quo, and he characterized Big Sur and its inhabitants as lacking pretense and conformity. What was more, Miller believed locals possessed kindness, an important "element of the American temperament," to a remarkable degree.[44] These desirable human elements, alongside Big Sur's beauty, compelled Miller to query after years spent in Big Sur: "This is Heaven enough, why ask for more?"[45]

Miller first arrived in Big Sur seeking isolation and instead found himself enmeshed in a satisfying community. Though certainly the best-known, Miller was one of several artists living along Partington Ridge. His close friends and neighbors, the Rosses, both produced notable work: Lillian, two well-known books; and Harry Dick Ross, numerous sculptures and hand-carved signs throughout Big Sur. Nicholas Roosevelt, a retired journalist and diplomat, was a prolific author, while other neighbors were proficient in pottery, ironwork, poetry, and screenwriting.[46] These artists flocked to Big Sur for reasons similar to those of other artists forming colonies: to find a beautiful place of inspiration, to escape the distractions of an urban area, and to make a political statement of sorts by rejecting certain aspects of contemporary society. In Big Sur, these artists both rejected certain aspects of modernity—namely the suburbs and the Cold War—while taking full advantage of the highway and telephones that afforded connections to the larger world.[47] In 1952 a local paper described the Ridge as a gathering of "artists, writers and simple-living escapists who by their own choice exist in a crag above Big Sur" because they view life as "too crowded and disturbing elsewhere."[48] It was called the "closest-knit" community within Big Sur, where the artists and those aspiring to become such were known to support one another's endeavors. Surplus game, fish, and other food found its way into neighbors' mailboxes throughout the year. Eve Miller, Henry's fourth wife, whom he married in Big Sur, ran a local kindergarten in their home. Her students arrived from farther up the ridge with the mailman, who picked them back up at the end of his route.[49] Big Sur served well those who embraced the idiosyncrasies of life along this coast and rejected those who could not make the break from mainstream America. It was a way of life that kept Miller rooted to this ridgetop home for nearly twenty years.

In 1957 Miller published a memoir that made a strong case for preserving this coastal community. The title, *Big Sur and the Oranges of Hieronymus Bosch,* linked Big Sur to the sort of pleasure and freedom that Miller perceived in Bosch's *Garden of Earthly Delights*. In this memoir, Miller exalted Big Sur as a place where "to give thanks to the Creator comes natural and easy. Out yonder they may curse, revile and torture one another, defile all the human instincts, make a shambles of creation (if it were in their power), but here, no, here it is unthinkable, here there is abiding peace, the peace of God."[50] Miller's praise for this undeveloped landscape ultimately succeeded in drawing enormous attention to Big Sur, but this was not the only paradox. Though Miller craved the peace that Big Sur offered, he envisioned a time when many more people could experience the joys of life along this coast: "I sometimes think how wonderful will be the day when all these mountain sides are filled with habitations. . . . This place can be a paradise. It is now, for those who live it."[51] Meanwhile, Miller's appreciation of Big Sur did not prevent him from tossing his trash down to the ocean, below his house. He even found that such a chore brought him good cheer, for "as always when dumping the garbage, I had been rewarded by a breathtaking view of the coast."[52] Miller apparently felt untroubled by the incongruity of such a practice with a high regard for the scenic wonders of Big Sur. And despite his disapproval of the American lifestyle, Miller too tended to overlook, or disregard, the environmental toll of his daily activities. Like the vast majority of his contemporaries, Miller saw nature as something to be enjoyed, used, by humans. The complexities that Miller confronted in Big Sur (consciously or not) resonated throughout the state. To an alarming extent, Californians in the postwar era degraded their prized environment in the process of carving out their own piece of the good life, all the while proclaiming to the rest of the country the wonders of their state.

It is ironic that Miller found his haven in California, a hyper-American state where defense-industry jobs and the temperate climate led to astonishing growth. In 1957 California gained a new resident every 55 seconds, while suburban sprawl, automobiles and highways, commercial values, and rootlessness undergirded its mainstream culture.[53] But California's popular image was much more idyllic. Countless Americans saw along the Pacific edge a carefree, inventive, nature-loving society. The beaches, Disneyland, Hollywood, San Francisco, and the Sierra Nevada Range drew millions to the Golden State. The majority of newcomers settled in the Los Angeles Basin. From 1940 to 1955, 700,000 new homes transformed the landscape of southern California. As one local wrote in 1954 of the San Fernando Valley: "When I came here 20-odd years ago only a few thousand ranchers lived down there. Land sold for $10 an acre, and the main highway you came into Hollywood on was a country lane. Now half a million live in the valley, and more are moving in all the time. You pass an orange grove one day; the next, it's gone and men are building houses there."[54]

Generations of Americans had put stock in the promise of the American West, seeing in this relatively young society the chance to improve their opportunities and happiness. Miller went so far as to envision Big Sur as the anvil on which to forge a more meaningful and responsible American character. "The place itself is so overwhelmingly bigger, greater, than anyone could hope to make it that it engenders a humility and reverence not frequently met with in Americans," reflected Miller. "There being nothing to improve on in the surroundings, the tendency is to set about improving oneself."[55] During his time in Big Sur, Miller himself strove for personal growth in his role of father to his young children, Val and Tony, and as a neighbor and friend.[56] By his own admission, he failed multiple times to achieve these goals, but he never stopped examining himself and his behavior. Given the reputation for lewdness that Miller developed after *The Tropic of Cancer,* it is noteworthy that he was so oriented toward domesticity while living in Big Sur. A typical week for Miller included walking to the hot springs to wash diapers and building forts with his children, as well as entertaining fellow authors, painting watercolors, and periods of intense writing.

His son Tony recalls his father taking them deep into the forest behind their home to the streams where the "mottled sunlight through the canopy of redwoods" provided the backdrop for his father's stories, "wonderful stories of flying Tibetans, soaring over the chasms of the Himalayas and so forth" that derived from Miller's deep personal interest in India and Tibet.[57] Big Sur was a refuge for Miller, certainly, but it was also a place of torment when he had to admit his own shortcomings. Miller and his children's mother divorced, and after a period of trying to raise Val and Tony on his own he admitted defeat and the children went to live with their mother. Perhaps parenting would have been easier in the postwar suburbs, with playmates in close proximity, playgrounds, and television, but such a life would have been stultifying for Miller's writing career. This latter point was not lost on his children: Tony later reflected, "I know that artists basically shouldn't have children or wives. . . . It is cumbersome and drains energy from the Art. And never forget which comes first. . . . And that is the way it should be. Otherwise, you just get TV sitcoms."[58]

Miller liked to assert that self-delusion, a quality he detested in the general American population, had little place in Big Sur. Throughout *Big Sur and the Oranges of Hieronymus Bosch,* Miller made no pretense about his inability to keep his family together or even consistently put food on the table. But he maintained that Big Sur was well suited to personal growth: "Here you get it quick and get it hard. . . . The result is that you either come to grips with yourself or else you turn tail and seek some other spot in which to nourish your illusions."[59] The opportunities for individualism, peace, and self-definition in Miller's utopia were not a far cry from the alluring frontier qualities of America's past. And Miller's vision of Big Sur as encompassing the best of American culture, made available to all who wanted to participate, was a reiteration of the promise of the American frontier: a place where good land was made even better by industrious (or, according to Miller, creative) individuals. In Big Sur, so it seemed, Americans could find redemption.

WRITING FROM THE EDGE

From this imagined frontier at the edge of American society, Henry Miller joined Robinson Jeffers in critiquing the rest of the country as entangled in a political and cultural morass. Both writers achieved success during a period of intense political division and what they perceived as cultural devastation. These two writers, whose work resonated with such wide audiences, claimed insight into humanity, including war and people's proclivity toward it. Jeffers in fact believed that it was inherent in human nature to seek conflict, so much so that "life seems to [humans] meaningless without it." In the preface to his 1948 volume of poetry, *The Double Axe,* Jeffers proposed that Americans "could take a walk . . . and admire landscape: that is better than killing one's brother in war or trying to be superior to one's neighbor in time of peace." However, Jeffers went on to query: "Do I really believe that people will be content" with these peaceful alternatives? "Certainly not."[60] Jeffers may have been pessimistic, but his poetry suggested ways for humans to fight violent or selfish instincts. Several decades earlier, as a young man, Jeffers had experienced conflicting feelings of patriotic duty and responsibility for his family, and finally enlisted for World War I (only to be turned away on account of his high blood pressure). He admitted that it was the condition of humanity to engage in war, and he did not see himself as a man apart.

Jeffers did not condone this belligerent behavior, even if he understood the motivations behind it. In a poem that his publisher excised from *The Double Axe,* Jeffers accused the former President Franklin Roosevelt of blowing "on the coal-bed, and when it kindled" deliberately sabotaging "every fire-wall that even the men who denied / My hope had built."[61] Jeffers essentially charged Roosevelt with the murder of thousands of Americans. Though Jeffers had been a well-regarded poet for more than two decades, his opposition to the war and his criticism of the president virtually ended his literary career.[62] *The Double Axe* appeared in 1948, at a time when Americans generally regarded their recent actions as necessary and even laudable, and yet Jeffers asserted not only that the war was wrong but that it had set the stage for a subsequent world war and an international political climate in which

FIGURE 9. Robinson Jeffers wrote all his major works from Tor House, situated in Carmel-by-the-Sea. Jeffers built Hawk Tower, to the right, by hand. (Photo: author.)

most of the world would unify against the United States.[63] At best, Jeffers's critique of society and war was too far ahead of its time to be popular or acceptable to most Americans.

Jeffers used the Big Sur landscape to create the setting for numerous tales of misery, seeing the region's elemental forces and severe landscape as an appropriate backdrop. Given that Jeffers's career spanned two world wars and a debilitating economic depression, neither his stance as a pacifist nor his ruminations on misery are surprising. Jeffers's friends, however, did not mistake this harsh depiction of humanity as an indication of his aversion to people. Indeed, the photographer Edward Weston felt compelled to say of his friend Jeffers, "I cannot feel him misanthropic: his is the bitterness of despair over humanity he really loves."[64] In 1948, just years after the United States deployed nuclear weapons against Japan, and as the USSR developed comparable armaments, Jeffers composed "The Inquisitors," in which he imagined three hills within the Santa Lucia Mountains as giant Indians squatting and examining the sad remains of human beings after an atomic holocaust. In Big Sur, more than most places, Jeffers must have been struck by the sort of politics that could bring destruction to this kind of beauty.

Miller, too, had developed a reputation for working outside the general bounds of acceptability. The United States government banned the sale of Miller's *Tropic of Cancer,* published in France in 1934, calling the book obscene for its sexually explicit content. This book, along with the follow-up *Tropic of Capricorn,* sat on the banned-book list in the United States until 1961, when, on the grounds of free speech, the government lifted the ban (though the Citizens for Decent Literature continued to label the work obscene). This restriction at least partly explains Miller's poverty in Big Sur and his dim view of politicians. Hitler's advance in 1939 forced Miller out of his home in Paris and back to the United States, where he nevertheless soon found himself surrounded by the politics of war. Such events led Miller to consider politics a "thoroughly foul, rotten world." He not only disagreed with politicians but saw their entire enterprise as futile and harmful: "We get nowhere through politics. It debases everything."[65]

In contrast, Miller portrayed life in Big Sur as uplifting—a place where residents and even visitors could transcend many of the demoralizing realities of the mid-twentieth century. In depicting his paradise, Miller ignored (at least in his memoir) several aspects of the government and a wealthy, technologically advanced society that he presumably appreciated, including the restrictive county zoning and court ruling that perpetuated Big Sur's pastoral landscape, the state highway, and the Department of Agriculture, which protected the vast forest. Miller, and countless others, depended on the highway built and maintained by government funds allocated in Sacramento and Washington, D.C., as well as the automobiles assembled in Detroit. The vast open spaces that to Miller reflected the work of the Creator had been very much shaped and protected by the U.S. Forest Service, California State Parks, and Monterey County planners. That such manipulations were nearly invisible only underscored how invasive they had become.

In a well-worn practice, Miller and Jeffers retreated to nature to critique a society apparently out of touch with the natural world. The lure of the open land in the West appealed to Miller and Jeffers much as it had done to Americans over the previous century. Both writers were born and raised in the East and spent considerable time living in Europe but ultimately chose to make their homes in the American West, where they could find seclusion, imposing natural elements, and a culture that seemed less set in stone.[66] Like other cultural critics, Jeffers and Miller did not feel comfortable with many aspects of modern-day society, yet these two artists did not call for a return to traditionalism. Jeffers's philosophy of inhumanism and Miller's loose sexual mores were rejections of the status quo, situating them more firmly in an alternative vision of modernity. Not that these artists had found a place truly removed from the society and government they critiqued but rather that in Big Sur they found encouragement and inspiration because human forces appeared subdued by the powerful landscape. In a sense, their sentiments aligned with the developing land management in Big Sur. Monterey County officials challenged prevailing American conventions by banning billboards in order to carve out for this coast a unique space that highlighted nature not as a rejection of modernity but as a measured response to and for its more superficial qualities.

Both these highly creative, introspective artists saw Big Sur as uniquely evocative of an American predicament. Here Americans could rediscover the totality of their connection to the earth and thereby save themselves from the worst aspects of modernity; and yet their praise for Big Sur threatened its prized separation from modern-day society in an era when reverence for nature became entwined with the automobile and commercialism. Miller and Jeffers retreated to the furthest edge of the United States, where they could experience, as late as the mid-twentieth century, a region little touched by the complex civilization they critiqued. Those who read these writers' work, and many, many others, flocked to this coast for these very same reasons.

At midcentury, more than fifty years after Frederick Jackson Turner's compelling epitaph "The Significance of the Frontier in American History," Americans felt drawn to this dramatic perch above the Pacific, a place glorified for its rugged individualism and its artistic inspiration. A state touring magazine featured Big Sur in 1948, arguing "there is no place in the United States which better represents the last frontier, the most western and the most wild."[67] As a growing number of Americans happily consumed this wild stretch of the California coast, multiple levels of government smoothed their entrance into Big Sur. Property values, potential economic endeavors, even the reach of wildfires, looked significantly different in the wake of the highway. Indeed, at midcentury Big Sur was on its way to becoming as popular as Yosemite, as government-managed as any western landscape, and as expensive as a coastal metropolis. This stretch of California coast fit many categories, but more notably occupied a hybrid category of its own: an inhabited space that was nevertheless perceived as wild.

THREE

Big Sur: Utopia, U.S.A.?

Whoever settles here hopes that he will be the last invader. The
very look of the land makes one long to keep it intact—the spiritual reserve of a few bright spirits. . . . Peace and solitude! I have
had a taste of it, even here in America.

HENRY MILLER, *Big Sur and the Oranges of
Hieronymus Bosch*

ON ANY GIVEN SUMMER DAY in the 1950s one might find artists Henry
Miller and Harry Dick Ross at the bar of Nepenthe Restaurant, down from
their homes on Partington Ridge. While sitting at the bar these artists may
have discussed the latest news or the likelihood of a forest fire. Alongside these
locals sat the tourists passing through from Los Angeles or San Francisco. Out
on the terrace of the restaurant sat the families, some of whom had likely come
from their campground at Pfeiffer Big Sur State Park to treat themselves to a
restaurant meal. The waiters and waitresses might be struggling artists trying
to make ends meet or descendants of longtime Big Sur families tapping into
the rare wage labor to be found along this coast. The tourists undoubtedly
remarked on the exquisite view down the southern coast, where the cliffs and
mountains, looking as wild as they did centuries earlier, poured right into the
Pacific. Some of these visitors probably wondered whether they could secure a
second home here. Other tourists likely appreciated the extreme beauty but
would not choose to inhabit such an isolated landscape. Big Sur stood in stark
contrast to urban and suburban life, and this was precisely why so many people wanted to visit the area and why so few would call it home.

Nepenthe, like all Big Sur's businesses, relied upon outside forces to flourish. The two hundred homes (some seasonal) scattered along the coast for
thirty-some miles in each direction could not support a business such as this.
As a result, Nepenthe closed its doors during the winter, waiting for the tourists to come again in the spring. In the restaurant's early years, a costumed
Halloween party drew people from all over California and beyond to officially
close the season. One year a La Jolla couple came dressed in nothing but fig

FIGURE 10. Three generations of the Fassett family have operated Nepenthe, a popular restaurant and gathering spot opened in 1949. Nepenthe has welcomed tourists, locals, and many famed visitors, including Elizabeth Taylor and Richard Burton. Their 1965 movie, *The Sandpiper,* included a scene filmed atop the terrace. (Photo: author.)

leaves, acting the part of Adam and Eve, prompting a local paper to inquire of its readers: "Now where else in the U.S. of the 1950s would that be possible in public?" Residents, too, cultivated this avant-garde reputation. The same journalist noted that local youth arrived at Nepenthe in bare feet and proceeded to "dance wildly to folk tunes and good modern music by the light of an open fire." These revelers provided entertainment to the "gag-eyed tourists" who may have seen in them "a picture of paganism, whirling fire worshippers on a terrace several hundred feet over the Pacific."[1] Henry Miller became a regular at Nepenthe, as did many other locals who appreciated the rare social atmosphere within the lonely Sur. These locals helped provide the mystique that made Nepenthe a quintessential Big Sur destination for countless visitors.

This collaborative construction of Big Sur as unconventional and exotic, and as a haven for "a few bright spirits," was increasingly underpinned by a growing sociological reality. The 1950s would prove to be a pivotal decade for Big Sur as postwar wealth and new technologies led to commercial and residential development alongside new ways of thinking about people's relationship to the environment. In the years after the war, Big Sur's population, like California's more generally, grew in size and demographic diversity. Although Big Sur had long been a place where people worked the land, it increasingly drew more artists than ranchers; it had exponentially more tourists than residents, and it had a growing wealthy class. Newly arrived residents were awed by the place and, not surprisingly, were happy to extol the beauty of their home. This only attracted more visitors and more residents, but in certain ways Big Sur seemed large enough for all this. This seventy-five-mile coastline had space enough for many more people than the five hundred it currently supported. Indeed, a 1960 planning document envisioned a population of 3,750 residents by 1980, or a density of one person per forty acres.[2]

But Big Sur's population would not reach two thousand by the end of the twentieth century, nor is it ever likely to, as a number of factors have converged to make such a plan unpalatable to residents and to county and state officials. Big Sur at midcentury was not a pristine or untouched landscape, and neither was it static; like other coastal California areas it too was being manipulated. But it was being managed in a manner that made it more exclusive and unique. Why such events occurred earlier in Big Sur than in almost any other community around the country speaks to the presence of forward-thinking residents and county officials, as well as to the fact that as late as 1960 Big Sur still appeared largely as a tabula rasa, a blank canvas upon which to experiment with creating a space entirely distinct from the metropolitan-suburban sprawl. Within just two decades of the highway's completion, Big Sur possessed a distinctive flair that arose from the unique combination of residents and tourists who occupied a space that together they constructed as unconventional. This was no Levittown or *Leave it to Beaver* neighborhood; bomb shelters, McCarthy's red baiting, and the Cold War were of little consequence here. Big Sur increasingly existed at the figurative and literal outer edge of the United States.

BIG SUR AND THE GOLDEN STATE

In a period when much of coastal California and metropolitan areas throughout the country were transformed by the bulldozer, Big Sur became all the more notable because of its vast open spaces and minimal pavement. To most observers, Highway 1 and the small number of homes and businesses did not overwhelm this landscape and could almost be overlooked, leading some locals and outsiders alike to take part in a sort of collective amnesia. During the 1920s and '30s, when workers had blasted through the mountainsides and hurled dirt and rocks down into the sea, many decried the project as shocking and destructive. Within a short period of time, however, the highway faded into the backdrop and ceased to be such a stark reminder of people's manipulation of this landscape. On the fiftieth anniversary of Big Sur's Highway 1, the director of California's Department of Transportation boasted that the state crews had worked "within the scope of the environment" throughout the entirety of the highway's construction.[3] And when Henry Miller reflected on Big Sur in the 1950s, he boldly proclaimed it "the California that men dreamed of years ago . . . this is the face of the earth as the Creator intended it to look."[4] Miller was hardly the first, nor was he the last, to feel this way about Big Sur, for this arresting coastline masked its intensively regulated nature.

National media frequently featured this coastline that had defied California growth patterns. In the 1954 *National Geographic* article that described the agricultural-to-suburban transformation of the San Fernando Valley, in southern California, the authors recounted a very different experience in Big Sur. They waxed poetical about their drive along this stretch of Highway 1: "Mile after mile, now high, now low, we skirted bold promontories standing in echelon against the pounding sea." The article omitted any mention of people in Big Sur, a stark contrast to the treatment of Los Angeles, where "a torrent of traffic filled the 8-lane highway. Eating places, gasoline stations, motor inns, supermarkets, used car lots, and shops by the thousands lined the road solidly for miles."[5] Seven years later, another journalist entered Big Sur and noted the impact of such a landscape on the observer: "This place is a myth-maker's paradise, so vast and so varied and so beautiful that the imagination of the visitor is tempted to run wild at the sight of it."[6] The growing dichotomy between most of southern California and the Big Sur country led to the latter's popularity for those who could afford retreat from a harried life.

Despite popular accounts extolling California's glorious scenery, there were no virgin lands left in California by the mid-twentieth century, nor even in the continental United States. Protected by fire management and antidevelopment regulations, even federally designated primitive and wild areas expressed an aesthetic ideal, not a primeval ecosystem. And yet the concept of wilderness held increasing allure for Americans, even more so as the country developed and grew rapidly. An event in 1955 brought this sentiment into focus. A proposal to create the Echo Park Dam within Utah and Colorado's Dinosaur National Monument became a rallying point for wilderness advocates who feared that allowing the dam would create a dangerous precedent for all national parks and monuments. Senator Richard Neuberger of Oregon argued against the authorization of the Echo Park Dam, declaring that wilderness was priceless because it served as "the last place where Americans can see what our country must have been like as the first white men camped there." Furthermore, according to Neuberger, wilderness provided an escape from "the tensions and anxieties of the civilization we have created."[7] Proponents of conservation and wilderness had long used similar arguments, but the nuclear threat of the Cold War created a new sense of urgency for maintaining such safety valves.

Many young families in the postwar era sought safe, happy excursions into nature, where they could forget their nuclear fears.[8] Modern conditions threatened to destroy all life, and idealizing the security of the home became one way to cope with this threat.[9] Setting up a temporary home in nature, far from the vulnerable metropolitan areas, could provide families with a sense of security as they participated in the long tradition of retreating into America's wealth of striking landscapes. At the same time, the contemporary American lifestyle, with its highways, air conditioning, and its proliferation of synthetic products, enabled Americans to grow increasingly disconnected from the natural world. Many sought to counter this disconnection by pursuing increased contact with nature. California was well poised to welcome these nature tourists, with its nineteen U.S. National Forests, four U.S. National Parks, eight U.S. National Monuments and 127 California State Parks. It was, as *National Geographic* pointed out, a veritable "vacationer's dreamland."[10]

Big Sur stood as a prime example of what these postwar nature tourists sought in their excursions. Beginning in the 1950s, hopeful summer campers far outnumbered local campground sites. The most popular destination in Big Sur, Pfeiffer State Park, reported that it turned away more than a hundred campers every day in the busy season and that this first-come, first-served campground filled before 7:00 A.M.[11] Campers loved Pfeiffer's diverse amenities: an outdoor theater, a swimming pool, and facilities for hunting, fishing, riding, and hiking, in addition to its campgrounds and lodge.[12] Its stunning redwoods, its idyllic tree-and-rock-lined river, and its many miles of mountainous and forested hiking trails all held vast appeal. State Park officials noted that every year's tourist count (including day visitors) substantially exceeded the prior year's, with close to four hundred thousand visitors in 1955. Of this number, nearly one hundred thousand were campers—a "testimony," according to a local paper, "of the new national pastime."[13] The vast majority traveled in the summer, when roughly three thousand cars a day ventured through Big Sur.[14]

Big Sur's scenic reputation was firmly established in the early postwar era, but its appeal began to extend beyond its landscape as local advertising helped paint Big Sur as a culturally rich destination as well. Beginning in the 1950s, a resident named Emil White (one of Henry Miller's closest friends) published an annual tourist guide to Big Sur. The guide read like a booster's account of the coast, describing Big Sur not only as a place where "all five senses come alive and alert" but as "a stretch of coast line of such virginal beauty and magnificence as cannot be found anywhere else. Its scenery is as varied as its inhabitants, its topography, and its climate."[15] White intended to explain the special features of the land and its people to those visitors who might otherwise miss the essence of Big Sur. Unlike national publications that mostly featured the coast's beauty or its tourist amenities, the *Big Sur Guide* incorporated the region's human community as if it was one more powerful natural element.

As a locally created publication, the *Big Sur Guide* was ostensibly an authority on the region, yet it was very much a subjective interpretation of the area and its community. White described the residents as a combination of the descendants of the "sturdy" pioneers who still worked the land and at times eschewed their cars for travel on horseback, the wealthy investors who owned "thousands of acres they have never set foot on," retired folk drawn by the temperate climate, and finally artists and craftsmen "who are always to be found where there is beauty and peace and cheap housing." In all, White described these few hundred year-round residents as "friendly, warmhearted, intelligent" painters, writers, ranchers, and woodsmen "all living compatibly and having in common a deep love for the place itself."[16] This was a rather uncomplicated version of the story, but, significantly, it was how many residents liked to view their community. White cast the residents (himself included) as a benign force on the land, enjoying the good life to be found along this coast. As a publication designed to entice tourists, the *Big Sur Guide* framed the community as intriguing, mostly respectable, and largely passive in their appreciation of the landscape. The *Big Sur Guide* read like a locally approved version of Big Sur, shaping how outsiders viewed the region and its inhabitants.

Another regional publication, the *Carmel Pacific Spectator,* echoed much of White's assessment of Big Sur, though with a slightly more critical tone. "Big Sur 1955," an article appearing in the *Carmel Pacific Spectator Journal,* described the Big Sur community as a "potpourri" of pioneering descendants, "well-to-do retired people, "some Sunday ranchers, a great many creative people and even more hangers-on, drifters and first-rate third-raters in the arts and crafts." The article introduced a new subset of the Big Sur community that would, in the next decade and a half, become almost synonymous with this coast. This Carmel journal asserted that Big Sur attracted "a number of outright bums, mostly the charming kind, who admit freely that they are out for the free, easy and uninhibited life they can still live at Big Sur."[17] Many of these were aspiring artists who followed in Jeffers's and Miller's footsteps, seeing in Big Sur an ideal place to live without steady income. Others arrived expressly in hopes of joining Miller's sex cult, for they assumed that this author of *Tropic of Cancer* must be connected to one.[18] In 1947 *Harper's Magazine* included a feature, entitled "The New Cult of Sex and Anarchy," that painted Miller as the bard of the bohemian literary scene and Big Sur as the new Paris, the destination for the "modern, the new, the truly creative" writers of the day.[19] As locals and outsiders alike forged a reputation for Big Sur, it took on the air of a place dominated more by its creative folk than by its wealthy landowners and investors, a community worthy of this place because of its demonstrated reflective and aesthetic inclinations. The idea of Big Sur as a place of inspiration and alternative thinking and living was coming more and more into focus by the late 1950s.

THE BEATNIKS AND BIG SUR

Some of the drifters who arrived in Big Sur were part of the Beat Generation—middle-class American youth who joined the emerging counterculture to challenge and criticize what they deemed a commercialized, conformist, and belligerent postwar culture.[20] "Beatniks," as they came to be called, consciously chose to dress, speak, and act in ways that would make a mainstream American uncomfortable. Allen Ginsberg, a leading poet in the San Francisco Beat community, bluntly asserted in his poem "America" that the country should "Go fuck yourself with your atom bomb." Ginsberg, along with Jack Kerouac and other writers, found San Francisco a conducive environment for developing a subculture of dissent. They strove for authenticity in their writing and, ostensibly, in their lives, finding in this Pacific-facing city and forward-oriented state the influences and inspiration they desired. Eastern philosophy, African American music, and Native American traditions all shaped Beat writing and were all a part of the San Francisco Bay Area's history.[21]

Tapping into the city's long bohemian literary tradition, Lawrence Ferlinghetti, a literary scholar and Navy veteran turned pacifist, opened City Lights Bookstore in 1953 in San Francisco's North Beach. His bookstore specialized in paperback books, making Beat writers available to a wide audience, and it even included a publishing adjunct to further spread Beat ideas. But it was more than the books alone that mattered; Ferlinghetti made the bookstore itself a force in the bohemian movement. A former student of the Sorbonne in Paris, Ferlinghetti fashioned the City Lights Bookstore as a literary salon of sorts. The store's affordable books, its encouragement to browse, and its author readings all cultivated a community of like-minded folk. Ginsberg and Kerouac were regulars, and Ferlinghetti published both these Beat icons. Ferlinghetti's decision to put in print Ginsberg's *Howl and Other Poems* in 1956 led to his arrest and trial on obscenity charges. To those not already acquainted with San Francisco's bohemian writers, the obscenity trial brought national coverage of this literary scene. Ferlinghetti received support from nine literary expert witnesses who all argued that "Howl" had literary merit by reason of the author's legitimate desire to present the world as he saw it, with language that was appropriate to his message. In the end, Judge Clayton Horn asserted that he did not "believe that 'Howl' is without redeeming social importance" and dismissed the charge of obscenity.[22]

Throughout the 1950s the media depicted the average "square" American and the Beats as occupying opposite ends of the social spectrum.[23] While leading radically different lifestyles, these two groups shared at least a few commonalities. They both feared the destructive power of the atom bomb; they both sought authenticity in their travels, and both saw in Big Sur's landscape and its culture something they could not find in America's cities and suburbs, where the sublime had little place.[24] Here in Big Sur, it appeared, was authentic nature, not shaped by post–World War II technology and wealth.[25] And so Big Sur attracted both groups and provided them a chance to express their desires and practice leisure.

In the summer of 1960, three years after his *On the Road* became the defining text for the Beat Generation, Jack Kerouac took leave again of his Long Island home. Tired of his fame, he traveled to San Francisco; there he planned to sneak into City Lights to make contact with Ferlinghetti, who had offered Kerouac the use of his Big Sur cabin. But Kerouac's penchant for drinking overcame his reluctance to be noticed, and he instead stumbled drunkenly into the bookstore, where he received a hero's welcome. His subsequent revelry meant that he missed his ride to the Big Sur coast, but he caught the bus and a taxi and finally hiked to the sought-after cabin. Kerouac was looking for isolation, to "be alone and undisturbed for six weeks just chopping wood, drawing water, writing, sleeping, hiking, etc. etc."[26] Big Sur was to be a place of escape and rejuvenation for this "king of the beatniks." For several weeks Kerouac felt he had found something akin to peace along this rugged coast, but his meditation next to the Pacific prompted a sudden perception of human cravenness and the pettiness of human endeavors that caused him to seek comfort in his familiar habits. Back in San Francisco he found companionship with old friends, who upon returning to the cabin with him enabled or at least did nothing to prevent his alcoholic stupors. Kerouac drank so heavily while in Big Sur that he experienced delirium tremens. Remarkably, he managed to produce a memoir of his manic summer. His 1962 *Big Sur* related the summer's events and shared with his wide audience an appealing image of life lived between the Beat nucleus in San Francisco and a Big Sur outpost.

Kerouac's memoir also laid bare the tension between the families visiting Big Sur and Beats like himself. Kerouac recorded his impressions of an effort at hitchhiking to Monterey in which thousands of cars (the majority family station wagons) passed by without giving him so much as a second glance. Kerouac imagined that these mainstream, middle-class Americans saw him in his tattered boots and rucksack as "the very apotheosical [*sic*] opposite of their every vacation dream." Nor did observing this endless stream of conformity (from the cars to the occupants, their belongings, and their behavior) bring any comfort or happiness to Kerouac, who categorized each family member into a distinct but equally contemptuous category. He considered the husbands as under the control of their wives while looking "witless and idiot," the women perpetually "sneering," and the "millions of children" simply spoiled and obnoxious.[27]

Such families likely sought a contrast to their suburban environment and may have spent little time seeking deeper spiritual revelation while in Big Sur. But plenty of people did arrive in pursuit of "finding themselves," and they did so because Big Sur had a history of alternative thinkers. Perhaps this tradition is what had drawn Kerouac to this coast. While sojourning in Big Sur, Kerouac sought out an opportunity to meet Henry Miller, whom the Beat admired; but Kerouac's carousing cost him his chance. On the day when they were to meet, Kerouac got lost in revelry, finally contacting Miller at an hour that Miller considered too late for an old man like himself. Though Miller saw value in Kerouac's writing, the elder writer likely would have seen in the Beat an artist who was struggling to come to terms with himself along this raw, forbidding coastline.[28]

More than anyone or anything else, Henry Miller drew this alternative culture to Big Sur. Miller himself admitted that he sometimes felt he had "disturbed the wonderful, intimate harmony that existed in Big Sur" by virtue of his presence there.[29] Throughout *Big Sur and the Oranges of Hieronymus Bosch*, Miller recounts numerous visitors, from those able to pay for his watercolors to the down-and-out writer wanting advice from this sage. Ten years after moving to Big Sur, Miller remarked that he had seen at least a hundred artists of all types try to establish themselves along the coast, many of whom, no doubt, had expressly sought out Miller's advice and guidance. Increasingly, at least to outsiders, these artists came to represent the essence of Big Sur. By the 1960s the side road to Partington Ridge, where Miller lived, displayed the hand-lettered sign CAUTION: CHILDREN, DOGS, HORSES, POETS, ARTISTS, AND FLOWERS AT PLAY.[30] These artists were proud of their hideaway colony, and such a sign not only fulfilled their need to proclaim their purpose in Big Sur but stood to please many a tourist who suspected that just such frivolity and creative productivity flourished along this coast. Increasingly, Big Sur's allure was the supposedly authentic experience that it offered inhabitants and visitors alike.

NURTURING A COMMUNITY

While the artists provided an aura of glamour and creativity, in the late-1940s descendants of Big Sur's homesteading families solidified their own close-knit group in the Big Sur Grange. Grangers initially met in one another's homes until they could afford to build a meeting hall, a place that would become an important gathering spot for the community. Two "sisters" of the Grange composed a song about this establishment situated along the Big Sur River. These lifelong residents highlighted their vision of Big Sur as a striking but hospitable landscape. Set to the tune "Church in the Wildwood" the lyrics are:[31]

> There's a Grange in the hills by the ocean; no lovelier place in the vale; no spot is so dear to us Grangers, as the Big Sur Grange in the dale.
> O come to the Grange in the valley, to the Grange with Big Sur running by; we have chosen to labor and frolic, and keep our ideals high.
> O how sweet on a clear Friday evening to trek to the Grange o'er the hill; to list to the voices of neighbors, and work out our problems with a will.
> From the Grange in the valley by the ocean, as the years swiftly come and go past, we hope our endeavors enduring will bear fruits of joy to the last.

These residents of Big Sur had their own way of expressing the beauty that they saw around them. They saw themselves as belonging in and to this landscape, a community of neighbors undertaking similar endeavors, not merely a scattering of individuals pursuing unrelated goals. Their words and images suggest how they viewed this coastline as a place suited to a community. Unlike outsiders with their depictions of the landscape that revealed feelings

FIGURE 11. The Big Sur Grange Hall, built in 1950, is nestled among stately redwoods midway along the Big Sur coast. It has long hosted community gatherings, ranging from the entertaining Potluck Revues to regional planning meetings, and for several years housed the Big Sur Health Center. (Photo: author.)

of awe and sometimes intimidation, these locals appeared secure and comfortable in Big Sur. This is not to say that they did not feel inspired by the beauty around them, for they sought to keep their "ideals high" in this beloved home that provided room for both work and pleasure. But they painted a more pastoral image of Big Sur than anyone else had. The Grange provided its members a platform from which to address community concerns, land management being of particular importance to this agricultural and ranching-oriented organization.

In a sense, a move toward the Grange seemed dated by the 1940s, when the highway meant that tourism, not agriculture and ranching, would define the local economy. Across the state, however, the Grange was increasing its membership in the 1940s. Partly this must have been linked to the rapid growth of California's population as a whole, but there were specific postwar issues that brought together rural residents. In the midst of a ravaged global economy, American farmers feared economic loss unless the government provided subsidies to support farming if prices fell below the cost of production. The California Grange cited this as one of its key concerns in 1945, as well as the rising taxes that accompanied rising property values in this popular state.[32] Those still working the land in Big Sur after the coming of the highway were well aware of this challenge.

In addition to membership in an organization pushing for government-supported agriculture, Grangers benefited from the Grange's low-cost fire insurance.[33] Those living in Big Sur understood the hazards of fire and the speed with which flames consumed the vegetation of these steep hillsides. The Grange provided practical benefits for locals while enabling them to hold on to a tradition of husbandry that had defined residence in Big Sur for more than a century. These were members of the early Big Sur families, and their collaboration enabled this important element of the community to persist in the midst of changing dynamics.

Though these longtime residents could have used the Grange to set themselves apart from the rest of the population and used their longevity as an excuse, the Grangers chose inclusiveness instead. One of the most notable traditions of Big Sur became the annual Grange potluck revue, an event that highlighted the talents and creativity of Big Sur's residents. Of course the old families were represented in this Grange affair, but so were Eve Miller and the author Lillian Bos Ross, among others. What began as a fundraiser in 1952 to pay the mortgage for the Grange Hall quickly became a popular theatrical evening for residents and outsiders alike. The revues received coverage in the newspapers of the Monterey Peninsula and enticed so many people south for the show that it became necessary to hold three nights of the revue by 1956.[34] In 1957 the Grange newsletter asked residents to attend either the Friday or the Sunday night performance, leaving Saturday night for the "out-of-towners."[35]

These revues created a sense of community for a very diverse set of inhabitants living in a vast and sparsely populated region. From the perspective of a Carmel journalist, the Grange and its activities could be credited with bringing the Big Sur residents together again as a community.[36] Henry Miller took a different stance on this point. In *Big Sur and the Orange of Hieronymus Bosch*, he argued that locals possessed "no common purpose, no common effort." Despite "remarkable neighborliness," Miller detected "no community spirit" as late as 1957.[37] This was a subjective evaluation, of course, and Miller himself had already identified the cause of what would soon become a serious community effort. Writing in 1948, speculating on the future of California in general, and of Big Sur in particular, Miller had queried: "Already it is rumored that Southern California can absorb no further influx of population because of the restricted water supply. Northern California steadily diminishes in population. Here is the golden mean: how long will it hold out against the invader?"[38]

Other residents also looked on in concern, some noting disturbing evidence of Big Sur's developing residential character. A 1948 *Monterey Peninsula*

Herald article entitled "'Down-the-Coast' Residents Worry over Building Boom: Big Sur Area Is Called 'Crowded'" highlighted the concern over twelve new homes built in the previous year. Changes such as "more partying and visiting" and the "dramatic architecture" of many newer residences prompted a debate among residents over how to manage matters such as residential and commercial zoning. As the article illustrated, "The Big Sur folks are worried over the future. They fear the hot dog stand, the subdivision and the neon-lighted cocktail bar as the rabbit fears the hawk."[39] This concern could help explain the popularity of the Grange, as at least some residents wished to counter modern development with a commitment to traditional pursuits.

The newspaper article noted what the author believed to be a division among residents, with those residents "lucky enough to acquire a spot of land for purposes of 'getting away from it all'" standing against the type of development that would endanger their peace and solitude, whereas "old timers and others who make a living on the spot welcome developments which mean more work and a bigger income."[40] This was an oversimplified distinction; at least a few members of the pioneer families consistently argued for preservation, and some newcomers were more interested in shaping Big Sur to meet their desires than in protecting the land. In fact, in 1937 one "wealthy Californian" had attempted to turn Partington Landing (which had once been used as a site for shipping timber) into a yacht harbor and to build a stone home on the rocky outcropping above. He did not move forward, as he could not secure the sale of the property.[41] A decade later another wealthy resident, Lathrop Brown, a former United States congressman, built a residence on either side of the highway, with a private elevator to reach his beachfront home.[42] New technologies converged with postwar wealth to allow development that challenged Big Sur's tradition of isolation and carefree living.

Opinions varied on whether Big Sur was indeed becoming crowded, but no one could deny that it was becoming more expensive to buy land along this coastline. As early as the 1950s real-estate prices in Big Sur kept out the average-income resident. In the somewhat rare event that land went on the market, one acre cost at least $1,000, and to clear the land and prep for building cost an additional $2,500.[43] The old homesteads often sold as large estates, such as the Circle-M Ranch, which in 1944 sold for $100,000—the largest real-estate transaction in central California in several years.[44] A decade later, a portion of Rancho El Sur sold for $900,000.[45] Increasingly, Big Sur attracted the very wealthy, who could afford second homes in this desirable location, or who could simply retire here. The actors Orson Welles and Kim Novak and the radio commentator John Nesbitt all sought a slice of this California good life. Novak told *LIFE Magazine* in 1964, "Maybe I should be in Hollywood studying acting, but here I have my Utopia!"[46] As Nicholas Roosevelt commented in 1956, Big Sur was home to more *Who's Who* celebrities than any other community its size.[47] Roosevelt himself was one such notable resident, as was also the longtime Sierra Club board member (later honorary president) William Colby, the architect Nathaniel Owings, the winner of the Nobel Peace Prize (and Nobel-winning chemist) Linus Pauling, the railroad heir Samuel Hopkins, the authors Henry Miller and Lillian Bos Ross, and undoubtedly others as well who attained anonymity. Such residents helped drive up real-estate prices, but they also introduced an important housing option for low-income community members. Many second-home owners employed local caretakers to watch after their property. These jobs provided much-needed housing and work for those not able to buy their own homes in Big Sur, including longtime community members who perpetually sought new ways to support themselves along this economically marginal coastline.

By the late 1950s Big Sur had a national reputation rooted in its scenic grandeur, its wide-open spaces, and its unique residents. New, even elegant private residences were unlikely to alter this reputation, but there were those within and outside Big Sur who, with a note of ambivalence, took each development into account. In 1959 a *LIFE Magazine* article entitled "Rugged, Romantic, World Apart" argued: "Some of Big Sur's primitive quality is disappearing. New homes are more elaborate. More and more tourists are poking their way into the canyons. But the fierce and the solitary beauty still remains."[48] A native resident reinforced the idea that Big Sur was too grand to be altered so easily; as late as 1965 Esther Ewoldsen reflected: "This country hasn't changed much since I was a girl." But, she continued, "Our biggest concern is keeping it as it is and to resist the blandishments of the developers. In my grandfather's time land was valued only for what it would provide in the way of food for cattle. Now, things are different."[49]

That so many newcomers could live in Big Sur without relying upon agricultural efforts indicated how much the economy of Big Sur changed in the decades after the highway's completion.[50] This change did not necessarily mean Big Sur would lose its rural flavor. Instead, natives and new residents began to discuss the distinctive qualities of Big Sur and how to maintain its wildness, even as they inhabited the space. Someone like Ewoldsen, who was a young adult when the highway arrived, had witnessed vast changes to her native home and yet never lost the conviction that this land was wild and should remain so. Many newcomers happily embraced a similar attitude, for they had sought a connection to the land in moving to Big Sur. At a time when most Americans praised development as progress, most residents of Big Sur defined a very different ideal for their landscape.

A common local response to the externally driven changes of the postwar era was to trust that natural limitations would protect against Big Sur's over-development. Almost as if Emil White was reassuring himself and, ironically, those whom he wanted to attract to Big Sur, his *Big Sur Guide* asserted as late as 1960 that Big Sur was protected from excessive development:[51]

> Many there are who fear that the increased traffic may also bring the real estate men whose signs usually proclaim the doom of all such paradises. This possibility, however, is still quite remote. There is hardly any land for sale. The water, though plentiful in the canyons, is not so easily piped to where it may be needed. And except for the summer months, there are but few opportunities for employment or for business.

White echoed Miller's assertion that this formidable landscape sought to remain uninhabited.[52] It would require a good deal of ingenuity to make the land accommodating, but Californians were proving that such natural constraints to growth could be overcome with substantial manipulation of water supplies and technology designed for hillside development.[53] Nevertheless, White's points were true for the time being: even during a statewide economic boom, few residents could count on earning an income derived from labor in Big Sur. Ranching and agriculture became increasingly challenging as property taxes rose to reflect the scenic and recreational value of the land; the only industry in Big Sur, tourism, operated for less than half the year; and unlike in the ubiquitous suburbs, one could not easily commute from Big Sur to a metropolitan center for work. It followed, then, that artists and the wealthy settled in Big Sur, as well as those who thought of Big Sur as the best place to live without employment. Such residents were predisposed to envisioning their home as an escape from the mundane and would feel compelled to protect their haven. They would find that government officials, too, sought to treat this landscape as exceptional.

MAINTAINING A PLACE APART

For its part, the U.S. Forest Service helped preserve Big Sur's scenery by restricting all but recreational development within Los Padres National

Forest, acknowledging the "continued growing importance" of this pastime.[54] Californians expressed an enormous interest in recreation in the postwar era. The state recorded the highest number of recreational national-forest visits in the nation, with 12,471,700 in 1958 alone.[55] In response, nearly every national forest in California grew in size in the 1950s, including the Monterey District of Los Padres. In 1956 the supervisor of Los Padres sought land acquisition in the Pacific Valley region of Big Sur with the intent to devote it "to the maximum extent for public recreation."[56] Foresters also prioritized additional wilderness lands through the acquisition of submarginal farmland from nearby homesteads and land exchanges to reduce inholdings, including swapping lands with the California Department of Parks and Recreation. The forest used its holdings along the western part of Highway 1 to exchange with landowners alongside the Ventana Primitive Area in order to provide continuity throughout the forest for such things as watershed protection and fire control.[57]

Across the country, national forests served a range of purposes, including meeting the skyrocketing demands for outdoor recreation and for lumber in the postwar era. The U.S. Forest Service accommodated the timber industry through "intensive management" designed to increase commercial timber production.[58] This was evident in northern California, where the forest service allowed an annual cut of 170 million board feet in Klamath National Forest, and 101 million board feet in Lassen National Forest during the 1950s.[59] Federal policy for Big Sur, meanwhile, further established the idea that this area would exist as a place apart from the profit-oriented forests throughout the West. With the forest service allowing no annual cut in the Los Padres National Forest, trees could be felled for control of insects and disease and for fire salvage only.[60]

In contrast to most forests in California, recreation was officially the "primary consideration" for Los Padres, However, the U.S. Forest Service chose not to pursue recreation on a large scale in Big Sur, as it did in other districts. During the 1940s the forest service planned to develop a portion of the San Gorgonio Primitive Area of the San Bernardino National Forest, east of Los Angeles. The plan included a road, a parking lot, and a ski lift, all designed to appeal to the growing population of southern California. But the forest service soon learned that many of the residents whom they sought to attract actually placed a higher value on the undisturbed forest than on the opportunity for intensive recreation. Local residents and other Americans "deluged" the forest service with letters arguing against the resort proposal, leading the agency to note that "These people have demonstrated that wilderness is a real value to them—merely by its existence."[61] An increasing number of Americans were so concerned by the forest service's commitment to timber and other commercial operations during and after the war that these policies helped intensify the push for a strong wilderness policy that would serve as a counterbalance to the ever-increasing commercial and residential development.

Such protection would seem all the more necessary in the wake of the 1956 Federal-Aid Highway Act, designed by President Eisenhower to improve and facilitate national transportation and provide for national defense by creating thousands of miles of highways throughout the country. These new conduits enabled a vast expansion of suburbia and the overall development of once-rural areas. California state legislators responded to Eisenhower's initiative with a highway plan that would link recreational areas throughout the state with new and expanded roads. In Sacramento, plans were under way to turn the highway through Big Sur into a four-lane freeway that would not only increase the capacity of this road but would make it a more efficient thoroughfare between the northern and southern portions of the state. The proposal also called for straightening the highway for travel at faster speeds, ignoring the lay of the land. Big Sur residents feared that the expansion of the highway would ruin the peacefulness and desirability of this coastline. Nicholas Roosevelt called the proposal "bureaucratic vandalism."[62] Local State Senator Fred Farr of Carmel immediately opposed the plan, and, despite his own zeal for development, even Governor Edmund "Pat" Brown supported the idea of protecting "scenic Highway 1 from crude exploitation."[63] Residents agreed, and they began to discuss ways to prohibit the expansion of the highway.[64]

This community effort would be the beginning of a decades-long local endeavor to preserve Big Sur's tradition of low-density residential and commercial development. A local Big Sur Advisory Committee formed to create several recommendations to facilitate travel along the highway in hopes of deterring the freeway. Nicholas Roosevelt, Harry Dick Ross, and Samuel Hopkins all worked on the plan. All were established and respected members of the community, but none was a native of Big Sur. The committee's recommendations called for widening mile-long portions of the highway to three lanes for safer passing opportunities, paving turnouts for slow-moving automobiles and more and bigger scenic turnouts, as well as better signage for speed limits, dangerous curves, slide areas, and turnouts.[65] It is difficult to know whether the residents who worked on this plan truly wanted these changes, or (more likely) saw such a proposal as the lesser of two evils when compared to a state freeway. In 1959, with the support of Governor Brown, Senator Farr led the vote to strike down the plan to incorporate Highway 1 into the state's freeway plan.

Residents of Big Sur understood that this was only a temporary reprieve and that nothing prevented Big Sur from being targeted in a future round of highway planning. As the highway debates unfolded in California, the U.S. Congress responded to the nationwide growth of outdoor enthusiasts by commissioning a comprehensive study of the nation's outdoor recreation resources.[66] This endeavor was premised on the idea that outdoor recreation and contact with nature "are not only a vital part of the American tradition of life and freedom, but are essential elements of a rich and well balanced life of our people for the future."[67] The report declared that the coastal stretch from Carmel to San Simeon "warrants preservation of its outstanding aesthetic qualities" and urged protection against encroaching development through zoning or even outright acquisition.[68] The report did not specify whether the county, state, or federal government should assume authority for this protection. But the point was clear: Big Sur held national importance, and residents should expect their home to be treated accordingly: that is, not as a community of five hundred but as a national playground and preserve. Concurrently, national and local news features echoed Robinson Jeffers's and Henry Miller's praise for Big Sur's beauty as well as its creative, nonconforming inhabitants and gave weight to the idea that this coast was both a great scenic *and* residential landscape. The task of maintaining these seemingly incompatible features in the face of Big Sur's growing popularity would fall to residents and county officials, who had never entertained the notion that this coast would be anything less.

FOUR

Open Space at Continent's End

I think that one may contribute (ever so slightly) to the beauty
of things by making one's own life and environment beautiful,
so far as one's power reaches.

ROBINSON JEFFERS

NINETEEN SIXTY-TWO PROVED to be a watershed year for the Big Sur
coast. Robinson Jeffers, the area's poet laureate, the first person to give Big
Sur a name around the nation and the world, passed away that year at the age
of seventy-five, twelve years after his beloved wife, Una, succumbed to cancer.
Around this same time, Henry Miller decided to leave his home in Big Sur
for southern California. After the United States lifted its ban on such risqué
novels as his *Tropic of Cancer,* Miller experienced newfound wealth at the age
of seventy-one. He left his mountain retreat for a home in Pacific Palisades,
still calling himself a patriot of Big Sur.[1] Miller's name would continue to be
linked to Big Sur in the collective imagination, especially after his friend
Emil White established the Henry Miller Library in a picturesque grove on
the eastern side of Highway 1. To this day, the library serves as a cultural
resource center for local residents and visitors, and a place to celebrate Miller
and the landscape that inspired him. That landscape drew the photographer
Ansel Adams to settle in Carmel Highlands in 1962, into a home with an
arresting view down the Big Sur coastline. Adams's appreciation of the Big
Sur country, and his admiration for Robinson Jeffers, would draw him into
discussions about Big Sur's future.

This artists' haven also attracted Jack Kerouac, whose 1962 memoir *Big Sur*
further enhanced the area's reputation as a favorable environment for nonconformists. Big Sur's backcountry and unconventional community beckoned to
the counterculture, which is partly why Michael Murphy and Richard Price
established a new sort of retreat celebrating human potential on the grounds
of the former Slate's Hot Springs. The Esalen Institute, launched in 1962,
sought to provide a space for the exploration and realization of such potential.

Throughout the decade the institute attracted a diverse group of celebrities. Musicians such as George Harrison, Paul Simon, Art Garfunkel, Ali Akbar Kahn, Joan Baez, and Bob Dylan, as well as the philosopher Alan Watts, the author Aldous Huxley, the architect and innovator Buckminster Fuller, the LSD advocate Timothy Leary, and Ansel Adams all offered their talents to the young institute and in doing so enhanced the mystique of Big Sur.

As noteworthy as each of these episodes was to Big Sur's community and its image, arguably the most important event for the region since the building of the highway was the adoption in 1962 of the Monterey County Coast Master Plan (CMP) to guide the future of the Big Sur coast. A locally driven and county-sponsored plan, the CMP severely restricted commercial and residential development in Big Sur during a statewide and national economic boom. It was no coincidence that this plan emerged in the same year that California surpassed New York as the most populous state. Significantly, however, Big Sur still appeared a near-wild space to most people in 1962. Indeed, electricity had reached the majority of homes only in the previous decade. Nevertheless, Big Sur joined in the open-space movement gaining popularity in rapidly expanding metropolitan areas.

In the early 1950s, concerned residents in the Santa Monica Mountains joined forces to resist additional hillside development by establishing a minimum lot size. They cited open space, increased fire and flooding hazards, and pollution as motivators for their activism.[2] In the San Francisco Bay Area, the earliest open-space measures addressed proposals to develop the Marin Headlands and to fill in portions of the Bay. Open-space proponents in the Bay Area stressed the environmental concerns of rapid development and looked for measures that would protect open space and recreational opportunities.[3] Advances such as these in two of the nation's fastest-growing metropolises made sense. But Big Sur, a place popularly perceived as nothing but open space, with a population density of one person per 250 acres, did not seem an obvious candidate for open-space planning.[4] Locals' decisions to protect against overdevelopment, to regulate design and landscaping, and to put in place measures to prevent erosion and unwise road building were premised on the idea that high-density development, common along other parts of the California coast, would cause chaos in Big Sur.[5]

City planners in the early postwar era set aside parks and green space in California's towns and cities, but to a much greater extent paved over agricultural land, created infill along bay fronts, and zoned for housing atop hillsides and other formerly undeveloped land. Although some people praised and encouraged this growth and the accompanying jobs and lifestyle, others began to wonder if these were good developments for the state. Earl Warren, the former governor of California serving as Chief Justice of the U.S. Supreme Court, remarked on California's new status in 1962: "I would not celebrate with fireworks or dancing in the streets. Mere numbers do not mean happiness."[6] The population boom of the preceding two decades challenged the state's and the counties' ability to provide adequate schools for the growing baby boomers, as well as to build and maintain necessary roadways and social services for the sprawling suburbs, or what some were beginning to call "slurbs."[7]

This growth was felt most acutely within California's coastal counties, where the bulk of new residents settled. With each passing year, coastal development expanded in size and ambition. Developers envisioned expansive residential spreads along the bluffs, hills, and coastal plains, regardless of topographical challenges, water limitations, or risks of erosion or fire.[8] Many county-planning departments approved large-scale development plans, with prospective residents eagerly awaiting their new slice of the California good life. This era was defined by hope, idealism, and a general belief that something new was unfolding in California, where social ills seemed minor and economic rewards great—not just for the fortunate few but for a broad and expanding middle class whose members could hope to own a home and a car or two and to take vacations in the state's diverse landscapes.[9]

Big Sur's striking landscape and welcoming campgrounds appealed to mainstream middle-class residents of the state, but this coastline also held meaning for people across the cultural divide of the 1960s. Indeed, Big Sur attracted countless members of the counterculture seeking to return to the land in the 1960s and into the 1970s, as well as vacationers in search of a scenic California destination. Nineteen-sixties tourism in Big Sur was characterized by families crowding the state-park picnic and camping areas, New Age visitors, ministers, teachers, psychologists, and social workers all exploring the mind-expanding and therapy-based retreats at Esalen Institute, and hippies flowing into the national forest and private ranchlands. The first two groups respected traditional tourist etiquette, whereas the latter group asserted that the land belonged to all, free of charge. They may have been attracted by Miller's and Kerouac's books, but hippies claimed deeper roots to this coastline with their admiration of Robinson Jeffers and his powerful verse. Big Sur attracted and satisfied a range of people as it sought to balance conservation with the demands of those who wanted to live in and visit this remarkable landscape.

Residents and county planners charted a distinct course for Big Sur in this era by nurturing cultural richness and remarkable scenery. Its dual appeal set it apart from the scenic state and national parks as well as such popular destinations as Disneyland. In protecting and promoting both the community and the land, Big Sur's version of improvement stood in contrast to almost any other place in California as population pressure drove rapid, even haphazard development ahead of long-term planning. Big Sur's approach did not come without a social cost, however. By simultaneously accommodating different types of visitors and implementing open-space measures to restrict the number of residents and commercial establishments, locals and the county presented the appearance of a democratic landscape open and available to all while in fact creating an increasingly exclusive residential landscape. This coastline served as a reminder of what California looked like in its early days and forecasted besides the elitist thrust that would come to define late-twentieth-century California.

BIG SUR'S CULTURAL SIGNIFICANCE

Perhaps nothing better illustrates the confluence of wealth and cultural meaning in California than the Esalen Institute, a retreat that would become a permanent fixture along the Big Sur coast and in American spirituality. The Esalen Institute, the New Age spiritual mecca of the 1960s, was first imagined by the Stanford graduates Michael Murphy and Richard (Dick) Price while living in San Francisco's East West house, an integral-yoga ashram. Murphy and Price hoped to create a new space for exploring the meeting of spirituality and psychology. The institute was forward-thinking and future-oriented, yet premised on the early Romantic tradition of retreating to nature in order to assess, and ideally improve, the human condition. Big Sur's well-preserved and accessible landscape made it an ideal location for this retreat, established on the grounds of Murphy's grandfather's property and the former Slate's Hot Springs. As Murphy noted, "I don't think it would have worked as well if we started Esalen in, say, New Jersey. The sheer magnitude of the land and the power of the elements are what shape lives in Big Sur."[10] Within its first decade of operation, the Esalen Institute drew widespread attention for its seminars on Eastern and Western philosophies, the human relationship to nature, and humanistic psychology. Its methods and ideas were discussed, analyzed, and at times emulated in universities, churches, and even on *The Tonight Show with Johnny Carson*.[11] Perched above the Pacific,

FIGURE 12. Drawing from the beauty and inspiration of its surroundings, the Esalen Institute in 1962 began hosting workshops to explore human potential on the family land of co-founder Michael Murphy. Esalen continues to offer seminars and workshops designed to enrich the individual and transform society. (Photo: author.)

at the continent's brink, Esalen stood at the cutting edge of the alternative spirituality gaining ground throughout the United States.

Esalen's seminars and publications purposefully avoided prioritizing one single religious dogma while spreading an essential message—that everyone possesses a spark of divinity, which when cultivated or harnessed can set a person on a path to realizing his or her full, human potential. Esalen thrived because it tapped into the experimentation that Californians embraced in this era. Indeed, Esalen helped lead this venture. The institute has been credited with no less than popularizing spiritual options and democratizing the religious marketplace.[12] Abraham Maslow, one of the founders of humanistic psychology, went so far as to call Esalen "potentially the most important educational institution in the world."[13] By 1971 Esalen's popularity spawned ninety-some offshoots in California and around the country. That such an institution evolved in Big Sur spoke to just how much Americans felt a spiritual stirring at this great meeting place of mountain and ocean.

Throughout the 1960s, an Esalen-seminar participant might find himself or herself soaking in a hot-spring tub with Allen Ginsberg, who was holding forth on spirituality and religion.[14] A visitor came to expect the far-out experience at Esalen, for it was rife with sexual experimentation, psychedelic drugs, and New Age pursuits.[15] Esalen also became an iconic tourist destination, where mostly well-to-do visitors could revel in California's seemingly never-ending potential. Those who patronized Esalen, like the beatniks, were by and large members of the middle to upper classes who were disenchanted with mainstream American culture, institutions, and politics, and had the funds to travel to Big Sur in search of meaning in a complex and often troubled society.

A contemporary California development, the second-home community of The Sea Ranch, established in 1963 along the Sonoma coast, sought to cater to a similar demographic. Lawrence Halprin, the San Francisco Bay Area landscape architect in charge of The Sea Ranch design, strove to create a space where these part-time residents could find community with other residents who valued a beautiful landscape. He envisioned attracting a particular population of homeowners—"the professor, the off-beat lawyer, other professionals who are not able to find what they want in the ordinary house tract or within the social set."[16] Like Esalen, The Sea Ranch was designed to make people feel that their presence in this place put them in harmony with nature.[17] In fact, it is entirely possible that aspects of Big Sur influenced The Sea Ranch design, as Halprin first served as a consultant to the Monterey County–sponsored draft master plan for Big Sur before beginning work along the Sonoma coast.[18]

Jeffers, Miller, Kerouac, and now Esalen brought attention to Big Sur as a place of nonconformity, a place where one could reject the materialism defining much of American culture and contemplate human nature while communing with the land. This would be the hallmark of the Big Sur experience: a connection to something intangible, but not what one encountered in a national park, which downplayed if not deliberately erased traces of human communities. Big Sur was a place to revel in nature and to explore human potential, a proving ground for artists and a space for locals and county planners to experiment with land management. Esalen was an innovation at the

FIGURE 13. The famed hot-spring-fed baths of Esalen first became a tourist destination as Slate's Hot Springs in the late nineteenth century. Before Esalen opened in 1962, Henry Miller was known to head down from his Partington Ridge home to enjoy a bath and use the flow of hot water to wash his children's diapers. (Photo: lewisha1990: https://www.flickr.com/photos/bluemandy/2809769895/in/photostream/.)

forefront of California developments, as was the Coast Master Plan. They both were inspired by the uniqueness of Big Sur.

THE FIRST MOVE

How and why did Big Sur residents and Monterey County develop the Coast Master Plan, an initiative that William Whyte, the leader of the open-space movement, highlighted as the signal example of open-space planning in the nation?[19] The motivations were many, but chief among them was to protect Big Sur's status quo. Locals and county officials feared that the burgeoning California population could prompt the establishment of a state or national recreational area along this coast or lead to considerable residential and commercial development.[20] By the late 1950s the state spoke of widening Highway 1 through Big Sur to increase the road's carrying capacity and efficiency.

President Eisenhower's 1956 Federal-Aid Highway Act expanded the nation's road system, transforming many areas that had previously provided visual and physical relief from residential, urban, or industrial landscapes. The emerging open-space movement sought to protect some of these undeveloped spaces, not just for aesthetic and recreational purposes but also as flood insurance and to protect farmland. This was especially important in California, where approximately sixty thousand agricultural acres fell under developers' blades each year throughout the 1950s and 1960s.[21]

Together, Monterey County officials and local residents took proactive measures to prevent overdevelopment in Big Sur. Beginning in early 1956, the county appointed a Coast Highway Master Plan Committee to create a long-range general plan for Big Sur to address the anticipated demand for development along this scenic coastline.[22] This committee solicited feedback and ideas from the Big Sur community, and in 1960 the county commissioned the architectural and planning firm Skidmore, Owings & Merrill (SOM) to draft a master plan for the Big Sur coastal area. Nathaniel Owings, a partner in the firm, and his wife, Margaret Wentworth Owings, had recently moved to Big Sur, where they built a stunning home, Wildbird, on a perch above the Pacific. For professional and personal reasons, Owings enthusiastically engaged with the novel task of crafting a county-led slow-growth plan for a world-renowned, largely undeveloped coastline.

Owings brought a distinct perspective to this planning project, for his professional background was undeniably urban and corporate, yet he embraced a remote, rural coastline as his home. For over two decades Owings had overseen large-scale architectural projects in which he gained a reputation for knowing how to get things done. He had much to show for his efforts: his firm had earned more top design awards from the American Institute of Architects than any other, and by the late 1950s SOM had established itself as the corporate architectural firm par excellence, having designed buildings for Heinz, Ford, and PepsiCo, among others. Owings's stature earned him an appointment from President Kennedy in 1962 to sit on the planning board for the redesign of Pennsylvania Avenue. One of the other board members, Patrick Moynihan, described Owings as "ebullient, competent, and devoted—and also a randy rogue, and a bandit and a buccaneer. His great ability is to get other people to do good work."[23] Owings exhibited the same sort of determination in his planning for Big Sur.

Owings set about creating a shared vision for Big Sur among fellow residents and found considerable support from Nicholas Roosevelt, who had moved from New York to Big Sur in 1946. Roosevelt served as the chairman of the advisory committee for the drafting of the SOM master plan and as editor for the report itself. One of them a leading architect and the other a member of one of the country's most prominent families, Owings and Roosevelt could have chosen any number of desirable locations for their homes, but they saw something unique in Big Sur and intended to do their part in maintaining the undeveloped character of this stretch of coast. Like many new arrivals to California, these two residents were well educated and looking to enjoy the advantages of living along a beautiful coastline. Their familiarity with the more developed eastern seaboard convinced them to employ their professional skills and political know-how to coordinate a viable plan for the preservation of their adoptive home. Owings and Roosevelt tapped into the nascent open-space movement gaining momentum throughout the country while also crafting a laudable model for this national movement.

Though postwar development pressure was at its most extreme in California, overdevelopment became a nationwide concern that prompted federal commissions and legislation. In early 1961, U.S. Senator Harrison Williams of New Jersey introduced a bill, "Urban Sprawl and Open Space," with the goal of providing financial support to states and counties for creating open spaces in urban and suburban areas. Williams noted that his was the first bill of its kind in Congress, driven by "a growing awareness—if not alarm—over the chaotic and enormously wasteful sprawl of our urban areas, and the consequent disappearance of our lovely old farms and pastures, quiet streams and wooded hills under the onrushing blade of the bulldozer." Senator Williams argued that preserving open space would not only help improve cities and towns and their environs but would also lessen the impact on the "limited and sometimes nonreplaceable [sic] human and material resources at a period in history when we need them most to meet our grave international and defense responsibilities."[24] In the tradition of utilitarian conservation, preserving open space was needed in order to fulfill multiple human benefits. Initiated at the peak of the Cold War, Senator Williams's bill proposed saving resources to save America.

Municipal officials, housing authorities, the American Recreation Society, and the American Institute of Architects (AIA) all endorsed Williams's bill. Each group recognized the pressing need to regulate urban and suburban sprawl while setting aside open space that would meet recreation and conservation priorities. The American Recreation Society asked: "With more income—more need for the wholesome recreation use of leisure—more citizens than ever before—will they have parks and open space resources for their recreation? Or will their only heritage in the future be the concrete slum, cloverleaf, and congestion?"[25] As the suburbs encroached upon open land and pushed it further and further from urban centers, those who worried about recreational space became increasingly concerned about this all-too-common pattern. It would take very deliberate preservation of such open space in order to keep it from slipping into developers' hands.

In line with the American Recreation Society, the AIA believed that all levels of government were obligated to meet the recreational needs of these urban and suburban Americans "within a reasonable distance of their homes. If we don't, the great wilderness and forest preserves that we treasure now will become the park slums of the future." The AIA reasoned that open space was more than a physical necessity; it provided "a certain psychic relief" that "cannot be underestimated. It gives us visual relief from the tangled, jarring, and often monotonous sight of urban development, and a sense of orientation and community identity."[26] The wide-open spaces of the West had once provided an escape valve for an industrializing nation; in the second half of the twentieth century open space provided the equivalent escape for a suburbanizing nation.

The AIA, having long contemplated how to provide order and purpose to the unbridled residential growth of the past two decades, provided an in-depth explanation of their multiple reasons for supporting Williams's bill. The organization highlighted the practical municipal concerns addressed by conservation, noting "the relationship of land to problems of water supply, and flood and water pollution control. . . . We are spending considerable sums for drainage and to avoid the costly destruction of floods, yet we have failed to realize that to adequately control floods we must have open land." With an ever-increasing amount of pavement and concrete applied to the earth, the land was losing its ability to continue basic precipitation cycles, while also accumulating excessive pollutants. Scientists could now weigh in on the importance of checking development and provide expert testimony on the need for open space. Aside from the eastern seaboard, the AIA argued that "most of our other urban areas in the United States still have an opportunity to be the masters of their future development and not the victims of it."[27] Such thinking was certainly optimistic, for it would require an immediate concerted effort by city and county planning departments to guide the residential and commercial development in the country's rapidly expanding metropolitan areas.

Williams's bill became part of the 1961 Housing Act, which encompassed open-space provisions and urban beautification and improvement. Once in office, President Lyndon Johnson furthered momentum for these measures, seeing in these natural landscapes and resources something important for the well-being of American society. Johnson's Great Society included antipollution efforts, highway-beautification measures, and additions to wildlife refuges, national parks, and wilderness areas.[28] He presided over the passage of the Wilderness Act of 1964, thereby securing more than nine million acres of public land as areas "untrammeled by man, where man himself is a visitor who does not remain."[29] Johnson and his administration emphasized the importance of timely attention to the degradation of the country's natural resources. Secretary of the Interior Stewart Udall published *The Quiet Crisis* in 1963 to encourage action:[30]

> There is an unmistakable note of urgency in the quiet crisis of American cities. We must act decisively—and soon—if we are to assert the people's right to clean air and water, to open space, to well-designed urban areas, to mental and physical health. In every part of the nation we need men and women who will fight *for* man-made masterpieces and against senseless squalor and urban decay.

Udall respected the architectural and planning goals of the open-space movement and hoped to encourage this trend throughout the country. His book included praise for Monterey County's forward planning.[31] Udall, Whyte, Senator Williams, and other advocates of open space received support from Americans who sensed the same urgency, who saw open space as they had once seen the frontier—as a bulwark of democracy and freedom—and were alarmed by its growing scarcity in proximity to their urban and suburban homes.

Nathaniel Owings, being an experienced architect with national scope, understood the appeal and the viability of the open-space movement. In Big Sur he sought to preserve not only the beauty of the land but a way of life for the people who were connected to this dramatic coast. Owings chose Big Sur as his home ostensibly because it provided a counterbalance to the hectic pace and settings of his professional life. In his autobiography Owings described Big Sur as more than just a beautiful spot but "a changer of one's point of view."[32] He believed nature's scale in Big Sur made humans think about their place in the scheme of things differently from what they would in almost any other place in the country. While working on the master plan Owings asserted: "There's a lot of loose talk about this being the most beautiful spot in the world. Well, it is."[33] His experience taught him what could become of a place that lacked appropriate planning, and Owings and his wife both feared what would happen to Big Sur as its population grew and the state considered modernizing it with a four-lane highway. Margaret spent years on the State Parks Board, founded the Save the Sea Otters program in Monterey, and was instrumental in pressing the state to remove the bounty on the mountain lion. An artist and activist, Margaret was very much at home in Big Sur.[34] The couple felt passionately that Big Sur needed wise future planning and therefore set out to drive development regulations for Big Sur.

In Big Sur, Nat (as he was called) tackled the interplay between the preservation and the property aspects of the open-space movement. Owings left little doubt that he wanted Highway 1 through Big Sur to be the finest scenic highway in the United States.[35] He knew that aesthetically Big Sur could not be improved; now it needed the proper protection to ensure that property owners (whether private individuals, the state, or the federal government) did not mar this beauty by overdeveloping the coast. Owings described his job as "primarily to protect the status quo of the highway," understanding that a two-lane highway had minimal capacity for increased residential and commercial development.[36] Supporting the planning efforts were county officials and Big Sur landowners and residents who agreed to serve on advisory committees. Residents, county planners, and Owings all strove to conform not to statewide growth patterns but to the local tradition of low-density development. The devil would be in the plan's details.

A MASTER PLAN PROPOSAL

The primary objective of the SOM plan was twofold: to preserve the scenic beauty of Big Sur through securing open space and to do so "without imposing unjustifiable restrictions on present or future property owners."[37] While the plan acknowledged the importance of private-property rights, it called for zoning that limited choices for property owners, especially those along the coastal side of the highway. If open space was to be secured for the enjoyment of the many, it would have to come at the expense of the few; but the SOM plan proposed to temper these sacrifices with a unique credit for an open-space system. Under such a plan, an owner of coastal frontage property could earn credits to build extra houses on the eastern side of the highway in exchange for dedicating the coastal property as permanent open space. For the well-being of the land, and to protect the open vistas, the SOM plan recommended density controls of one home per ten acres on the west side of the highway, and one home per twenty acres to the east of the highway.[38] With scenic value of primary importance, the plan recommended "the land adjacent to the road should be kept as free as possible from residential or commercial developments."[39] The SOM plan would likely have met with immediate resistance had Owings been the first to propose such restricted property rights, but for decades Monterey County had carefully zoned the coast for minimal development.[40] Big Sur, therefore, was suited to testing open-space measures.

The SOM plan focused primarily on residential planning, but it necessarily grappled with the implications of Big Sur's popularity. In response to the increasing "hordes" demanding additional development, the SOM plan recommended the expansion of Pfeiffer Big Sur State Park.[41] The plan outlined adding five thousand acres to this popular park in order to offer sufficient camping spots and day-visitor parking spaces.[42] With the frame of reference of a resident, Owings believed that an expansion of Pfeiffer was a better option than creating several smaller parks along the coast, what he called "fragmenting." He saw this latter option as detrimental to residents, for it would place new parks in the "foot of many of our canyons," thereby creating congestion and intruding upon the privacy of the residents tucked away in these canyons.[43] The SOM plan cited the seasonal nature of tourism to assert that the demand for additional lodging and eating establishments was "relatively restricted," and it applied the open-space principles for any new commercial developments: one hotel unit per acre.[44] Such measured commercial growth was in keeping with the restricted residential growth. Neither form of land use was to dominate Big Sur. The SOM plan consistently outlined a slow-growth, conservation-oriented framework that protected the value of the current properties.

In concert with the SOM proposal, California State Senator Fred Farr of Carmel introduced a bill in the state legislature to create a new category of roads called "scenic highways," based on Monterey County's management of Highway 1. For the past decade, even before entering the state senate, Farr had collaborated with other concerned citizens such as Nat Owings and Ansel Adams on state conservation issues as part of a group called the Foundation for Environmental Design.[45] Farr used his accumulated knowledge to argue successfully for the need to protect the byways along the state's growing highway system from billboards and other clutter. These roads were to serve "as leisurely travel lanes for vacationists [sic] and tourists, rather than as arterials dedicated to speed."[46] Highway 1 through Big Sur would become the state's first official scenic highway in 1966, designated as a thoroughfare meant to remain a two-lane road. Farr's legislation brought him into dialogue with national figures. Lady Bird Johnson invited Farr to join her on a tour of scenic roads and historic places, during which he used this opportunity to highlight the measures for protecting Highway 1. He was soon asked to sit on the President's Task Force on Natural Beauty, alongside Secretary Udall and William Whyte.[47] Farr was part of a select group of people who wished to temper the era's transportation boom, and he understood conservation's appeal for many of his constituents and fellow legislators. Protecting Big Sur's highway as a two-lane road would preserve the status quo for residents, while the twisting scenic road would become an increasingly popular destination in itself.

In 1960 SOM submitted its master-plan proposal to the Monterey County Board of Supervisors. County planners then began a review process that encompassed public opinion. Roughly a third of Big Sur's residents attended the multiple town-hall meetings to weigh in on the plan's details. Despite offering general support for the spirit of the plan, residents raised points of contention. The most immediate protest against the SOM plan concerned the expansion of Pfeiffer Big Sur State Park. Most residents argued that the expansion was out of character with the plan's professed purpose of limiting traffic and development of the area. Hans Ewoldsen, Esther (née) Pfeiffer's husband, an ecologist and a longtime resident, believed that increasing the park's size and camping sites would "crowd the park and defeat" the plan's purpose.[48] It came as no surprise, furthermore, that many residents opposed the condemnation of the Sycamore Canyon homes falling under the proposed boundaries of the park's expansion.[49] This single proposal, to expand the state park, created a constant roadblock at planning meetings. The Monterey County Board of Supervisors made a point of not intervening in the discussion about the expansion of Pfeiffer Big Sur State Park, with the chairman of the board insisting that this was a dispute between the residents of Big Sur and the state. Community resistance to the park-expansion proposal succeeded, and SOM planners scrapped the idea.[50] Two decades earlier the state had asked residents to donate or sell parts of their land for the coming highway, and most residents had agreed, seeing the potential benefits as outweighing the costs of ceding land to such a project. Even though the purpose of the highway was largely recreational in nature, it offered as much to locals as it did to tourists. In the early 1960s residents resisted the proposed alterations of Pfeiffer Big Sur State Park, viewing this as a tourist-oriented project likely to come at the expense of the community and landowners.

The other common criticism that locals leveled against the master-plan proposal was the discrepancy between the proposed zoning in the northern and southern portions of Big Sur. The plan included a five-acre minimum for new residential construction in the northern half of Big Sur, and ten acres in the southern half. Open-space planning was often like a balance sheet: development could proceed, but nearby areas would be kept underdeveloped to counter this growth. The SOM plan argued that the southern portion of Big Sur was the natural choice for a greater commitment to open space, for this half of Big Sur, situated farther from the Monterey Peninsula, supported only a third of the area's population. Some of the residents in this portion of the coast had long considered their lands as distinct from the larger region called Big Sur. Chafing against government planning in general and zoning in particular, John Harlan, a descendant of a pioneering family in Lucia, wrote to the Monterey County Board of Supervisors in response to the plan: "No official of Monterey County would allow an official of some other county to dictate to him what he should do to solve his problems. Therefore, why should I allow someone in Big Sur or Carmel or further to dictate to me in the Lucia area what to do with my land?" Drawing a distinction between a native like himself and county planners and key figures like Owings, Harlan stated unequivocally: "I am opposed to selfish non-indigenous persons entering into a master plan which does not concern them."[51]

Harlan stood opposed to more than regulation of private property. His concern extended to the social and economic impact of Big Sur's increasing popularity. Harlan echoed the opponents of wilderness policies who disagreed with the premise that preservation and recreation took priority over using the land to produce income. Harlan's family had worked the land in Big Sur for nearly a century and had rented or sold portions of their land when expedient. His family had helped maintain the striking landscape that tourists admired along this coastal stretch. Harlan's lifelong perspective on land management in Big Sur was guided by the requirements of making a living from the land and its resources, and the government was likely only to hamper his personal success. This backcountry mindset among some Big Sur pioneer families was being overshadowed by those like Owings who wished to harness the regulatory power of the state to secure specific local benefits of open space and high property values.

Certain other landowners also believed that the proposed master plan's zoning stood in the way of the particular benefits that they hoped to enjoy from the land. Clarence Petersen, a former motel owner in Big Sur who now lived on the Monterey Peninsula, owned twenty acres that he had hoped to develop into homes for "ten happy families," but under the new restrictions he could sell or build on only one or two sites. Petersen led a meeting in which he spoke against the need for such a preservation-minded plan. "The ocean can't be changed and the mountains cannot be greatly changed. There is nothing that is going to mar it. Without homes, the rocks are uninteresting." Petersen thought primarily of the residents in this land-management equation, arguing that locals should fight any plan "that is going to deprive anyone of anything." Petersen organized a committee of residents to resist the restrictive policies of the proposed master plan and even argued in favor of a four-lane highway.[52]

Petersen found support from residents who framed this fight as a matter of economics and personal freedoms. The Kobuses of Big Sur expressed their opposition to limited property rights in a letter to the board: "Scenery is alright [sic], although it sure isn't putting any beans in *our* pot, but it seems to us that human rights should come first, and of these, the property owner's rights to the use of his property are among the most sacrosanct."[53] Katherine and John Brazil, owners of the large Brazil Ranch, also chafed against preservation-oriented planning that required high-minimum-acre building sites, seeing such measures as opposed to American freedoms.[54] Another resident pleaded with the board not to be "too blind to civil rights in the name of conservation and beauty."[55]

To those who opposed the master plan's proposed zoning, it was particularly galling that the general public's welfare seemed to matter more than the landowners' right to develop their property. Instead of seeing open-space preservation, these landowners interpreted the zoning as passing the land to a public that did not pay for the benefit. As one resident noted in a letter to the board: "If so much land is to be channeled off to 'the public' then the public should pay for it by buying it and supporting it with taxes, not by having a few landowners sign over their rights and still be burdened with taxes on it through the years."[56] Such residents as these did not feel compelled to restrict property rights in the name of the public good. They saw the large national forest and state-park lands as sufficient for visitors and believed that bounding off additional land from development could potentially lead to a time when the property owners of Big Sur were an insignificant presence in an area of vast open space. Clarence Petersen, the Kobuses, and John Harlan all appealed to private-property interests at a time when a small but growing sector of society articulated a challenge to the authority of a powerful government.[57]

Although open to the criticism of economic self-interest, residents like Petersen and the Kobuses could turn the tables to argue a similar point against Owings.[58] In the midst of the debate over the proposed master plan, one resident of Big Sur voiced his resentment for the "damn newcomer in the fancy glass house" telling everyone else what to do.[59] Implicit in this attack was the idea that first Owings got what he wanted with his property and was now looking to protect his investment. Years later, Margaret Owings admitted the validity of this argument, though she explained that she and her husband hadn't realized when they built their home just how much they would come to believe in the need for Big Sur's preservation.[60] It is impossible to know the Owings' inner convictions, but it is clear that in preserving vast open spaces they also protected the quality of life that they had sought along this coast.

Nat Owings believed that county zoning measures provided the best protection for Big Sur, and he found support from the editorial board of the *Monterey Peninsula Herald*. The editors acknowledged that the proposed master plan required private-property owners to forgo certain rights to their land but downplayed the significance of these restrictions alongside the perceived benefit: "No dream of this sort involving many ownerships can be carried out entirely by voluntary relinquishment of traditional property rights, but requires the support of the law." The editors appreciated the plan's high standard for preservation, based on the strength of the law to preserve as a people what "otherwise men as individuals may destroy." The *Herald* gave ample coverage to the master plan, publishing in August 1961 an entire eight-page spread detailing and promoting the plan, and dedicating that section of the paper to the "Big Sur country" and to "a dream."[61] In a region known for its beauty, Big Sur was a source of pride for many locals.

The paper also provided space for Nicholas Roosevelt, an ardent supporter of conservation, to publish his opinion on land use. In this forum Roosevelt drew from personal experience to stress how opposition to preservation was merely a part of the "standard procedure" when substituting planned development for unrestricted individual initiative. He shared his cousin's opinion on this matter, telling of a camping trip with Theodore in 1913 when the former president explained how each of his executive proposals for a national park or monument met opposition from some group—most often the lumbermen or cattle associations. Nicholas asserted that opposition always occurred, usually driven by reasons of self-interest, and that such considerations should not stand in the way of environmental planning.[62] By the late 1960s, after twenty years of living in Big Sur, Roosevelt penned *Conservation: Now or Never* to argue against unchecked commercial and residential development. Neither Roosevelt nor Owings conceded that his vision for Big Sur, like his opponents', derived from financial and aesthetic self-interest, although with a different conviction regarding the proper relationship between people and nature.

As the master plan moved forward, a number of Big Sur residents understood that its focus on large lot sizes would very likely turn this region into an area where only the wealthy could afford to buy property. This was a goal in other open-space initiatives and an expected outcome of minimum-lot-size planning.[63] At a meeting held in the Grange Hall, one landowner criticized the zoning of Big Sur as for "the rich man only." Chairman Hudson of the Monterey County Board of Supervisors responded that it was actually the wealthy property owners along the coast who had to make the "biggest sacrifices since they will be asked to give up development rights for the sake of maintaining the natural character of the coastline." When pushed, however, the chairman also had to admit that this new zoning would keep the "small man" from building in Big Sur, which he called the "harsh answer" of economics.[64] In an era of extraordinary statewide growth, the proposed master plan appeared based on the idea that Big Sur's best hope for remaining undeveloped was to entrust it to those who could afford the privilege of residing along this coast.

Owings knew the power of planning and understood that someone's vision would trump the rights of others. In his memoir Owings reflected on how "planning imposes uneven restraints, requiring disciplines and sacrifices from some, granting unearned benefits to others, and therefore involves battles of sorts." Owings also understood the visceral dislike for government regulations in Big Sur and realized that those on either side of the planning debate "were resolved on only one point: they wanted to be left alone, free to do each as they saw fit." This individualistic ethic, long common in Big Sur, challenged a cooperative stance toward land management. According to Owings, it was the middle-income landowners who enabled the plan to pass, because they recognized the danger of an unregulated landscape, whereas it was the lower-income and very wealthy residents who generally distrusted any level of government control and saw it as their "God-given American heritage" to do with their land as they pleased.[65]

Generally speaking, the proposed master plan presented financial drawbacks for each class of residents. The largest landowners could not hope to aggressively subdivide, and small landowners were also circumscribed in their options to develop their lands. Those who had not yet entered the ranks of homeownership in Big Sur saw the plan as narrowing their chance of ever affording such a scarce and increasingly expensive commodity. Letters to the board from members of the Dani and Plaskett families reflected this concern, as they did not yet own land and believed the proposed ten-acre minimum for the southern coast a prohibitively high requirement.[66] And so while there were supporters and opponents on both ends of the economic spectrum, it does make sense, as Owings suggested, that the middle-income sector would be most in favor of the plan. It was this middle group that saw the plan as containing roughly equal personal benefits and sacrifices. Although they might be losing some ability to develop their land, they would gain protection against overdevelopment, which would hurt not only their property values but the exceptional quality of Big Sur's scenery. Reaction to the master-plan proposal was not merely a factor of wealth or landholdings, however; support for the plan cut across income levels.

In the end, the majority of residents agreed that some form of planning was necessary in order to maintain Big Sur's distinction. Several respected native residents approved of and endorsed the master plan's restrictive regulations. Bill Post and Esther Ewoldsen, both of whose families homesteaded in Big Sur in the nineteenth century, argued in favor of the plan.[67] Esther and her husband, Hans, had long been known as conservationists and viewed the plan as appropriately protective while also in the economic interest of landowners.[68] Esther Ewoldsen explained that she knew "that things don't stand still." She recognized that "development will come in," but she hoped to see this development controlled in such a way that Big Sur did not take on the character of the Santa Cruz Mountains—an area, she believed, that was once as beautiful as Big Sur but now was compromised by billboards and houses built too close to the highway.[69] Bill Post also worried that Big Sur could go the way of once-beautiful spots that had become overdeveloped. Post sincerely hoped that Big Sur would avoid resembling Carmel Valley, which was "getting to be just another town up there."[70] Post stated he would like the master plan if it could help retain the character of the landscape and the community without any further commercialization. Post was a large landowner and no doubt could have profited from additional commercial development. Support for the plan from these particular residents contradicted the idea that only relative newcomers with environmentalist sensibilities wanted to see growth restrictions for Big Sur. Post and Ewoldsen's convictions grew out of their lifelong ties to the land in Big Sur, leading them to argue that developers' money in their pockets was worth less than the land's beauty. They were following in their parents' footsteps, hoping to retain the special character that they attached to Big Sur.

One well-known resident of the southern coast of Big Sur, an area in which the United States Forest Service owned over three-quarters of the land, also became an advocate for government preservation efforts. Mabel Plaskett moved in 1898 at the age of two to the Mill Creek area, where her father bought a sawmill.[71] Mabel lived the rest of her life along this coast and served as a columnist for the *King City Rustler* and its supplement, *The Land*. In her column, Plaskett shared the history of the southern coast as well as her views about land management. She argued in 1961 that the USFS's ownership of her family's original homestead "clear to the coast" was "right and proper as this insures the preservation of this recreational area for the people's use."[72] She seemed delighted, even, with the transfer that would protect the land from harvests and would instead allow it to serve as a domain for wildlife: "We leave Mill Creek to the silence, broken only by the cry of the Blue Jay, the scurrying feet of the tree squirrels, the occasional scream of a mountain lion or perhaps the shadow of a California Condor as it ventures out from its last stand in the craggy fastness of Cone Peak." Plaskett never lost her awe of Big Sur and had an unusually nonproprietary view of the land. Instead of pining for the freedom of a less-regulated era, Plaskett reflected happily on recent developments, exclaiming: "What vast changes in the last fifty years!"[73]

Two other pillars (but not natives) of the community also weighed in with their support for the master plan. Esther's husband, Hans Ewoldsen, viewed the plan in terms of what it would mean for the future of Big Sur. He appreciated the restrictions and planned development, which served "the welfare of the community as a whole." Because the plan intended to preserve the undeveloped character of Big Sur, he saw it as essentially benefiting even more "the people who will come after us."[74] The beloved resident Harry Dick Ross stated that he believed the master plan was "the only way the charm and wonderful beauty of this area can be preserved." Two business owners approved of the plan, understanding that Big Sur's appeal depended on its open vistas. Bill Fasset, the owner of Nepenthe, called the plan brilliant for its flexible approach in trying to restrict development while still allowing a "safety valve" for those instances in which "development seems right or necessary."[75] Esalen's Michael Murphy shared with the board how often visitors from Los Angeles and San Francisco praised what they found in Big Sur and lamented that such preservation was no longer possible in their metropolitan homes: "If something had only been done where we live!"[76]

In addition to these well-known residents, other noteworthy supporters of the proposed plan included residents whose opinions often reflected not only their love for Big Sur but a background that had given them a broader perspective on the price of preservation and development. Samuel Hopkins, a descendant of Mark Hopkins, of the Big Four of the Southern Pacific Railroad, moved with his family to Big Sur in 1945. The Hopkins family became respected members of the community, known among neighbors for their kindness and generosity.[77] In a 1961 letter to the board, Hopkins wrote of Big Sur: "In the long run, its beauty is its greatest asset, and the interests of landowners will be most protected if this scenic quality can be preserved." Hopkins's study of the plan's details led him to assert "that its acreage limitations are fair and designed to meet the needs of both tourists and residents, by protecting the natural beauty of the coast and preventing too much unsightly development."[78] Like Post and Ewoldsen in their comparisons, Hopkins's wife cited Lake Tahoe as an example of what can happen without planned development, essentially seeing this Sierra destination as "one big hot dog stand."[79]

Another prominent resident of Big Sur, William Colby of the Sierra Club (who had helped convince the Pfeiffers to sell a portion of their land to the state in the early 1930s), lent his support to the plan. At the age of 86 Colby drew upon his decades of involvement with the Sierra Club, dating back to the battle for the Hetch Hetchy Valley, and his tenure as chairman of the California State Parks Commission, to argue in favor of the focus on establishing a scenic highway in Big Sur that protected the current road configuration. Colby explained his experience of fighting with highway planners to conserve California parkland. The problem, as Colby saw it, was that highway engineers "want to build roads wide and run them straight and they don't care what's in the way." He implored the board to act: "For over 60 years my life has been largely devoted to the preservation of the unrivalled scenery of the West and I am urging you now to do what you can to keep what is generally recognized as the finest coastal area in the world from being unnecessarily destroyed and mutilated."[80] Of all the stunning landscapes Colby had encountered in his long career, it was Big Sur that commanded his loyalty. His praise for Big Sur's beauty was all the more meaningful for his broad perspective, and the Monterey County Board of Supervisors likely looked upon Colby's opinion as the nearest to expert that they were going to find in Big Sur.

Though not a resident of Big Sur, Ansel Adams weighed in on the proposed master plan just after moving to Monterey County. He praised the plan for considering the effects of development upon the land and people's quality of life. He argued that the plan was "good for the community and its enterprise," because its zoning regulations would "elevate property value more than any uncoordinated development can possibly assure." Ultimately, Adams supported the plan out of his conviction that it served "the citizens of the State and the Nation."[81] Adams and Colby approached Big Sur's preservation not in isolation but within the context of careers that sought to preserve wild spaces. They appreciated the role that Big Sur played in the larger landscape of the West; the frontier had closed long ago, but here at the continent's end it was still possible to experience the wide open spaces that evoked the promise attached to America's great natural wealth.

As the master plan was refined in the first years of the 1960s, and as California's phenomenal growth in these same years captivated the nation, the popular media reflected on the state's meaning to the nation. George Leonard, the editor of *LOOK Magazine* and Murphy and Price's soon-to-be unofficial partner in Esalen, published a feature issue on California in September 1962. In it, Leonard argued that this fastest-growing state in the nation was a "window into the future." Like the respected California author Wallace Stegner, who saw California as "the national culture, at its most energetic end," Leonard held up the state as a leader of what was, and of what was to come for the nation. The journalist posited that in California people were leaving behind the traditions of the past to create a new society based on the "original American dream" of opportunity and self-definition.[82] Leonard, like Adams, understood the aesthetic and cultural significance of California, and, as they gravitated closer to a particular stretch of its coastline, the special significance of Big Sur.

Situated in the midst of this land-management debate was a group of residents who formed a property-owners' association to call attention to the needs and desires of landowners. The Coast Property Owners Association of Big Sur (CPOA) formed in 1962 "to protect and defend the rural and residential character, and to preserve the natural and esthetic beauty of the Big Sur coast; to provide for the health, safety, and welfare of the Big Sur Community."[83] As residents of an area where a majority of the land was public property, CPOA members wanted to ensure that any land-management plan considered people as at least as important as natural resources. Members feared that individual rights were lost when the government promoted such policies as using government oversight to protect Big Sur for the enjoyment of the many. They used the CPOA to voice concerns of the property owners throughout the master-plan proceedings. Ultimately, Petersen, Owings, and all property owners in Big Sur were privileged residents of the state beginning to see their interests through distinct lenses. The range of their opinions toward property rights and preservation revealed a tension that would show itself more prominently in the coming decades.[84]

By early 1962 the master-plan proposal had been tweaked and altered by the county's Planning Department to better suit the demands of local residents. Ultimately, the Monterey County Coast Master Plan (CMP), approved by the Board of Supervisors in November 1962, was a weaker version of SOM's proposal. With smaller minimum-acre requirements (in the northern half of Big Sur a minimum of two and one-half acres per home to the west of the highway, and a minimum of five acres in the southern half) and no transfer-development-credit system, the master plan did not meet Owings's original vision for Big Sur.[85] Nevertheless, Owings emphasized that preservation could still be achieved if the minimum-acreage requirements stayed in effect. The features of the original plan that did make it into the final draft were the "meander line," which required architectural control for all buildings visible from the highway, as well as the commitment to cluster new residential or commercial development so as to maximize open space. The Coast Master Plan also supported the use of scenic easements to preserve open space and protect watersheds.[86] The final plan indicated that the county intended to use the CMP not to prohibit development but as a guide for creating a local and flexible preservation plan that catered to tourist demands and local priorities.[87]

By protecting the two-lane highway, by limiting residential growth in the areas most visible from this highway, by imposing a certain setback requirement for all buildings, and by monitoring signage, the Coast Master Plan essentially created a blueprint for a recreation area that also managed to contain a community. With annual visitors numbering in the hundreds of thousands, it would have been impossible for the six hundred residents of Big Sur to convince county planners to consider only local concerns. What is remarkable, however, is that such a small community, in such a prime destination, managed to secure a master plan that stated as its primary intent preserving the beauty of the Big Sur Coast "without imposing unjustifiable restrictions on current and future property owners."[88] Monterey County was firmly committed to maintaining both habitation and county governance for Big Sur. The CMP was a unique plan for a revered scenic destination.

Owings asserted that the CMP's careful zoning would enable Big Sur to "become a major economic asset of the county."[89] If this was to be the case, it would be indirect, for the commercial and residential development regulations in the Coast Master Plan in no way maximized county revenue. Severe restrictions on homes and lodging establishments meant that the county would not reap property and hotel taxes to the extent that it could under denser development. Perhaps the Monterey County Board of Supervisors felt that increased visitation to the peninsula would offset this lost revenue, but the county must be credited with putting the welfare of Big Sur's natural resources at least on a par with development opportunities. And they did so well ahead of any state mandate. Big Sur and Monterey County pioneered a new preservation approach somewhere between national parks and land trusts, not just with the guidance of experts like Colby and Owings but through a negotiation between local government and its constituents. In an era of increasingly centralized power, the CMP asserted the rights of a community to define its future, even when that community oversaw a national treasure.

The Monterey County Coast Master Plan received approbation from Stewart Udall and William Whyte, national figures who ultimately shaped planning for other places of beauty. In *The Quiet Crisis* Interior Secretary Udall highlighted Monterey County's use of the scenic easement to protect against development along the coast as a successful response to the resource challenges of the postwar era. He noted this as a creative approach to conservation, one that he recommended other areas should follow because of its cost efficiency. In Big Sur, as Udall explained, many residents voluntarily gave up their right to development and in return gained tax benefits for placing some of their property in scenic easements.[90] William Whyte, the nation's leader of the open-space movement, visited Big Sur during the revision of the Coast Master Plan and reprinted the CMP in his federal report on open space. Whyte conjectured that Big Sur's example could prove beneficial to other areas looking to restrict development. He also called Monterey County's Coast Master Plan the earliest plan of its kind for establishing slow growth and scenic protection.[91] As a place long recognized for its extraordinary beauty, Big Sur, by the early 1960s, possessed a national reputation for sophisticated land management, bolstered by its long history of local zoning ordinances.[92]

BIG SUR IN ITS CONTEMPORARY CONTEXT

How did Big Sur compare with other popular California destinations in this era? Point Reyes and Lake Tahoe provide helpful counterpoints as places of comparable beauty with similar natural and demographic features. The U.S. Department of the Interior's 1958 study of the Pacific coastline noted Big Sur as an area worthy of preservation but did not call for turning it into a federal landscape. The study did identify Point Reyes, situated just north of San Francisco, as a place well suited for federal preservation. Key likenesses linked Big Sur and Point Reyes in the early 1960s, including a largely undeveloped beautiful coastline and seashore habitat, as well as a ranching and residential heritage. But unlike Monterey County, Marin County embraced a pro-growth plan that worried residents who appreciated the pastoral quality of Point Reyes. It is likely that Marin Congressman Clem Miller lobbied for federal attention on Point Reyes, for this was one of his campaign priorities in 1958.[93] The Department of the Interior's recommendation to preserve Point Reyes saw its way through Congress, and in 1962, the same year as the Coast Master Plan, Congress and President Kennedy created the Point Reyes National Seashore.

Because of opposition from local ranchers and residents, Point Reyes became a designated national seashore rather than a national park, so that twenty thousand acres could remain pastoral. The area had long supported a small dairy industry, but the dairy operators had felt the impact of rising property taxes as suburbanization spread into Marin County after World War II, and they were hit again by declining market prices, increasing labor costs, and the advent of environmental regulations in the early 1960s.[94] Such conditions led to the consolidation or closing of many dairies in the area. With the coming of the federal seashore, observers assumed that dairy operators would now "take their time about pulling down their cowsheds and moving into the more efficient cow-feed economy of California's Central Valley."[95]

Federal ownership in Point Reyes meant a permanent change toward non-development under a new landlord not known for flexibility.[96] But in Big Sur, the CMP meant that locals could expect some growth and the opportunity to have the ear of those who drew up the planning documents. Why did these two similar areas face such different futures? The principal difference was Point Reyes's proximity to the Bay Area. Situated fewer than fifty miles from San Francisco, Point Reyes was subject to the needs and desires of the burgeoning metropolitan population. In the congressional hearings for the creation of Point Reyes National Seashore, Undersecretary of the Interior James Carr promoted the federal acquisition, stating that "no other large area in the United States near a dense population center has been left so unaltered by man until now" and that given the anticipated growth of San Francisco and the enthusiasm for recreation and open space, California needed this seashore park.[97]

As if to underscore the point, Point Reyes continued to face development threats throughout the decade. By 1969, seven years after Point Reyes's designation as a federal seashore, the park had spent all its purchase money and had only ten parcels of scattered land to show for it. Loggers were active on a scenic ridge; new homes had been built at the seashore, and Marin County had approved new residential subdivisions. These developments touched off another round of protective measures sponsored by park advocates and preservation-oriented locals.[98] Monterey County's CMP followed a different trajectory. Under the Coast Master Plan, Monterey County supported careful growth for Big Sur in keeping with nature-oriented tourism and modest residential development. The Coast Master Plan's aesthetic focus meant that visitors to Big Sur experienced close to a seamless landscape from national forest, to state parks, to residential space. In Point Reyes this residential backdrop remained but would be subservient to public lands and needs. In contrast, Monterey County treated Big Sur's local culture as an asset alongside the scenery.

If in 1962 Big Sur locals and Monterey County did not like the federal model that Point Reyes portended, neither did they find acceptable the other end of the development-preservation spectrum. Lake Tahoe, another prime California destination, shared with Big Sur a scenic shoreline that contained roughly equivalent amounts of private land. Up from the water, national forest lands covered over half the acreage in both locations.[99] In contrast to Big Sur, the Tahoe area experienced substantial degradation by the early 1960s through residential and commercial development. New highways made it easy to access this prime winter-sports spot, and the arrival of casinos in the 1950s gave this tourist destination year-round appeal. As host of the Winter Olympics in 1960, Lake Tahoe became a world-class recreational area. This status came at an ecological price, for development destroyed once-important wetlands, while new roads, hillside home sites, and golf courses all brought pollution to the lake just as loss of these wetlands hindered its ability to cleanse and restore itself.[100]

Unlike Big Sur and Point Reyes, six counties and two states held jurisdiction over the Lake Tahoe Basin, increasing the complexity of land management. Added to this was a continuous history of development and resource extraction. During the nineteenth century a number of timber companies felled trees in this area in order to provide lumber for the Comstock Lode mineshafts in nearby Virginia City, Nevada. By the early twentieth century, several luxurious resorts had opened to cater to the wealthy San Franciscans who saw this Sierra destination as a beautiful and comfortable retreat from urban life. Though some residents began to press for zoning regulations in the late 1930s to limit the sizes and types of buildings that could be erected around the lakeshore, pro-development and property-rights interests won out and resisted such regulations. In hopes of revitalizing tourism after World War II, local boosters promoted growth over resource protection.[101] County supervisors allied with developers to increase tax revenue and, some argued, to create a base for county salaries.[102] In the 1950s new roads allowed Tahoe's year-round residential population to grow significantly, and a 1959 master plan envisioned as many as fifty thousand permanent residents around the lake. Pro-growth policies had their effect: whereas 47 students attended Tahoe schools in 1945, by 1965 there were 4,432 students enrolled.[103] Arguably, Tahoe's skyrocketing population was its own environmental crisis.

Just as the 1956 Federal-Aid Highway Act echoed in Big Sur, Tahoe also faced a proposal to widen to four lanes the highway ringing the lake. This highway, ultimately unsuccessfully promoted, would have included a bridge over Emerald Bay, additional casino districts, and heavily populated urban centers around the lake.[104] The League to Save Lake Tahoe developed in order to challenge this proposal and established itself as a community watchdog working to thwart environmentally unsound projects. It was not until 1968 that Tahoe received more comprehensive protection with the Tahoe Regional Planning Agency. The major impetus for creating this organization was the scientific data linking the growth of the past few decades to the degradation of the lake, which of course threatened tourism.[105] It took such information as this to create the groundswell of support for bringing the booming commercial and residential development under regulation.

In Big Sur, the Coast Master Plan was designed and established ahead of any such drastic deterioration. In recognition of this distinction, a consultant to the U.S. National Parks Association observed these two tourist destinations in 1969 and called commercialism "tomorrow's problem" for Big Sur, where "superlative grandeur . . . envelops the visitor" in a "different world." In contrast, the consultant described Tahoe as "a prime example of what neglect and heedless pressure of population may do to natural beauty across the nation. Spoliation is visible everywhere."[106] These observations were striking not only for their difference but for the fact that they were made regarding two of the state's greatest natural treasures. To many—probably to most—Tahoe exhibited world-class beauty. That Big Sur could seem so vastly superior (in the eyes of a national park consultant) to this Sierra lake basin suggests that something in the quality of the experience in Big Sur captivated the visitor, a melding of the human and natural community to an unusually agreeable measure.

In the early 1960s Tahoe and Point Reyes, two areas of esteemed beauty, sat on either end of the spectrum of land management, and neither's approach appealed to the majority of Big Sur's residents. Instead, locals in Big Sur forged a distinct response to development and the environment at a time when these two issues were just beginning to be spoken of together. By 1962 Big Sur's residents must have realized that few other land-management options existed than what was outlined in the Coast Master Plan. If residents chose to fight the local CMP they could probably expect that environmental protection would come in the form of state or federal control, as in Point Reyes. Or, if they avoided this intervention and rejected protective zoning, Big Sur could go the way of Lake Tahoe and other fast-developing recreational areas. Because the majority of Big Sur's residents agreed that Big Sur needed some form of protection in order to maintain its wild, peaceful qualities, this latter option seemed inappropriate as well.

Any plan would increase bureaucracy and decrease landowners' freedoms, but the CMP's goal to preserve the natural character of the landscape, control future growth in order to maintain harmony with the scenic setting, and to accomplish both "without turning the land over to a government agency" most likely seemed like the best deal they were going to get.[107] As Nathaniel Owings described it, the "beauty of this plan is that it can be done on a county level. . . . We want to try and preserve this beautiful coastline without large-scale federal subsidization. Nobody wants a national park along the Big Sur coast."[108] A national park might protect the scenery, but it would bring admirers to Big Sur in ever-greater numbers and impose considerable restrictions on landowners. If the Coast Master Plan succeeded, outsiders would continue to admire Big Sur's culture and scenery without experiencing the regimentation of a federal park or the high-density development of a suburban space, whereas residents could enjoy a measure of autonomy that ironically came from harnessing the regulatory power of the county and state governments.

AN ENVIRONMENTAL AWAKENING

The Coast Master Plan represented an early effort to grapple with the long-term impact of development. In its first iteration, as a draft produced by Skidmore, Owings, & Merrill in 1960, planners quoted Rachel Carson's 1951

The Sea around Us to argue that the present generation must take responsibility for the long-term well-being of the land: "Man often forgets the true nature of his planet and the long vistas of its history in which the existence of the race of man occupied but a mere moment of time."[109] Such thinking was uncommon in 1960, but Carson's seminal 1962 publication, *Silent Spring*, prompted widespread support for the idea that people should act as stewards, not consumers or manipulators, of the natural world. This idea gained stature throughout the decade, as science and public sentiment both supported a more informed understanding of people's impact on nature. Increasingly Americans became aware of the negative consequences of the liberal application of manufactured pesticides, the proliferation of synthetic materials, and new building techniques that enabled people to establish themselves within sensitive habitats. More and more, people were coming to understand that natural resources were limited and overtaxed, and could not be counted on to sustain indefinite growth for the burgeoning population. It took reframing for Americans to see an alternative path that considered the well-being of the Earth as well as its inhabitants. Big Sur's 1962 Coast Master Plan emerged at the cusp of the national discussion about the environment, and judging by Udall and Whyte's praise, it may have even helped inform this national conversation.

To those interested in conservation, California was a particularly alarming case. The state led the country in population growth while also containing more than its share of natural beauty. In 1962 one observer asked in anguish: "How polluted can a bright land become?"[110] By 1965, the field biologist and leading conservation scholar Ray Dasmann characterized the state's recent developments as destruction at the hands of the people who could not or would not question the dominant pattern of growth:[111]

> The threat comes essentially from all who do not know what California was, cannot see what it is, cannot dream of what it could be. The enemies are those who have looked so long into the blast furnaces of civilization that they can no longer appreciate a sunset—those to whom growth is progress and progress is good, regardless of its direction.

But Big Sur refused to conform to growth patterns. The cultural impact of Esalen, Kerouac, Miller, and Jeffers lent alternative ideas to a place that had not yet overcommitted to development, a place where residents remained open to forging a unique path for their community that did not resemble the nation's status quo. San Francisco had embraced such thinkers, but it was too late to put all these ideas into practice in a major metropolitan center. Instead, Big Sur served as a reminder of why these sentiments still mattered. Nat Owings and many others felt that Big Sur was one of the last, best places within this great state, and they were determined to retain this distinction. The rapid growth of the postwar era meant that if they failed, they were unlikely to find a similar quality of life elsewhere along California's central coast. But, more important, California would lose a stretch of coastline that held immense cultural and aesthetic value. Big Sur projected what many considered the best of California—the beauty, the creativity, the cultural allure, and the future-oriented land management—all in one unlikely package. It was an idea and a place that was important to preserve.

Big Sur managed to avoid the type of development so common throughout California in the postwar period not because all locals were environmentalists, who put the welfare of the Earth above economics, but because a majority placed high value upon the area's beauty and feared that it would diminish without a communitywide effort to preserve Big Sur. Supporters of the Coast Master Plan indicated their belief that people did not absolutely compromise nature by their presence. Instead, the plan asserted the local belief that humans and nature could coexist in a mutually beneficial manner. After six decades of management under the U.S. Forest Service, two and a half decades with a state highway, and finally the Coast Master Plan in 1962, Big Sur had become a highly governed landscape that earned the praise not only of countless visitors but of national figures, as well as the fierce loyalty of its residents.

By most accounts, the open-space experiment in Big Sur had succeeded. Owings and other residents not only sensed the need to preempt development but could also read the growing support for preservation among the general population. Owings had drawn upon Robinson Jeffers's verse in the introduction to the SOM master-plan proposal to reiterate the importance of preserving a place of wonder such as Big Sur:[112]

> I gazing at the boundaries of granite and spray, the
> Established sea-marks, felt behind me
> Mountain and plain, the immense breadth of the continent,
> Before me the mass and doubled stretch of water.

Jeffers felt the natural elements most intensely in Big Sur, and his dream was to maintain this area as a monument to nature, with limited human edifices.

Jeffers understood the development pressures of his time, as did Owings of his own era. Owings and others saw the Coast Master Plan as a realization of the long-held belief that Big Sur should not be subjected to the same treatment as more commonplace environments. In his final year, it must have pleased Robinson Jeffers tremendously to know that the people of Big Sur believed enough in its special character to work to preserve it in the face of encroaching development.

Decades after Jeffers first recorded his impression of this coastline, Joan Didion, an admirer of Jeffers and a writer who also spoke bluntly regarding the perils of her beloved home state, remarked of California: "The mind is troubled by some buried but ineradicable suspicion that things had better work here, because here, beneath that immense bleached sky, is where we run out of continent."[113] Didion wrote in 1968, in the wake of California's new distinction as the nation's most populous state. At a time when many remarked that California's realities embodied the nation's future, those in Big Sur felt a particular urgency in halting the march of material progress characterizing much of the state's coastline. Paradoxically, while a slow-growth measure like the Coast Master Plan ran counter to California's dominant land-use patterns, the county plan portended many soon-to-develop California trends: coastal conservation, promotion of property rights and minimum-lot-size protection, soaring real-estate prices, and the impact of wealth on the land and its human communities. To a remarkable degree, Big Sur was a bellwether for a state forecasting nationwide trends, all the while appearing as a timeless landscape.

FIVE

The Influence of the Counterculture, Community, and State

Big elbows of Rock rising everywhere, sea caves within them, seas plollocking all around inside them crashing out foams, the boom and pound on the sand, the sand dipping quick (no Malibu Beach here)—Yet you turn and see the pleasant woods winding upcreek like a picture in Vermont—But you look up into the sky, bend way back, my God you're standing directly under that aerial bridge with its thin white line running from rock to rock and witless cars racing across it like dreams! From rock to rock! All the way down the raging coast! So that when later I heard people say "Oh Big Sur must be beautiful!" I gulp and wonder why it has the reputation of being beautiful above and beyond its fearfulness, its Blakean groaning roughrock Creation throes, those vistas when you drive the coast highway on a sunny day opening up the eye for miles of horrible washing sawing.

JACK KEROUAC, *Big Sur*

IN 1964 THE *SATURDAY EVENING POST* ran an article on Big Sur entitled "A Utopia Is Turning into Paradise Lost." The author asserted that Big Sur was engaged in "a losing battle against modernity," in which many of the newly arrived residents—"escapists" from modern society who had settled into the Big Sur hills—were "now appalled to find that life is in hot pursuit." The author conjectured that Big Sur remained quite possibly the most beautiful spot in the country but left no doubt about his opinion on the future of the area. The main culprit, according to the article, was the new type of resident: "Among the population of some 600 there seems to be a disproportionate number of sexual athletes and exhibitionists, alcoholics, addicts and eccentrics of various milder persuasions."[1] A year and a half later the *San Francisco Chronicle* also featured Big Sur but drew a very different conclusion. The *Chronicle* asserted that "in a population-swollen California Big Sur is still the domain of the golden eagle, the osprey, the bull-voiced sea lions, the gulls and the sea otters."[2] In the eyes of the California journalist, the truly noteworthy aspect of Big Sur was its departure from the ubiquitous suburbs that had in recent decades subordinated the needs of wildlife to those of the family. In the end, these articles provided little insight into the complexities unfolding in Big Sur and instead revealed the fascination and alarm with which contemporaries viewed California's rapid cultural and environmental changes of the 1960s.

The *Saturday Evening Post* article hit home on one point in particular: by the 1960s Big Sur's demographics had come to include members of the counterculture. But the article put undue weight on their presence, ignoring the numerous residents who effectively worked to stem certain advances, namely overcrowding, overdevelopment, and commercialization. This latter group's successful efforts to maintain Big Sur's separation from mainstream America belied the article's assertion that locals fought a losing battle with modernity. Beginning with the creation of the Coast Master Plan in 1962, and throughout the next two decades, those in Big Sur shrewdly adopted contemporary tools, including a property owners' association, a land trust, and the government's resources and environmental guidelines to retain a rural, seemingly traditional landscape in Big Sur. In so doing, locals created something that was actually quite modern—a hybrid space that encompassed American ideals of settlement and the wild. And they did so seemingly against the odds. Those in Big Sur and in the Monterey County offices had no precedent to follow to maintain a place as popular as Yosemite through local measures while still safeguarding private property.

Despite, and in some cases because of, the vast government holdings in Big Sur, residents refused to abdicate responsibility for land management. Living in a region dominated by public land, residents faced a constant tension between their rights as landowners and their responsibilities as stewards of a national treasure. They sometimes stressed the perceived injustices of regulations designed to retain open space and at other times led the county's efforts to preserve their remarkable coastline. In an act of restraint rarely seen in that era, residents of Big Sur subordinated at least some human desires to the needs of the land. Rather than retreat from modern society, residents and county planners continued to pioneer environmentally oriented land management at a time when Americans were just beginning to acknowledge the need for long-term planning in that direction. Residents and county officials may have talked of maintaining the rural status quo in Big Sur, but they were in reality creating a new framework for a place that incorporated carefully chosen aspects of modernity set within a wild landscape. Arguably, for those fortunate enough to call Big Sur home, this coastline was on its way to becoming a paradise established, not lost.

THE COUNTERCULTURE IN BIG SUR

By the mid-1960s Big Sur held enormous appeal for those of the counterculture. Just a few years after Kerouac left his mark along this coast, no one could ignore the number of disaffected youth who flowed down the highway and into the Big Sur mountainside. Ironically, as a place that held its shape largely because of the multilayered government regulations, Big Sur appealed to hippies, those youth who rejected on principle America's dominant governing and social systems, including engagement in the Cold War, postwar consumption, and to a lesser degree, environmental destruction. Though Henry Miller had for years attracted struggling artists and nonconformists, this new wave of arrivals far exceeded anything Big Sur had yet experienced, leading a good number of residents to feel exasperated by these transients hoping to "find themselves" within this landscape. Prior to this influx, some residents had acknowledged the rights of such "freeloaders," claiming "these kids are here for the same reason we are—to get away from it all."[3] But this new set, the hippies, rejected even the loose norms of the Big Sur community.

Hitchhiking down the coast from San Francisco or further, with no more than they could carry, or arriving in vans with friends, the hippies did not come prepared to establish long-term homes, for they generally lacked the will or inclination to do so. They felt drawn by the region's reputation and expressed familiarity with its poet laureate. As one state park ranger noted of these youths: "All of them quote Robinson Jeffers."[4] Hippies came to Big Sur hoping to find meaning for their lives amid a troubled world. They resembled Robinson Jeffers, Henry Miller, Jack Kerouac, and countless others who embraced Big Sur for its distance from America's technological, commercialized mass culture, and these youths inscribed their own feelings about place upon Big Sur just as locals had long done. Settling on national forest or state park lands, these transients asserted that they had the right to dwell on any of the thousands of acres of public land because "it belongs to the people. We're the people too."[5] State park officials noted that many transients rejected the established campsites and settled outside allowable boundaries, thinking "that here you have all this open space, it ought to be free."[6]

Pfeiffer Big Sur State Park drew the bulk of these youths, for the park had not only the warmest public swimming hole but many unoccupied cabins in the offseason also, and plenty of secluded land not far from the highway. Partly because of low river levels, and partly because of the number of young folk frequenting the pool, the county health department condemned the swimming hole in 1967. The state park supervisor quoted a staff member in his log following the pool closure: "Thank goodness the pool is closed with all these filthy jerks upon us; also the closure of the pool has most noticeably cut the hoodlum type of element."[7] Instances such as the pool closure stood as a clear reminder that these were not free lands. Instead, Big Sur was subject to careful management, especially in the wake of the hippies' arrival. Nevertheless, the young transients did not take this development as a sign to move on and move out of Big Sur.

The presence of so many hippies prompted the Big Sur Grange Master to write to fellow landowners in 1965 encouraging action against the further incursion of these outsiders. H. C. Fleenor believed that the growing number of arrivals hoping to escape "the law and censorship of more populous areas" practice an "'unconforming' [sic] way of life [that] is offensive to the local citizens." In response to what he perceived as the youths' intention to develop a culture that ran counter to Big Sur traditions, Fleenor bluntly argued of the hippies: "These non-conformists contribute nothing to our taxes, beautification, or a socially acceptable way of life. They care absolutely nothing for the welfare of our community. Their manner of living contributes to fire hazards, to sanitary problems, and to anxiety on the part of tourists."[8] Residents like Fleenor worried that the hippies' desire to reject Big Sur's norms would end up ruining the very place that residents had fashioned as a retreat from conventional communities.

Of particular concern to residents was the fact that so many transients also encroached upon private lands. One rancher noted that in the course of one summer the trespassers had shot twenty-three of his sheep. These challenges made some residents consider an Old West tradition: vigilantism. Another rancher claimed he would "shoot the britches off" the next squatter he found on his land. Clearly frustrated, one local noted: "There isn't a law in Monterey County that says you can't shoot a predatory animal, and what else are they [the hippies]?" By 1968 residents informed the police at a town-hall meeting that "a gun club has just been formed down here. Last week some of the members spent two nights out looking for sheep-killers."[9] Local ranchers were nearly pushed to their limits by the hippies, but no recorded violence transpired between the two groups.

Residents attributed numerous problems to the hippies and sought to mitigate these issues through conventional methods as well. One effort included a petition to the Monterey County Board of Supervisors for no-parking signs along a popular three-mile stretch of Highway 1 in the hope of controlling or stopping "littering, trespassing, illegal fires, violations of health regulations and an assertedly [sic] rising crime rate."[10] Residents expected the patrolling police officer and state park and national forest rangers to stay on top of the problems in Big Sur, but this was a tall task in a region with thousands of forested and inaccessible acres. Indeed, the very attributes that made Big Sur such an inspiring place to live and to visit also made it susceptible to evasion of the law. In an age when hitchhiking was an acceptable means of transportation, locals pressured the county to enforce no-hitchhiking laws. With only one part-time police patrol for all of Big Sur, state park and national forest rangers became key law-enforcement officials in these years. By 1970 an average weekend could see upwards of twenty-five arrests for illegal camping, fire building, and nudity.[11]

State park employees could attest to the ordinary tourist's aversion to these transients. By the late 1960s the supervising ranger at Pfeiffer State Park reported that he regularly received phone calls from potential visitors wondering whether it was safe to visit Big Sur.[12] Concern only increased as the area developed a national reputation as a hotbed for the use of LSD and other drugs. Hippies, who were known to embrace psychedelics as a way of life, lent this reputation to Big Sur.[13] Of course, some of these drugs prevailed in Esalen (which the hippies called "the country club"), where LSD served as a tool for exploration into other states of mind.[14] Esalen catered to the well-to-do, allowing for drug experimentation for those who could afford a weekend retreat in this landscape before returning to their regular lives. With regard to the hippies, however, adding hallucinogenic drugs to the mix merely amplified the disorder wrought by hundreds of homeless residents.

The impact of these transients on the area's reputation, and ultimately its economy, seemed clear. When hippies did frequent local businesses, their disheveled appearance was likely to offend well-to-do tourists whose money fueled the local economy. Several Big Sur business owners posted signs in their windows to ward off hippies and more generally to discourage their presence in the area. Such signs went further than the typical No Shoes, No Shirt, No Service to include No Entrance for Those Who Are Barefoot, Dirty, or Unkempt or more simply We Do Not Serve Hippies or Beatnicks [sic]. One business owner claimed that he would not allow "vernal equinox festivals or any other such happenings" on his property and that his campground would be used by "decent folk" or he would shut it down. The co-owner of the Big Sur River Inn tersely described the problem with the hippies: "They are bad for business. We try to keep them out. They camp out on your property."[15]

The hippie invasion was not a fleeting issue for the Big Sur community or for the landscape. By the end of summer 1971, the Monterey County Health Department declared the water of the Big Sur River unfit to drink because of contamination by *E. coli* bacteria from human feces that the supervising ranger claimed came from the "long-haired vagabonds." Meanwhile, Pfeiffer Big Sur State Park officials felt compelled to reduce the number of campsites near the redwoods as a result of damaged soil caused by illegal parking and overuse. Once again, the hippies were to blame.[16] In 1975 the chief ranger for California's national forests suggested a symposium to discuss vandalism, noting that "outdoor recreation facilities may be taking their share of some of the sociological ills that beset our cities." Of the nineteen national forests in California, it was the Big Sur section of Los Padres that experienced by far the largest influx of hippies and related challenges.[17] As the local state park ranger noted in 1971: "For some reason, Big Sur has magic in its name. Groups of kids just flow up and down Highway 1."[18] Open land was not enough to trigger the influx of transients; these youth craved what Big Sur had to offer, or at least what its image suggested they would find.

For more than seven years, residents and officials spoke of the problems brought by the hippies. And then, on 1 August 1972, a raging fire dwarfed earlier concerns. An illegal campfire started by transients in Molera State Park sparked a fire that eventually spread to more than four thousand acres. It took nearly two thousand firefighters to put out the conflagration, which fortunately burned only two structures, neither one a residence. In the fire's aftermath, residents immediately criticized state park officials for opening the campground before "better patrols could be provided." Though the state parks division added two patrols, many residents felt that this coverage was still insufficient for a 2,200-acre park.[19]

Even after the flames were extinguished, there was, as usual, still an ecological price to pay, as the denuded slopes gave way to landslides during the winter rains. Landslides are common along this coast, where heavy rains pound on the frequently burned-over, steep mountainsides. Geologists have mapped more than fifteen hundred landslides in Big Sur.[20] Residents, of course, understood the causal connection between fires and landslides, and

FIGURE 14. The Big Sur River meets the Pacific Ocean in Andrew Molera State Park, once part of the Mexican land grant Rancho El Sur. Frances Molera, who inherited the southern half of her grandfather's ranch, bequeathed 2,200 acres on the western side of Highway 1 to the Nature Conservancy; the land later passed to the State of California. (Photo: author.)

knew what the impact could be on the community. Not only did Highway 1 close on three occasions after particularly heavy slides, but flowing debris wrecked the post office and Big Sur Grange Hall, and led to the death of a highway worker trying to clear the slide. Because of the contaminated water supply, the Point Sur Naval Facility opened its water lines to area residents.[21] Residents' fears about careless campfires were clearly grounded in serious considerations for the well-being of the landscape and its people. Of course, a large fire could have happened without the presence of hippies, but residents knew that most fires in Big Sur began at campsites.[22]

Regardless of locals' inclination to proclaim their independent lifestyle in Big Sur, the labors of state and federal firefighting crews and highway workers meant residents were perpetually beholden to the government to maintain a functioning community. In the wake of the slides, locals expressed resentment and frustration over the loss of business; one business owner felt compelled to sue the state for nearly half a million dollars in damages, claiming that the highway department had "failed to maintain ditches and culverts properly." The Big Sur Garage had lost two tow trucks and needed to perform nine thousand dollars' worth of cleaning after the storm. These events prompted the owner of the garage to exclaim: "They call it an act of God. Well maybe two-and [sic] one-half inches of rain in a half hour is an act of

God. But that mud slide was an act of man." The garage owner's stance blurred two basic facts about Big Sur's landscape: that the original cutting of the mountainsides for the highway initiated a permanent challenge to keeping the hills intact during especially wet winters and that fire frequently races through Big Sur from natural causes alone. To hold the state responsible for damages that ensued from mudslides would be an expensive precedent; the Monterey Superior Court jury ruled in favor of the state.[23]

Other residents pointed out that it was disingenuous to blame the hippies or government employees for troubles without admitting that along with the privilege of living in Big Sur came certain risks and discomforts. A columnist in the local Grange newsletter offered his perspective on the problems with hippies and expansive public lands in Big Sur:[24]

> Come hell or high water, the State Park and the National Forest are here to stay, and are an essential part of the local economy and way of life. They have urgent responsibilities in terms of extending every effort to prevent their operations from being a threat to the area, be it fire, flood, traffic, garbage or whatever, but beyond that, the matter of fires and trespassing on private property are strictly local problems, the handling of which is a matter among ourselves and the law enforcement authorities. If we choose to live and earn our living here, knowingly and deliberately in an area of high risk where fire, storms, floods, power outages, trespassing, and other disagreeable phenomena are an ineradicable part of the picture, then we certainly can't pass off all the responsibility and blame for our woes on government agencies.

This resident addressed the predicament in which locals found themselves. They had long worked to maintain an exceptional landscape and community but in doing so had attracted dropouts from society who threatened Big Sur's peace and beauty.

Big Sur's allure extended to another counterculture group of this era. The back-to-the-land movement in Big Sur provided a counterpoint to the influx of hippies. Across the country, those moving back to the land, like the hippies, questioned and challenged the standard American, suburban lifestyle. And like the Wilderness Act, the back-to-the-land movement acknowledged the destruction of the environment, but with a different prescription. Those moving back to the land in the late 1960s and the 1970s believed they could better address environmental degradation, unsustainable farming, and industrial pursuits by reinhabiting rural America and working the land, not by bounding it off for preservation. They looked to the example set by people such as Scott and Helen Nearing and M. G. Kains, who had moved back to the land during the Great Depression as a critique of the faltering capitalist economy in which they lived.[25] Published accounts of their experiences provided a guidepost for those wishing to emulate these modern-day pioneers.[26] And in Big Sur, back-to-the-landers also followed in the path of the region's famed writers, like Miller, who retreated to Big Sur out of disgust with mainstream society. In an old tradition, these members of the counterculture saw the land as a place where they could seek personal freedom.

Nearly two centuries earlier Thomas Jefferson had glorified the independent farmer as the bulwark of democracy and as a virtuous citizen mixing his labor with the land in order to provide for his family. Though the country inexorably moved away from this social model as it industrialized, as late as 1862 the federal government's Homestead Act encouraged rural life with affordable ownership of 160 acres of surveyed public land. As the United States became a predominantly urban society in the early twentieth century, there were those who continued to lift up the agrarian ideal as an alternative to modernity.[27] Those moving back to the land after World War II felt it especially important to disconnect from the technological, materialistic, and hierarchical ideology that pervaded America.[28] Increasing concerns about the environment, energy, and the economy led many to challenge the predominant mentality that had promoted unbridled growth in the postwar era.[29] The act of returning to the land drew on tradition to make a contemporary social statement.

In 1970, Wendell Berry, an American writer and advocate for moving back to the land, sought to heighten Americans' consciousness by pointing out what was wrong with modern American society: "We have made our false economy a false god, and it has made blasphemy of the truth." Berry then proposed an alternative way of life that acknowledged scarcity and limitations. He admonished:[30]

> If one deplores the destructiveness and wastefulness of the economy, then one is under an obligation to live as far out on the margin of the economy as one is able: to be economically independent of exploitive industries, to learn to need less, to waste less, to make things last, to give up meaningless luxuries.

Berry criticized the American economy for thriving on dysfunctional relationships among people and between people and the land.[31] Big Sur appealed to hippies, back-to-the-landers, and Americans wary of modern society because this coast had a tenuous connection to the mainstream economy. Though the highway provided an easy route into and out of Big Sur, it was still inconvenient to participate in the consumer economy. Big Sur contained few shops, and electricity, and therefore televisions and telephones, had not spread to all homes along this coast. In contrast to the growing metropolitan areas of California, Big Sur's distance from town required resourcefulness and neighborly exchange in lieu of easy access to groceries and consumer goods.

Despite its rustic appeal, it is difficult to see Big Sur as a congenial environment for back-to-the-landers. After the construction of the highway, landownership along this coast increasingly became linked to privilege and prestige. A 1963 real-estate ad in *The New Yorker* listed a four-acre home in Big Sur at $87,500 (and noted its below-market listed price), when the median price of a home in the United States was $17,500.[32] Yet despite the rising cost of land, a small number of people in this era did have the means to return to the land through settlement in Big Sur. Most came from urban areas hoping to establish entirely new lives for themselves in the ruggedness of Big Sur. A local publication noted in the summer of 1967: "Each year there is a migration of young couples. Up from Los Angeles, down from San Francisco, looking for the good life. Into the cabins vacated by last year's seekers. Many come each year. Very few stay."[33] These recent arrivals were, in short, beneficiaries of the economy Berry critiqued, as were the bulk of the people who could buy land and disengage from the economy.[34]

Those whose tenures were brief along Big Sur's coast may have been discouraged by the daily rigor of rural life regardless of their chosen landscape, but there is little doubt that Big Sur offered special challenges in terms of terrain, inaccessibility, and powerful winter storms. Big Sur had never proven itself a likely spot for productive farms. Even the pioneer families who had grown a good portion of their food in the early twentieth century often had to find outside work to provide the means to buy certain necessities and food staples. Now, in the second half of the twentieth century, high land values and property taxes made this endeavor even more difficult, and modern residential comforts were not always viable in Big Sur. Life in Big Sur was simply not for everyone.

The actress Jane Fonda, for one, felt the strong appeal of an alternative life along this coast. Fonda traveled to Big Sur in the early 1960s hoping to meet Henry Miller. During her sojourn she found herself surprised by just how keenly she felt the allure of living on the land. Staying on the grounds of what was soon to become Esalen, Fonda got to know the women who lived and worked there—women who, as Fonda remembers, "had hair under their arms and tie-dyed skirts." She felt the contrast between someone "so straight" as herself and these women, who gave birth and raised their children in the woods and simple cabins of this coastal retreat. Fonda later recalled thinking, "I could stop right here. This is very appealing to me." And she did indeed stop for a while, finding romance with Esalen's co-founder Dick Price before returning to her career. Fonda was one of many celebrities who arrived in Big Sur with an aura of her own and felt caught up in the power of the land, its history, and its potential.[35]

The postwar back-to-the-land movement can perhaps be understood as a sort of culminating social movement at the close of the vibrant sixties. Instead of protesting in the streets or in town halls, back-to-the-landers demonstrated their dissatisfaction with government and traditional society by seeking to live in harmony with the land and its resources as a way of contributing to a healthier, more balanced society.[36] Those who rejected the comforts of suburbia to return to the land made a powerful statement about wanting no complicity with what they deemed a damaging and irresponsible government and economy.[37] Back-to-the-landers who established farms with the hope of living largely removed from the mainstream economy exhibited an alternative lifestyle that was both productive and against the grain. For a minority of these baby boomers who critically evaluated their own condition and that of their country and those less privileged within it, there was much to protest during a time of complacency and conformity. Troubled race and gender relations, high levels of poverty within the world's wealthiest country, the deteriorating environment, and the war in Vietnam all suggested that those leading society had abdicated their responsibilities and could no longer provide moral direction for the nation.

The back-to-the-land movement was one strain of the environmental movement that sought to address the deterioration of the environment through human habitation rather than through traditional preservation. Such an approach blurred the growing boundary between wild and inhabited lands, which explains why back-to-the-landers saw Big Sur as an especially attractive destination. For years, residents had maintained that they could better protect the landscape by living on the land, not by bounding it off as public land. This sort of approach hinged on the growing belief that a real change in society would have to come through collective but ultimately individual efforts and choices. Government alone could not solve the problems of the day (and according to some, government was the source of many of the problems); instead, individual Americans would have to practice more responsible interactions with each other and with the land on which they lived. According to some, only through such grass-roots advances would society be able to tackle the fundamental problems that threatened everything from racial equality to healthy ecosystems. A well-known saying at the time, "The Personal Is Political," held true not just for gender relations, but also for choices in the realm of habitation.

As California's population boomed in the postwar era, Big Sur residents and county officials made land-management choices that ultimately influenced the number and types of tourists and residents along this coast. With increasing property values and a growing tourist reputation, residents in Big Sur had much to lose by allowing transient youth to wander continually through the landscape. If the Wilderness Act was meant to keep the nation's wild places from falling under the developers' reach, residents of Big Sur found that society's dropouts could at least temporarily alter the character of a place nearly as much as those with money and ambitious designs. For reasons of safety, economics, and general preference, many locals sought to make it difficult for the hippies to remain in Big Sur. Consciously or not, residents felt increasingly under pressure to exclude a group of people who claimed, at least, to champion the idea of universal access to the same public goods—beautiful land and a creative, nonconformist cultural environment—that many of those same residents had worked to preserve.

By 1970 an important demographic shift had occurred in Big Sur. in which professionals now defined the area's makeup. The 1970 population census reported that the single largest class of workers in Big Sur, comprising 30 percent of the population, was service employees, catering to the tourists. But added together, the next two groups indicated a larger and new white-collar set: 17 percent professional and technical workers, and 20 percent managers and administrators. Only 0.5 percent of the population listed themselves as agricultural laborers.[38] Of the nearly seven hundred residents in the Big Sur census tract, all but ten were white.[39] Rising property values and resistance to society's dropouts meant that by the late 1960s a place that had long been known for its nonconformity was becoming solidly linked to the privilege of affluence.

A GROUNDSWELL OF SUPPORT FOR
THE ENVIRONMENT

Big Sur's unique land-management strategies became increasingly viable as a growing number of Americans sought open spaces and well-preserved landscapes as retreats from the ever-expanding metropolitan areas. Big Sur's hiking trails indicated just how popular such a retreat was, as the trails through Los Padres National Forest (LPNF) saw an increase in use of 260 percent between 1967 and 1970.[40] In response to this remarkable demand, LPNF indicated that it would continue to seek opportunities to purchase private land within national forest boundaries as it became available. Moreover, national forest administrators decided that logging in this district was on a salvage basis only, and that "further development of commercial timber resources is likely to meet with strong public resistance due to the significance of these timber stands as an aesthetic resource for the region."[41] It was as one observer said of Big Sur while writing for the National Parks Association: "Here is proof, if any were needed, that a national forest can justify its existence on other than traditional purposes"—that is, "the production of logs and the grazing of livestock."[42]

Big Sur's flora and fauna both benefited from the common perception among residents and tourists that this coastal environment should have the look and feel of the wild. Margaret Owings, Nat's wife, played a critical role in the protection of two keystone species that symbolized the power and wonder of nature in Big Sur. She established the Friends of the Sea Otter in 1968 to advocate for the southern sea otter, which had increased modestly in number since the discovery of fifty otters living along the Big Sur coast in the late 1930s. The five hundred–odd otters now stretched beyond the borders of their state-protected refuge and at times met with violence at the hands of the growing number of commercial and sport fishermen who competed for the valuable abalone.[43] In the midst of the state-led debate about the future of sea-otter protection, Margaret Owings's group gathered fifteen thousand signatures to help thwart state legislation to allow the taking of sea otters found outside their refuge. Friends of the Sea Otter was instrumental in bringing sustained national attention and support to the cause of this marine mammal, helping it make great strides toward reestablishing itself along California's central coast.[44]

Margaret Owings also invested in the cause of the mountain lion, working to successfully remove the state bounty on this cat.[45] Owings was not alone in championing the rights of Big Sur's nonhuman residents. In response to the sanctioned killing of a mountain lion outside a Big Sur home, a local resident articulated the perceived value of this elusive creature and its habitat: "We are living on the edge of the wilderness. We are the intruders. We are taking a risk living here and we have chosen to take that risk. . . . When the Fish and Game warden pulled the trigger, he shot a much-loved neighbor of mine. He shot the reason I live here—he shot beauty and coexistence and respect."[46] Such sentiments informed the statewide debates regarding the extent of the sea-otter refuge, the protection of the mountain lion, and the wider goals of preserving open space and wildness, all the while reflecting the changing perceptions of nature early in the postwar era. Margaret Owings was instrumental in helping to forge a stronger link between an aesthetic appreciation for Big Sur and respect for its individual parts. An artist by training, Owings believed in the influence of beauty on the human psyche and crafted her wildlife campaigns accordingly. Owings described a 1971 *National Geographic* article on the sea otter accompanied by a Friends of the Sea Otter–produced photo spread as "the way to open the eyes of the nation. This was news and science as well as beauty."[47]

Margaret Owings was in close step with President Lyndon Johnson and his wife, Lady Bird. Johnson's Great Society program posited a link between nature's health and beauty, and the social challenges of crime and mental health. Johnson characteristically remarked, "Beauty belongs to all the people," and he stood in support of open-space measures and environmental design that would protect the nation's natural wealth and provide a healthy and supportive environment for all Americans.[48] In 1965 he pushed successfully for the creation of the Highway Beautification Act to limit roadside signage and clutter. In such a national climate, proponents of a special highway designation for Big Sur found success in 1966. A critical component of Big Sur's slow-growth measures was the designation of Highway 1 through Big Sur as California's first Scenic Highway.[49] Lady Bird, a symbol and leader of the beautification movement, traveled to California to dedicate Big Sur's Scenic Highway. Margaret Owings helped prepare the first lady's remarks, asserting that establishing the Scenic Highway represented "the maintenance of a trust—a trust for ourselves and a trust for the generations to follow. It is a partnership of open space and man's use—a heritage of landscape to be shared by all."[50] The first lady acknowledged Big Sur's unique dedication to open space within a treasured and inhabited landscape. Scrawled on a large boulder next to Lady Bird was an antiwar message possibly left by one of the transients in Big Sur. In the heightened tension of the event, Secret Service guards protecting Lady Bird nearly tackled Ansel Adams as he stooped under his camera's black curtain to record the event.[51] With the backdrop of this anti-Vietnam message, Lady Bird addressed a different but comparably powerful movement in America dedicated to environmental protection.[52] In the late 1960s, in an era when few issues received bipartisan support, the environ-

FIGURE 15. McWay Falls, part of Julia Pfeiffer Burns State Park, plunges eighty feet into the Pacific Ocean and draws millions of admirers each year. This view can be appreciated from the shoulder of Highway 1 or from a short trail through the state park. (Photo: Edward Dickinson.)

ment was one of them. Americans of all stripes were coming to view their quality of life as linked to the health of the nation's resources.

In Big Sur, residents had already created a bulwark against environmental degradation with the Coast Master Plan. The "Scenic Highway" designation further reduced the chance that Big Sur would face a substantial increase in development, because the carrying capacity of a two-lane highway would not support extensive housing developments or a significant increase in commercial activities.[53] The scenic road represented an effort to champion environmental priorities by maintaining certain areas as underdeveloped in a time when the highways increasingly linked together the country in urban and suburban growth. Like the recent Wilderness Act, the principles behind the scenic-road protection declared that some landscapes were simply inappropriate for commonplace development. But there was more to it than environmental preservation. Though the National Highway Beautification Act was intended to benefit all Americans regardless of financial status, the Scenic Highway in Big Sur stood to benefit first and foremost the fortunate residents of Big Sur. In contrast to some of their wealthy peers throughout the state and country who were beginning to resist a powerful regulatory government, Big Sur residents took a unique approach by working within government channels to secure desired outcomes.

Meanwhile, California voters on the whole indicated their displeasure with the big-government approach of Governor Pat Brown in 1966. This was a significant shift. Just two years earlier a large majority of Americans voted in favor of Lyndon Johnson's Great Society, a program centered on the belief that the federal government could and should provide the leadership for improving multiple aspects of American society. Beginning in the mid- to late 1960s, an increasing number of white, working-class, middle-class and middle-to-upper-class Americans turned to conservative politicians. Their displeasure with the Great Society included a desire for lower taxes and a smaller government that supported greater individual and local autonomy rather than large-scale government projects that sought to regulate social dynamics.[54] Ronald Reagan would capture the nation's support in 1980, but it was California where he first found political success by tapping into this political shift. In 1964 Reagan campaigned for the Republican presidential candidate, Barry Goldwater, establishing himself as an effective speaker against the Great Society and liberalism in general. He lamented: "We have so many people who can't see a fat man standing beside a thin one without coming to the conclusion that the fat man got that way by taking advantage of the thin one." Reagan derided such thinkers for believing they could "solve all the problems of human misery through government and government planning."[55] Support for Reagan and other conservatives came from Americans who disagreed with the idea that it was an appropriate role of the government, and therefore of taxpayers, to champion social causes such as antipoverty and civil rights.

Reagan also latched on to an important source of discontent with liberal government by asserting that it hampered entrepreneurialism. He argued that in a country such as the United States people should be free of government constraints when working to achieve profit from their homes or businesses. Reagan contended that the architects of the Constitution had put ultimate faith in the efficiency and effectiveness of individual citizens: "They also knew, those Founding Fathers, that outside of its legitimate functions, government does nothing as well or as economically as the private sector of the economy."[56] Economic libertarians disagreed fundamentally with the wide scope of the liberal state and threw their support behind candidates such as Goldwater and Reagan, who called for greater autonomy from the government.[57] As governor of California from 1967 to 1975, Reagan considered himself the guardian of the rights of local interests, the protector of "home rule."[58] Over the previous decade certain residents in Big Sur had voiced similar small-government sentiments and had therefore resisted the Coast Master Plan. They had helped ensure that private-property rights would remain in the forefront of the discussion. But an even greater number of residents saw government regulations as a means to sustain their quality of life—not just with the policies of the CMP but throughout the coming decades as well. These latter residents used their wealth and know-how to protect what they saw as the area's key resource: its beauty and appealing natural environment.

Governor Reagan often stood at odds with California's growing number of environmentally conscious residents, who saw environmental protection as too big a task for the local level alone. In the early years of Reagan's governorship, Californians became increasingly concerned over such issues as air and water pollution. A Gallup Poll in 1965 indicated that 28 percent of Californians expressed concern over air pollution, and 35 percent over water pollution; by 1969 these numbers had jumped to 69 percent and 74 percent, respectively.[59] As environmentalists stressed the linkage between the quality of the environment and Americans' quality of life, many citizens were willing to support preservation measures, even if such policies increased government bureaucracy.[60] Reagan, however, spoke of running an economical government, without the big spending of New Deal Democrats. He gave minimal attention to the environment and issues of resource protection, usually preferring to allow local governments to maintain control over their own environmental affairs. He had promised as much in his campaign: "As governor, I would work to return to the cities and the counties those powers usurped from them in recent years by the state." Reagan cut by 90 percent the amount spent for park acquisition and development, even cancelling plans to buy sites for nine new state parks.[61]

As lumber companies and environmentalists debated the creation of a Redwood National Park in the northwestern part of the state, Reagan thought first of lost jobs and decreased revenue if logging was reduced. In a cabinet meeting over the issue he exclaimed: "I'll be damned if I take away all this privately owned land for no reason. I owe that much to those people in these counties [where the redwood park would be created]. I wonder, has anybody ever asked the Sierra Club if they think these trees will grow forever?" Part of this sentiment echoed a statement Reagan had made earlier at a conference of wood producers: "A tree is a tree—how many more do you need to look at?"[62] As the national environmental movement gained momentum in the 1960s it had to work against leaders like Reagan, who were inclined to see the integrity of an ecosystem as subordinate to economic concerns and property rights.[63] A journalist who published a biography of Reagan in 1968 argued that the governor dragged his feet in supporting a regional protection agency for Lake Tahoe and acted only after the federal government threatened to intervene to protect the lake. It appears that when Governor Reagan did move to protect California's natural resources, the impetus came largely as a result of the concerted efforts of Norman ("Ike") Livermore, Reagan's Resources Secretary. It was Livermore who encouraged Reagan to ultimately lend his support to a decent-sized redwood park, to reject damming the middle fork of the Feather River, and to make the Tahoe Regional Planning Agency an effective organization by including nonlocals on its board and strengthening its building and pollution standards.[64]

And then, in 1969, an industrial disaster brought into sharp relief the cost of environmental degradation, spurring a statewide commitment to the protection of the coast and a renewed preservation effort in Big Sur. On 28 January 1969 a Union Oil drilling accident spilled a quarter-million gallons of oil off the coast of Santa Barbara. The despoliation of nearby beaches and certain wildlife was a call to arms for those who believed the coast was suffering from overdevelopment. Exposure to toxins had long been common in industrial areas where working-class Americans lived. The 1969 oil spill stained the landscape for wealthy Americans, bringing national attention to the issue and moving the environmental cause even further into the mainstream.[65] From the time of the Santa Barbara oil spill in 1969 until the passage of Proposition 20 (the forerunner of the Coastal Act) three years later, an important shift occurred, as environmentalists moved from piecemeal conservation efforts to forcing institutional changes at the federal and the state level. On the heels of the oil spill, President Richard Nixon signed into law on 1 January 1970 the National Environmental Policy Act. Though Nixon lacked any personal interest in protecting the environment, he nevertheless understood its political potency and wished to be associated with this popular effort.[66] The legislation created the Environmental Protection Agency to oversee the nation's air and water quality, solid-waste management, pesticide use, and nuclear-radiation criteria and standards.

In a show of enormous support for these federal measures, and to sustain the momentum, twenty million Americans gathered in their communities on 22 April 1970 in observance of the first Earth Day. Senator Gaylord Nelson of Wisconsin spearheaded the event after observing the destruction caused by the Santa Barbara oil spill, and he drew on the antiwar movement to fashion a teach-in to raise awareness about the country's deteriorating air and water quality, and to push for a commitment to environmental protection. The event resonated with the counterculture and many ordinary Americans, all of whom recognized that the nation's economic growth threatened the air that they breathed, the water that they drank, and the landscapes that they saw as part of their heritage.

THE CALIFORNIA COASTAL COMMISSION
TAKES FORM

In the early 1970s Californians were still up in arms over the Santa Barbara spill, and the time was ripe for galvanizing statewide support for coastal protection. California politicians responded in the two years after the oil spill by proposing eleven coastal-preservation bills; but when none passed, voters took the issue into their own hands. Ellen Stern Harris, who would come to be known as the mother of the Coastal Act, developed the idea for a state coastal commission with regional offices from the local- and state-level structure of the Los Angeles and Ventura regional water-quality control board, of which she was a member. She later reported that she felt compelled to address coastal preservation after observing the cancerlike growth along the California coastline that polluted coastal resources and diminished public access to the beaches. Harris consulted friends up and down the coast about her idea for a coastal commission. She started with Margaret Owings, whom Harris considered a great heroine for her work on behalf of wildlife and other environmental causes. Apparently Owings had high praise for Harris's plan, as did California State Senator Fred Farr.[67] In 1971 concerned citizens formed the Coastal Alliance, which grew to encompass some 1,500 member organizations such as the Sierra Club, the Planning and Conservation League, and the League of Women Voters.[68] These organizations all saw a need for a state commission to check development along the coast by setting standards for the appropriate use of natural resources, including offshore oil drilling. The Coastal Alliance was responsible for placing on the 1972 ballot the Coastal Initiative, with the goal of creating a state commission tasked with overseeing the development and conservation of California's 1,072-mile coastline.

Members of the Coastal Alliance were spurred on by well-grounded fears that California's treasured coastline was rapidly deteriorating, and in some places disappearing altogether. Private development blocked access to and views of long stretches of the coastline, while breakwaters and other construction eroded beaches. By the time Californians were asked to vote on coastal protection, only two hundred miles, just one-fifth, of the state's coastline could be accessed by the public.[69] This was despite the fact that by law the public had the right to enjoy the strip of beach below the mean high-tide line. In the face of the powerful anti–Proposition 20 campaign driven by PG&E, Gulf Oil, real-estate developers, and other large corporations warning of higher energy and building costs, the majority of Californians were not to be deterred and demanded access to clean, beautiful beaches as part of their California citizenship.[70] In the end, Proposition 20 passed with over 55 percent of the votes.

In Big Sur, residents voted in favor of Proposition 20 by a margin of three to one.[71] Monterey County voters on the whole saw the need for this state regulatory agency. Two developments—a recently built multistory hotel perched in the sands of Monterey Bay and a proposed oil refinery to the north, in Moss Landing—caused locals to vote in favor of Proposition 20. Local residents Ansel Adams and cartoonist Hank Ketcham donated their talents to promoting Proposition 20, and the local Sierra Club chapter also galvanized residents to back preservation.[72] Support came from those who felt that their landscape, and therefore their quality of life, was under threat. Proposition 20 was a slow-growth measure, just as the Coast Master Plan had been, and promised to put the power of the state behind development restrictions.

The passage of Proposition 20 was certainly not a foregone conclusion. Californians had long shown a proclivity for local jurisdiction over zoning and land-use controls, and hence weak state regulations. For more than a century, local land-preservation groups formed throughout the state in response to concern for particular areas threatened by new development. In the San Francisco Bay Area, local concern over infill of the bay and the region's deteriorating environmental quality prompted the creation of a regulatory agency to oversee development of the increasingly valuable real estate. In 1965, the state legislature created the San Francisco Bay Conservation and Development Commission and gave it the authority to minimize infill of the San Francisco Bay, conserve natural resources, and maximize public access to the coast. By the end of the twentieth century, Californians had created hundreds of nonprofit environmental groups and a substantial number of land trusts to protect areas of great natural wealth.[73] But local policies could not address federal oil leases or tackle broad regional pollution and could only rarely resist corporate development. Comprehensive coastal protection required the power of the state.

The success of the Coastal Initiative in 1972 meant the creation of a temporary California Coastal Commission, subject to legislative approval within four years. Also in 1972, the U.S. Congress passed the Coastal Zone Management Act (CZMA), calling for a "comprehensive, long-range, and coordinated" national program to balance competing land and water issues. The federal program provided support for states to develop coastal-zone management programs, including financial assistance for the acquisition of estuarine sanctuaries. The CZMA was meant to encourage and assist, not preempt, state efforts at coastal management in an era when disasters like the Santa Barbara spill stood as a reminder of how vulnerable these resources were.[74] In 1976 the California legislature passed the state's Coastal Act, establishing the Coastal Commission as a permanent agency to oversee and certify each coastal county's land-use plan, which, along with implementing ordinances, would become a Local Coastal Program (LCP).[75] Some counties, like Monterey, developed multiple LCPs to accommodate the needs and demands of distinct areas within their borders. Also in 1976, the legislature created the California State Coastal Conservancy to operate as a nonregulatory agency to further the work of coastal management. Under the federal CZMA, the California Coastal Commission, the California State Coastal Conservancy, and the San Francisco Bay Conservation and Development Commission, were authorized to lead the state's coastal zone management.

The California Coastal Commission set out to protect and even enhance coastal resources by guiding land management with an eye toward environmental sustainability. Per the Coastal Act, each coastal county was tasked with defining acceptable levels of growth while protecting "rural lands, agriculture and open space" and limiting "urban sprawl."[76] After the Coastal Commission certified a county's LCP (which often took several years), the county then had the authority to grant or deny development permits. This framework was a compromise between local leaders who felt that less-centralized regulation was key to proper protection and groups like the Sierra Club that worried local governments would likely kowtow to development pressure.[77] In the case of Big Sur, its local land-use plan became one of the most restrictive in the state.[78]

Though Big Sur had operated for ten years under its own Coast Master Plan, residents and the county now had to rethink local land-use policies to conform to more stringent environmental guidelines. The Monterey County Board of Supervisors chose to create a Citizens Advisory Committee (CAC) made up of Big Sur residents in recognition of "the uniqueness of the Big Sur

Coastal region, its unsurpassed beauty and the distinct life styles it now supports" and because the county wanted to ensure that the final plan would reflect "concern for the area's particular conditions and the needs of its people." Nineteen residents, with a collective four hundred years of experience living along the Big Sur coast, brought to the committee a broad range of opinions regarding the proper balance of private and public property.[79] County officials intended the CAC to share "its special insight" to recommend any and all ideas that seemed appropriate for the LCP.[80] Clearly, Big Sur residents had succeeded in earning the respect of the county government during the last decade and a half of cooperative planning for the area's future.

In addition to the CAC members, a substantial number of residents took an active role in drafting the new land-management plan. The small number of residents in Big Sur meant that the ratio of residents to CAC members was one of the smallest in the state, which ostensibly made for the creation of a plan that represented the majority of residents' opinions.[81] But the diversity of these opinions often led to points of contention. CAC meeting minutes indicate that the committee could not come to unanimous decisions regarding critical preservation and development issues. They all agreed in principle that Big Sur required comprehensive protection, but as with the Coast Master Plan, they expressed distinct opinions on the various details.

One of the more controversial measures among locals was the concept of a critical viewshed, a concept first proposed during the creation of the Coast Master Plan to discourage new construction within the highway corridor. The current viewshed proposal was meant to prohibit development that could be seen from the highway or major public viewing areas such as beaches, turnouts, and other popular locations on either side of the highway. CAC Chairman Gary Koeppel and many of his fellow committee members felt that such a prohibition was too restrictive for the affected landowners and was also unnecessary for maintaining an exceptionally scenic landscape. They called such a viewshed policy far too rigid, believing it would represent "an illegal condemnation of private property if adopted." Koeppel went on to state that the committee "shares the resolve to protect the scenic beauty of Big Sur, but feels that the Community's expressed goal of supporting slow, controlled development which is low-profile, unobtrusive, and carefully screened with appropriate landscaping would better serve all concerned," especially the residents who appreciated that Big Sur existed for more than the tourist who drove down the coast.[82] These residents came to see preservation as a double-edged sword: it could protect their treasured landscape, but as residential desires were subordinated to public priorities, preservation also threatened to come at the expense of a dynamic community.[83]

Roughly half the CAC members held a different perspective on the matter of the viewshed, believing that they represented a "substantial segment of Big Sur residents" in seeing viewshed protection as the "only means to preservation" of the landscape. Given that the "recreational experience for millions of people is visual" within Big Sur, these committee members reasoned that it would be impractical for the planning commission to determine which new developments were acceptable and which offensive within sight of the highway.[84] Throughout the development of Big Sur's Local Coastal Program, residents grappled with the extent to which the landowner and the community demanded careful safeguarding, or the landscape and the views, and what exactly this protection should look like. But engaged residents on either side of the debate believed that they had the tools and the wherewithal to address the issues facing Big Sur.

ELEMENTS OF A COMMUNITY

Despite the passionate divisions among Big Sur residents on matters of land management, they came together to build a much more organized and vital community in the 1970s. Although Big Sur residents had shown solidarity in resisting the widening of Highway 1 and in sensing the need for the Coast Master Plan, and though they gathered occasionally at the Grange Hall for potlucks and other events, by 1972 this was largely the extent of their community along the seventy-five sparsely populated miles of the Big Sur coast.[85] There were residents who feared that outside initiatives to protect the land would end up threatening the people of Big Sur, and they warned that the outcome of such efforts might lead to the "eventual exclusion of man himself from the Big Sur Coast."[86] But population numbers continued to grow over the course of the 1970s and 1980s, and though some of the unprecedented interest in civic organizations and community services during this era can be explained by this growth, residents' desire for a strong local voice in Big Sur's Local Coastal Program very well may help explain this community cohesion.[87]

The Big Sur public library acquired its first permanent building in 1974, and the first volunteer fire brigade formed in that year also. By 1978, residents hoping to preserve their pioneer heritage formed the Big Sur Historical Society. That year also saw the creation of a community softball league with local rules and teams that thrive to this day. Meanwhile, Gary Koeppel, concerned about the lack of knowledge among residents in regard to the drafting of the Local Coastal Program, founded a community newspaper, the *Big Sur Gazette,* in 1978. This paper ran for three years, covering crucial events in Big Sur while defining a community stance toward outside intervention. The following year locals formed an additional fire brigade and a local health center for the residents of this isolated area. The Friends of the Big Sur Coast, a group committed to keeping local autonomy for the community, was also created in 1979. It was also during this decade that Esalen developed its own elementary school for the institute's residents. By the end of the decade, Big Sur was more than a place with creative residents; it was a dynamic community that coalesced regardless of divergent opinions on issues of land management.

One important effort to influence future management developed in 1978, when a consortium of Big Sur families developed the Big Sur Land Trust (BSLT) to conserve land through nongovernmental means. This idea was not new. Land trusts had secured conservation for thousands of acres across the United States by the late 1970s.[88] The BSLT drew on technical support from the national Trust for Public Land and found financial support from Big Sur residents and property owners who were looking for alternative measures to address the pressures of land development, public-land acquisition, and the economic burdens of private property.[89] Understanding that some residents cared deeply about preserving the land but opposed government acquisition, the BSLT stressed its role as an organization that could solidify protection for a parcel of land without involving the government.[90] The BSLT did not take an ideological stance against the government but operated out of concern that government agencies did not have the necessary funds to protect and indefinitely conserve Big Sur's natural resources. Moreover, the trust feared that preservation-oriented legislation could be overturned with a change in political leadership and wished to secure open space not governed by revocable laws.

The BSLT immediately gained stature when Michael Murphy of Esalen donated a portion of his land just north of his retreat in 1978, followed by a gift from the David and Lucile Packard Foundation to allow the trust to create a conservation easement on its three thousand acres within Big Sur. The trust utilized the tax incentive of conservation easements in order to encourage residents to forgo development rights to their land. This strategy was particularly effective with ranch owners who wanted to maintain their rural lands but could not afford to do so as property values soared.[91] In late-1970s California, the pressure to develop and the pressure to preserve lands commanded significant attention, with proponents on both sides able to claim the public's best interest. Not all Big Sur residents appreciated the BSLT's goal of establishing conservation easements and therefore restricting future development on onetime private property. But the BSLT empowered at least some locals to decide which land should be preserved, and in what form, and within ten years of its founding the BSLT protected from development five thousand acres along the coast. The BSLT became one more piece of the land-management matrix in Big Sur.

The BSLT was a private organization made viable through donations from individual landowners. Concurrent with the trust's founding was an effort to establish a collective approach to local land management by way of seeking town incorporation for Big Sur. Gary Koeppel proposed the idea of incorporation in 1978 with the aim to "achieve democratic representation, authentic local control and self-determination."[92] Koeppel and others established a committee made up of members from the Grange, the Coast Property Owners' Association, the Chamber of Commerce, and the Big Sur Citizens Advisory Committee that included such figures as John Harlan and Frank Trotter, members of the area's homesteading families. This committee studied the economic feasibility of incorporation and determined that turning Big Sur into a town was possible based upon revenue from local sales taxes and lodging taxes.[93] Residents reflected on what township status would mean for Big Sur. Certainly Big Sur would not resemble most towns, for it had no downtown, the largest landowners were the federal and the state government, and the town budget would be based on tourist dollars. The proposal commanded the attention and focus of representatives from most groups within the community. Ultimately, a majority of residents indicated their desire to maintain a rural status for Big Sur. Some residents voiced concern that incorporation would encourage concentrated development along the coast and would add an unnecessary layer of government.[94]

Certainly the appeal for town incorporation was an explicit attempt to maintain local autonomy, and it seems plausible that the newly created community organizations were meant not only to provide services to residents but to indicate to outsiders that Big Sur was carefully guarded by locals who not only possessed a history of belonging to this coast but a vibrant present as well. Perhaps the community organizations were also meant to show (to outsiders and to the residents themselves) that Big Sur was more than a hippie hangout, but was instead a place with residents who had roots they intended to nurture and strengthen, and that they valued such traditional services as a library and a health center, and were capable of organizing sophisticated organizations such as a property-owners' association and a locally established land trust.[95] And by the late 1970s, the hippies who had recently seemed ubiquitous had faded from the Big Sur landscape just as they had from the broader culture. (They had left remnants behind, though, leading one observer to imagine that someday "the last flower child will be found wandering, stoned, in the hills above Esalen, like a counterculture Rip Van Winkle.")[96] Now that hippies no longer demanded attention, residents turned to developing community ties that would strengthen their hand at the negotiating table with state and county officials.

The shape and direction of Big Sur's new community-oriented developments in this era was telling. The fact that these developments suggested middle-class priorities indicates that Big Sur's residents by the 1970s included people with an economic stake in society who wanted to secure practical services and certain aspects of the mainstream culture within their secluded landscape. In a matter of just several decades, Big Sur had come to mean something important to a diverse set of Americans—from dropouts to Hollywood stars. Situated somewhere in the midst of this set were the residents, who carefully guarded their unique claim to Big Sur's rewards. Notably, the Big Sur community commanded a role in management of one of California's—really one of the nation's—most treasured coastlines. Far from being engaged in a losing battle against modernity, residents were passionately involved in planning Big Sur's future.

Was it a utopia lost? It is true that by the late 1970s it was much harder for struggling artists to arrive penniless, as Miller had done, and establish a home in Big Sur. Gone were the freedoms associated with a remote and inaccessible location, namely inexpensive land and minimal government oversight. But Big Sur managed to retain the nostalgic qualities of the earlier frontier—the wide-open spaces, imposing landscape, uncommercialized stretches—while its residents relied on the government to secure their rights and opportunities within this landscape. Residents navigated the state's rapid postwar development with aplomb. In response to the *Saturday Evening Post*'s skepticism regarding Big Sur's future, locals expressed "disappointment and amused condescension, but with no feeling that Big Sur won't survive its latest unsolicited analysis."[97] Residents were indeed appropriately optimistic about their influence over land management. Through a concerted community effort and in partnership with state and federal officials over the coming decade, Big Sur residents would find considerable success not only in maintaining their privileged status as inhabitants of this prized coastline but also in preserving a public good for millions of admirers.

SIX

___

The Battle for Big Sur; or, Debating the National Environmental Ethic

I have been conscious for nearly fifty years of the extraordinary quality of the Big Sur Coast but only within the past decade have I become aware of the very real dangers facing its future. I have searched my soul for a logical explanation of why I have so dedicated myself to the protective aspect of the land-ethic. I find that I can explain it only as a form of religion, or religious experience.... I am deeply concerned with the possible many small groups (regional and county) who might enter into the management picture and be incapable of an adequate inclusive management and funding program. Hence, my strong personal conviction that only National Park Service support and management could achieve the desired objectives.

ANSEL ADAMS

I resent not being grouped in the category of environmentalists. The people who've lived here—we are environmentalist by birth and training. We were environmentalists before anybody found it in vogue to be one. We've done pretty good keeping the place for more than one hundred years.... I don't see why it should go to hell in a hand basket just because the federal government doesn't own it.

JOHN HARLAN, *third-generation Big Sur landowner and resident, 1980*

BY THE LATE TWENTIETH CENTURY no one disputed Big Sur's reputation as one of the nation's most exceptional landscapes, and yet agreement over how best to steward this land proved elusive. The Big Sur Local Coastal Program (LCP) was meant to ensure that preservation and development follow a deliberate course in Big Sur, but Ansel Adams, in particular, did not trust that this was sufficient protection for a national treasure. In 1977 Adams advanced the idea of federal oversight for the entirety of Big Sur, an arrangement that would supersede the LCP. Adams's perspective stood in stark contrast to those held by locals like John Harlan, who argued that Big Sur's special qualities had been protected by generations of residents' stewardship, a system being worked into the local land-use plan. As the quotations presented above as epigraphs to this chapter reveal, on one side of this debate stood a near-local, Ansel Adams, and on the other side a Big Sur native, John Harlan. Each was in his seventies, each possessed an intimate relationship to the land, and each came to very different conclusions regarding ideal land management. The priorities of Harlan's tourist business on his family's hundred-year-old property and Adams's photography can explain some of this difference, no doubt, but, as Adams points out, it went beyond a material explanation. Like Americans of all stripes, these two men saw the land as representing promise and hope and perhaps redemption. But to what end, and for whom? Here is where they diverged.

Adams envisioned preserving for all time in Big Sur a near wilderness, not unlike his beloved Yosemite, where government officials made land- and resource-management decisions according to environmental and tourist priorities. Harlan appreciated what the land had provided for his family and wanted to secure a working landscape with residents committed to conserving the land and its resources, with an eye toward aesthetics. Despite a professed appreciation for the place of Big Sur residents, Adams ultimately believed that Big Sur's inspirational qualities would be diminished by further residentially based developments. Harlan thought about the well-being of the land in terms of its ability to continue in what he saw as its primary function: providing a varied set of human experiences ranging from work to pleasure. Most locals, like Harlan, believed that preserving Big Sur meant protecting it from excessive bureaucracy and tourism. Residents generally regarded county regulations, along with the natural constraints of topography and access to water, as sufficient protection from overdevelopment.[1] Harlan and Adams could not see eye to eye on the issue because their ideals for Big Sur prioritized different conceptions of land use.

Although it is tempting to paint the battle over Big Sur's future in the late 1970s and 1980s as essentially a reiteration of the West's long tradition of utilitarian-versus-preservation commitments to the land, that framework does not entirely describe this debate. The showdown in Big Sur hinged as much on exactly who should have authority over resource regulation as on the issue of development itself. Neither side pushed for development. Instead, both called for maintaining Big Sur's landscape "as is." Those in favor of increased federal ownership, as well as those opposed to it, all claimed a deep love for the beauty and power of nature in Big Sur. Neither side entrenched itself in the traditional preservation-versus-development arguments. Ultimately each side believed a different level of government could provide the kind of protection that all agreed was necessary.

Big Sur seemed an appropriate setting in which to debate the national environmental ethic, for it had long held a reputation as a place apart, a natural haven in the midst of an ever-developing California coast. For generations, people within and outside Big Sur invested meanings in its nature that suited their own needs and desires. By the early 1980s Big Sur drew three million visitors annually, making it more popular than Yosemite National Park.[2] By any measure, Big Sur's land management was of national importance. Big Sur's environment sometimes embodied the politics of autonomy, rights, and privilege in the late twentieth century, but at its heart the debate over Big Sur centered on the proper place of people within nature, especially within a landscape long thought of as wild.

WHEN THE SPARKS FLEW

Big Sur captured national attention in July 1977 when a lightning storm sparked a fire that burned 177,866 acres, much of it in the Ventana Wilderness. The two preceding winters saw less than half the average precipitation, with 15.28 inches and 16.94 inches, respectively. Foresters attributed the Marble-Cone Fire's massive scale to the considerable buildup of underbrush and dead fuel caused by the drought and a 1974 snowstorm that left oak and madrone branches scattered on the forest floor. The fire ignited amidst a ratio of dead to live fuel that was nearly seven times the point at which the U.S. Forest Service considered the fire threat critical.[3] Remote fire stations, difficult terrain, and a scarce water supply all contributed to the extent of the fire's reach.[4] A journalist who helicoptered into the center of the firefighting efforts held the forest service accountable for failing to mitigate the fire danger, reporting that "in my experience, when officials tell you that a natural disaster was an 'act of God,' they are merely making excuses for their failures to anticipate and minimize the damage."[5]

Some locals, too, questioned the forest service's policies, specifically the prohibition of mechanical equipment and fire roads through the Ventana Wilderness. They worried that rigid regulations prioritizing wilderness could come at the expense of the landscape or their homes in order "to please extreme conservationist groups."[6] Residents' displeasure with federal policy, however, belied their dependence upon the forest service. For most of the twentieth century, residents had the reassurance that forest rangers would work to protect neighboring homes and properties. In the case of the Marble-Cone Fire, federal aid to the tune of $18 million went to fire control and mudslide prevention in the fire's aftermath.[7] Los Padres National Forest, though a bureaucracy charged with the management of the forest's natural resources, was also a neighbor to the Big Sur community, and for good or ill its policies had long shaped local realities.

The Marble-Cone Fire was just a recent reminder that living in Big Sur entailed not just physical hardships but at times danger. Residents willfully embraced this aspect of life in Big Sur, and they proved to be equally tenacious in the face of a manmade threat. On the heels of the Marble-Cone Fire, Ansel Adams rocked the community with his proposal to turn Big Sur into a federally protected seashore. From his nearby residence in Carmel Highlands, Adams observed sizeable population growth throughout the 1970s in Big Sur and worried that such growth, if sustained, would spell ruin for this spectacular coast.[8] At the peak of his fame, Adams now placed his substantial influence behind the argument that only the federal government could protect Big Sur from local and corporate development interests.[9] Although he was unlikely to witness Big Sur's degradation himself, Adams saw his efforts as part of a legacy: "I am nearly 78 years old. . . . Perhaps the greatest joy I will ever find in my lifetime is the opportunity to protect the unsurpassed natural beauty of our coastline for our children and grandchildren."[10] Despite his allowance that Big Sur's "most unusual feature of land use planning over the last forty years is how well the County and State have protected this coast," Adams argued in early 1980 that "this exemplary record must not obscure the present inability of the LCP to continue to do so in the face of rising pressures for both private and public use."[11] Local and state management had kept Big Sur from overdevelopment during the state's enormous postwar boom, but Adams thought that the worst was yet to come, contending that "*No* zoning is safe" in the face of "sufficient pressure." And though he claimed to respect locals' place within Big Sur, Adams maintained: "We can't allow local feelings to intrude" in matters of land management.[12]

Adams identified the same threats to Big Sur as those facing national parks: "The pressures of a growing population, self-interest, and shortness of vision."[13] Despite Big Sur's continuous history of habitation, Adams essen-

FIGURE 16. Ansel Adams along Highway 1 in 1980. Adams spent the last twenty years of his life as a resident of Carmel Highlands, just to the north of Big Sur. He worked passionately for the creation of a national seashore along the Big Sur coastline, believing federal ownership was critical to preserving Big Sur's unique beauty. (Photo: *Los Angeles Times,* UCLA Special Collections.)

tially held Big Sur to the same standards of preservation as a place like Yosemite. Undeterred by local opposition, Adams projected confidence that perseverance could bring about his desired results, and he made clear that he intended "to fight very hard" to achieve federal protection for Big Sur. This effort would include up to fifty thousand dollars' worth of free legal services to forward the proposal pledged by the Los Angeles law firm, Latham and

Watkins, that had often represented Adams.[14] Four months after the Marble-Cone Fire, Adams drew what most residents considered a battle line across the landscape. In a statement to a local newspaper, Adams implied that he could be as formidable as Big Sur's topography: "We had the whole San Joaquin Valley against us at the outset of Kings Canyon National Park, but in the end they all came to realize its value and we got the park."[15]

Privately, Adams grappled with the fact that his proposal would restrict residents' freedom in Big Sur. In a letter to Big Sur's U.S. Congressman Leon Panetta (D-CA), Adams admitted that "I find myself in a certain complexity of logic; I wish to be supportive of the human effort in all constructive directions and, at the same time, protective of the precious resources that are of equal validity, but perhaps less obvious immediate practical value (if you limit 'practical' to material profit)."[16] For this reason, Adams told Panetta that he was considering an arrangement that would acknowledge residents' place in Big Sur, a "plan perhaps similar to the Cape Cod National Seashore, the Golden Gate National Recreational Area, etc., where the inherent character of the land and its culture are considered together."[17] But publicly Adams took a firm stance, telling the papers that: "It always happens in such cases—people with financial interest getting panicky, worried about being thrown off their property. We heard it in Yosemite, Kings Canyon, Golden Gate Highlands, Point Reyes—everywhere."[18] Adams anticipated opposition between locals wishing to retain autonomy and someone like himself, who was committed to preservation, as if the two were mutually exclusive and preservation was free from any sort of self-interest. Perhaps Adams was not so disinterested as he appeared to be. There were those who accused Adams of allowing his rising popularity in the 1970s to alter his stance toward allowing more concessions in Yosemite Valley. Some Big Sur residents feared he had the same plans for this coastline, and nearly every resident believed Big Sur would face enormous tourist pressure if Adams's plan succeeded.[19]

PLANNING FOR THE FUTURE IN AN ERA OF LIMITS

A majority of Americans questioned the efficacy of big government in the latter part of the twentieth century yet nevertheless recognized that in certain cases only comprehensive management at this level could bring about desired objectives. Adams's proposal was premised on this perplexing situation. At the heart of his campaign was a paradox that Adams had previously acknowledged in regard to national-park land: "Unfortunately, in order to keep it pure we have to occupy it."[20] Adams intended for government, not residents, to occupy these landscapes as stewards of the natural resources. Whereas Adams maintained confidence in the national park service to manage lands and in some cases communities, residents of Big Sur believed that their community, certainly, but their landscape too would be better served if locals partnered with, and did not subordinate themselves to, government entities. Contemporary political realities challenged California's residents to find a role in helping to shape the growing state regulations governing the coast.

Proposition 20, which led to the Coastal Act, was a clear indication that individual Californians, and even cities, could not garner the resources or create the policies that would protect the vast California coastline from overdevelopment and degradation. The same was true nationwide, as the federal government took responsibility for dwindling and deteriorating natural resources by creating the Environmental Protection Agency in 1970. Despite voter frustration with government, the complexity and broad implications of the many issues facing California (and the nation) in the 1970s seemingly left few options but to place greater reliance upon the government's resources, power and reach. Complicating all of this was reduced government revenue in the wake of California's antitax initiative, Proposition 13.

Proposition 13, like Proposition 20, led to the transfer of local power to the state (though this was far from its intent) and changed the possibilities related to land preservation. Rapidly rising property taxes and a large state-budget surplus helped contribute to the "tax revolt" of 1978, when 65 percent of California voters approved Proposition 13 to roll back property-assessment values and cap property tax at 1 percent of sale price. Ironically, in capping property taxes and reducing county revenue, the effect was to decrease local control and give the state legislature the responsibility for allocating funds for county services, such as public schools.[21] In Big Sur, roughly two-thirds of residents voted in favor of Proposition 13.[22] Despite the association of tax reform with Republican values, this measure succeeded in a Democratic state, and in a heavily Democratic Big Sur.[23] In 1970 California contained close to twenty million residents, and by 1980 the population had grown by nearly four million more. Both propositions 20 and 13 benefitted the state's middle to upper classes, voters who looked to secure the good life in California by slowing down the development of the coast and increasing disposable income for property owners. The economic downturn in the 1970s led many to discuss the limits to growth, and it appears that certain among these advantaged property owners and residents also sought in fact to impose these limits to growth.

As Big Sur residents united to resist the extension of federal management, they had to reckon with the same issue that Adams had identified: that the state's economy challenged effective local land management. Reduced county revenue in the wake of Proposition 13 meant constricted funds for preservation (along with nearly all local governmental services). By 1980 Monterey County struggled to provide sufficient funding for its local parks, leading a county supervisor to lament what he saw as the parks department being forced "to turn itself into a prostitute": that is, encouraging private development of public lands to protect park boundaries.[24] Locals and Monterey County planners only added to this financial challenge when they wrote into the Big Sur land-use plan a critical viewshed component to prohibit any new development within view of Highway 1. The initial plan provided an option for transfer development credits to the affected landowners, but if owners demanded market-value compensation for lost development rights, the viewshed measure could ultimately cost Monterey County $77 million.[25] Although the state's Coastal Commission endorsed this viewshed component, neither the state nor the county had the means to guarantee its success, and few people believed the county could enforce this viewshed policy without the necessary funding.

Ansel Adams's response to the financial dilemma was to identify the federal government as "the only realistic source of funds" for Big Sur's preservation.[26] The Coastal Commission's executive director, Michael Fischer, felt compelled to agree, viewing federal funds as not only necessary but appropriate in Big Sur. Fischer argued that he would consider it "a dereliction" if the federal government failed "to recognize a shared responsibility in the protection of this priceless area."[27] Meanwhile, Governor Jerry Brown's chief of staff, Gray Davis, also expressed support for federal funding.[28] Certainly California officials understood the financial constraints placed on counties and the state after Proposition 13, and therefore remained open to, even solicitous of, outside funding.

California, like the nation as a whole, continued to experience a political shift in the late 1970s as a group of voters articulated a set of conservative values that formed the New Right. This coalition included a diverse set of constituents who felt passionately about constraining government, protecting the role of religion in American life, and promoting a traditional society in the face of changing social mores. Economic libertarians and the Religious Right found common ground in their desire for a less powerful federal government and came together to challenge Democrats and their more expansive economic agenda and its social implications.[29] Likely reading the shifting political sentiments that would usher in a more conservative administration, Adams decided to push for federal legislation for Big Sur in advance of the 1980 election. Any political discussion, including the expansion of federal control over Big Sur, would take place among this increasingly polarized electorate.

Ansel Adams's strategy for Big Sur derived from his involvement in decades of large-scale conservation measures. His influence with the country's leadership and national conservation organizations went back as far as the 1930s, when his photography and lobbying helped convince Franklin Roosevelt to establish Kings Canyon National Park. He served in the leadership of the Sierra Club for nearly forty years and helped publish the club's *This Is the American Earth* in 1960, a work that helped define a conservation ethic for the rapidly growing group of wilderness supporters in the postwar period.[30] In 1975 President Gerald Ford extended an invitation to Adams to visit the White House, and Adams used the opportunity to press for tougher regulations for the preservation of national parks.[31] In November 1979 Adams traveled to the White House to create Jimmy Carter's official portrait. During the course of this photo session Adams passed a memo to Carter highlighting two current Wilderness Society priorities: preservation in Big Sur and in Alaska.[32] Adams's former business manager, William Turnage, had recently become the executive director for the Wilderness Society. Turnage devoted a subsequent issue of the society's newsletter to honoring Ansel Adams as an artist and as an advocate for environmental causes, and he used this platform to promote Adams's endeavors to preserve the Big Sur coast.[33] Adams and the Wilderness Society proposed a model of land preservation that had been common over the previous century. Now, in the midst of growing political conservatism and a sustained economic downturn, when even the Democratic Party called for "fiscal restraint," such expensive federal plans gained less political traction.[34]

PRESERVATION AND POLARIZATION

It would take a legislator with a firm commitment to environmental protection to further Adams's ambitious plan for Big Sur. In January 1980, U.S. Senator Alan Cranston introduced S.2551 to establish the Big Sur Coast

National Scenic Area. Cranston, a Democrat from California, had long supported measures to extend and protect wilderness boundaries, wildlife refuges, marine sanctuaries, and other environmentally sensitive areas. Cranston's bill recognized Big Sur as "a national treasure" and "the most beautiful scenic drive in the United States," and was premised on the belief that only the federal government could afford to protect this coastline from overdevelopment. S.2551 called for the appropriation of $100 million over ten years for land acquisition and management under the U.S. Forest Service (under the umbrella of the Department of Agriculture). Cranston outlined a plan in which land would be acquired from willing sellers, with condemnation utilized only if the secretary of agriculture deemed a change in private land use incompatible with a scenic area, or if the secretary identified specific private-property holdings as "necessary for public access and recreational use." The bill stipulated that only 5 percent of private property could be acquired for recreational use.[35]

Although Big Sur residents agreed that Big Sur was exceptionally beautiful and should remain so, the majority of them disagreed that only the forest service could adequately protect this coastline. They instead put faith in the developing land-use plan and the natural constraints of topography and limited water. They disagreed fundamentally with the concept of condemnation to achieve tourist priorities, and many feared that federal status would increase public use and therefore conflict with preservation efforts.[36] The intensity and shape of local resistance to Adams's plan varied, but Big Sur residents found near-unanimity in opposing Cranston's legislation.[37] Their arguments against the bill took many forms and revealed just how politicized resource protection had become by the latter part of the century.

A well-organized and vocal group of Big Sur residents aligned with the emerging property-rights movement, employing this movement's language and resources to question the very philosophical and legal concepts of federal ownership and land management.[38] This particular group of residents foresaw the worst: that the federal government would "hound the residents out and turn Big Sur from a community into a museum," and they queried whether the government had the "right to wipe out a way of life." They pointed to numerous examples of communities that had been broken apart when a newly established national park or recreation area superseded local government.[39] Big Sur residents poured themselves into the battle, investing countless hours and considerable resources to thwart the federal legislation. They formed the Friends of the Big Sur Coast and raised $100,000 over a period of six months, earmarking $6,000 to bring in Charles Cushman, the property-rights activist, Wise-Use Movement leader, and founder of the National Inholders Association, to rally residents against the Senate bill.[40]

Cushman had united neighbors in and around Yosemite National Park in the late 1970s to file a lawsuit against the National Park Service. His National Inholders Association communicated with 1,800 national groups all aiming to protect private property from federal encroachment. While touring Big Sur, Cushman announced: "There are many well-meaning but naïve folk here who have never lived under federal management. Proposing federal intervention in Big Sur is like leading the lambs to the slaughter."[41] Cushman described himself as "a tank commander in the war against environmentalists," and his strategies earned him a national reputation as a "rent-a-riot" personality.[42]

Cushman's audience gleaned antienvironmental arguments from those around the country who furthered the property-rights movement, and they could even turn to its National Rights Library for information and inspiration.[43] While the more prominent Wise-Use Movement called for opening public land for corporate use and resource extraction, those advocating property rights sought to curtail any additional federal lands. They felt government acquisition stood in opposition to private initiative by removing land from the realm of private property ownership. Both groups saw as a threat the environmentalists who called for government regulation of resource use and an ever-increasing amount of parkland. In a statement that rang true for the more extreme opponents of Adams's proposal, Ron Arnold, one of the founders of the Wise-Use Movement, excoriated the National Park Service as an "empire designed to eliminate all private property in the United States."[44]

Western property-rights advocates took multiple approaches throughout this era, and in California an organization of those with financial interests along the coast formed to resist the impact of the state regulations developed under the Coastal Act. The California Coastal Council cited a membership in 1980 of eight thousand individual property owners, with affiliate members totaling two hundred thousand, including unions, construction and real-estate groups, agricultural associations, utilities, and oil companies. The council's intent was to construct a legislative, judicial, and media response to what they deemed "excessive and unreasonable government regulatory activity."[45] The council's executive director, Joseph Mastroianni, declared that the private landowner "must not be unfairly burdened in the noble name of the public good with a de facto moratorium, under which he must still continue to pay taxes." Though Cranston's bill for Big Sur was unrelated to Coastal Act regulations, the Coastal Council decided to take a stance on the federal proposal, linking it to the "consistent and not-so-subtle conspiratorial efforts between the Burton/Cranston federal park machine, the California Coastal Commission, and groups of radical self-proclaimed environmentalists who seek the elimination of private property holdings, not the protection of the environment." In case its message was unclear, the council went on to argue: "Over one-third of the nation is now in federal ownership. . . . This process must end."[46]

Gary Koeppel, the editor of the *Big Sur Gazette* and a member of Big Sur's Citizens Advisory Committee, chose to run the council's statement in his paper. Koeppel himself bluntly exclaimed: "The environmentalists are using the logic of hysteria and hyperbole. Big Sur needs saving. It needs saving from the radical environmentalists and from government domination."[47] Residents like Koeppel felt duty-bound to stand up against what they perceived as an overreaching government.[48] Such thinking was reflected in Big Sur's voting rolls: elections of the late 1970s revealed that as many as a third of Big Sur residents shifted their votes to the Republican Party.[49] These were western individualists, and they had found a place where it seemed relatively easy to live outside the reach of mainstream society and government. They took pride in this distinction: "Hell, we could do just fine without the government," said one resident. "We've got timber, we've got water, fish in the ocean, deer; we could raise cattle, pigs. There are a lot of people on this coast who have expertise in almost anything you'd need to know."[50] Such thinking may have been a holdover from the frontier mentality, but like the homesteaders who were inherently reliant upon the federal government's establishment and protection of private-property parcels, by the late twentieth century residents in Big Sur relied upon services such as highway maintenance and fire protection provided by their county, state, and federal governments.

Despite (and to some extent because of) this reliance, these residents prioritized private-property rights. In 1980 the *Big Sur Gazette* ran an excerpt from the Republican National Convention Platform, asserting that "the widespread distribution of private property ownership is the cornerstone of American liberty. Without it neither our free enterprise system nor our republican form of government could long endure."[51] Residents who adhered to this view would not support preservation that increased public-land acquisition, for they believed firmly that the end result of such preservation would be the erasure of all inhabitants of Big Sur. Their fears were grounded in some real data: by 1980 the state had a long-range proposal to add 27,085 acres to park holdings in Big Sur; the 1978 U.S. Forest Service land-management plan for Big Sur called for acquisition of up to 2,500 acres of private land within the forest; and an increasing number of privately owned acres were held in scenic easements, thereby putting this property off-limits to future development.[52] Cranston's proposed legislation not only called for acquisition of additional acres for public access but allowed for the further removal of private property deemed out-of-step with the overarching land-management goals established for the Big Sur National Scenic Area. These stipulations caused alarm even among residents with no particular affinity for the property-rights movement but who nevertheless opposed federal management for Big Sur because increased public holdings threatened the community's ability to perpetuate its long tradition of isolated creativity.[53]

In the months preceding the Senate hearing on Cranston's bill, residents and interested figures primarily used the newspapers to forward their respective opinions on land management, but on one memorable occasion, on a beautiful day in early March 1980, they convened at Nepenthe Restaurant. Nothing about the warm, sunny day or the glorious setting seemed to jibe with the passionate battle unfolding on the terrace. Bill Fassett, the restaurant's owner, acknowledged the heightened emotions that characterized the debate: "We turned Nepenthe over to you today as our contribution to this pending civil war." Throughout the afternoon, hundreds of Big Sur and Monterey County residents, their elected officials, and representatives from Los Padres National Forest and national organizations debated Big Sur's future.[54] A meeting drawing the likes of Representative Leon Panetta and Ansel Adams spoke to the considerable importance of Big Sur and was also an indication that state and national figures felt a measure of respect for the residents who had helped to foster and maintain this iconic coastline.

Panetta encouraged the audience to consider concrete measures to address the increasing pressures to develop Big Sur's popular coastline, reminding them that "Whether we like it or not, we are at a crossroads in deciding which direction to take." Jim Josoff, head of Friends of the Big Sur Coast, argued on behalf of residents like himself: "We simply want to be left alone by the federal government to enjoy our lifestyles. We don't want to see development." Ansel Adams retorted by characterizing Josoff's view as parochial. Charles Cushman was quick to respond, raising his voice in anger against Adams for failing to support the residents who had fought to keep their homes in Yosemite. Though Cushman admitted that federal funding might have some role in protecting Big Sur, he thought residents should first have the opportunity to attempt preservation on their own terms: "I damn well think they ought to have a chance to fail before they roll over and say the feds will have to manage us."[55]

Representative Panetta, who was generally well respected and well liked throughout his district, maintained a friendly tone throughout the debate as he continued to press for forward movement. He pointed out that the federal government, by owning Los Padres National Forest, was going to have some role in the developing land-use plan regardless of the proposed federal legislation, but he voiced agreement with most residents that a national park was inappropriate for Big Sur: "We may not want the park service here, and dammit, we can say that. I personally don't want the park service." Panetta nonetheless encouraged residents to work toward legislation that would respect private property (such as disallowing land condemnation) while also protecting the area's beauty and tranquility through federally funded regulations. Ron Tipton of the Wilderness Society also argued in favor of federal legislation, asserting that Highway 1 was already a de facto national park. Tipton's remarks drew hisses from the crowd, and at one point someone in the audience offered a solution to halting the steady stream of tourists: "Blow up the Bixby Bridge!"[56] No resolution was reached that day at Nepenthe, but no one anticipated that such a meeting was going to run smoothly when everyone present felt emotionally invested in the Big Sur landscape.

DEBATING THE LAND'S MEANING

During the many months of the federal-legislation debate, people on both sides heightened the stakes by casting preservation in nonmaterial terms. Like the public morality debates over issues such as abortion, busing, and prisoners' rights, the realm of the environment became value-laden in American political discourse as it was linked to individual and community rights.[57] According to Charles Cushman, the disagreement between environmentalists and people like himself was no less than a "holy war between fundamentally different religions. The preservationists are like a new pagan religion, worshipping trees and animals and sacrificing people."[58] John McClaughry, a leader of the property-rights movement who had served as a Vermont state senator and was soon to be a senior policy advisor in Ronald Reagan's White House, explained the dichotomy as "two different world views at work here between us and the environmentalists. . . . They [environmentalists] think anything that increases comfort or convenience should be banned. It's part of what I call the Green Church, this religious compulsion to make people suffer for our sins against nature."[59]

In Big Sur, most residents tended to associate freedom with the enjoyment of the land in all its varied functions. Skeptical of an environmentalist approach to land management, residents like John Harlan advocated for reducing government regulation. Harlan and others firmly believed that they served as the rightful arbiters between the land and the opportunities it promised and that private stewardship was appropriate for the health of the community and the land. Harlan maintained: "There's nothing on God's green earth that wasn't put here for man to use, and he has the ability to control his destiny, providing he use it judiciously."[60] Other residents believed that in Big Sur their freedom and well-being was tied to the less tangible, inspirational qualities of the landscape. Nat Owings queried: "I look at the great sweep of earth and sea and mountain that is Big Sur—and I ask, what are the economics of wonder and of harmonious living?" He posited that personal growth could come from time spent in Big Sur, where "there is something beyond the boundaries of the limited human intellect to lead us toward truly creative energy."[61] After serving a sixteen-year stint on the advisory board of the National Park Service, Owings assessed Big Sur in 1980 and argued that allowing the federal government control over land management in Big Sur would be "a form of dictatorship and authoritarianism that's appropriate if an area can't solve its own problems. You pay the penalty of facelessness, ineptness, lack of ability to get something done."[62] Owings, like most residents, believed that in Big Sur an unusual combination of commitments to the land and its people could best be achieved through local control. John Harlan and Nat Owings approached the land-management debate with distinct convictions but could still agree that life in Big Sur offered exceptional liberty that was best guarded by local management.

It was notable that similar convictions led Adams to argue in *favor* of federal protection for Big Sur. Adams himself attached weight to the creative impulse that Big Sur inspired in an artist like himself.[63] Well before he moved to the central coast, Adams drew artistic inspiration from Robinson Jeffers (whom he photographed, with results Jeffers admired, for a published collection of poems in 1928).[64] Adams appreciated Jeffers's verse for its fine representation of the Big Sur landscape and its effect on the reader. For Adams, Jeffers's poems "sound more music and pile more mountains in the spirit than almost anything I know of." In 1945 Adams wrote to his friend and fellow photographer Alfred Stieglitz, claiming that he planned to "do my best to call attention to the simplicities of environment and method; to 'the enormous beauty of the world,' as Jeffers writes. Pray for me."[65] Adams did indeed succeed in calling attention to the enormous beauty of the world through his masterful photographs. Significantly, Adams accomplished something more than sharing this beauty with a worldwide audience. His work glorified a conception of wilderness that held these landscapes as separate and implicitly superior to, say, an urban area. Adams's most popular photographs reveal few signs of human habitation; he must be credited with reinforcing the conception of wilderness as a place without people and their trappings. And his enormous and enduring popularity meant that Adams's photographs spread these wilderness ideas not as an argument per se but as an apparent natural reality.[66]

It is reasonable to imagine that Adams's early impressions of Big Sur and its poet laureate helped spur his conviction to preserve the beauty that he and so many others saw in this coast. Adams's career flourished on capturing and representing such beauty. He did not need to harvest resources or develop his property to earn a living; his particular work depended upon the earth's wild places remaining wild. Clearly though, Adams engaged with the earth around him for reasons beyond work alone. Through his photographs Adams sought to sanctify a religious idea and to "inquire of my own soul just what the primeval scene really signifies. . . . In the last analysis, Half Dome is just a piece of rock. . . . There is some deep personal distillation of spirit and concept which molds these earthly facts into some transcendental emotional and spiritual experience."[67] Adams used photography to transmute his ideas about the inherent worth of nature into the scenes that he admired. When Adams sought to preserve nature, he saw himself preserving something sacred. Like John Muir before him, Adams believed that to destroy such beauty was comparable to desecrating a religious edifice. If he likened his land ethic to a religion, then Adams was an evangelical in the conservation movement, with a vast congregation of followers who understood implicitly his message that wild lands deserved to remain unaltered.

It is hardly surprising that in Big Sur, a place often considered an Eden, locals' and outsiders' stance on land management reflected their feelings about the intangible value of the land and their personal convictions about how society and its landscapes should look and operate. The debate over preservation, therefore, became as volatile as any other political issue in this era, and particularly complex in Big Sur, where people across the political spectrum all sought to retain an image of Big Sur that fit their particular ideas of the ideal relationship between people and nature. Despite their considerable influence and experience, neither Adams nor Owings, nor anyone else, had the final answer for Big Sur. But in a battle of values, it mattered very much who expressed which values. Adams not only helped create the impression of this coast as a place apart but sought to set people apart from Big Sur as temporary admirers and to minimize their presence as permanent consumers of, or residents in, its beauty. Locals who opposed him sought to do something unique: secure a place for residents in a landscape widely recognized as worthy of national-park status. If they succeeded, they would buck the tradition of removing the most appealing tourist locations from local control, but, more significant, they would reshape the long-held perception that wild lands were incompatible with human habitation.[68]

WASHINGTON WEIGHS IN

A contingent of Monterey County residents traveled to Washington, D.C., in April 1980 to testify in the Senate Committee hearings on Cranston's federal proposal for Big Sur. Monterey County Supervisor Barbara Shipnuck sat before the senators and emphasized that she and her fellow supervisors recognized that "in preserving the Big Sur Coast, we hold a public trust that transcends our usual responsibilities to our own local constituents." Supervisor Shipnuck detailed the county's long track record of preservation dating back to the 1930s, well before federal and state mandates, and explained how in the years following Proposition 20 Monterey County became one of ten jurisdictions to undertake a special pilot planning program to pioneer appropriate land-management coordination between the county and state. In all, Shipnuck sought to convince the Senate that Monterey County had the intention and the wherewithal to preserve the Big Sur coast, and that the county's developing Local Coastal Program (LCP) should serve as the first step in defining land management. Only after the LCP was in effect, Shipnuck argued, should the role of federal assistance be assessed.[69]

Aware of the national interest in Big Sur, Shipnuck highlighted the county's commitment to protecting the characteristics valued by tourists and environmentalists. These included retaining open space, protecting the highway viewshed, safeguarding water supplies, preserving local flora and fauna, managing Highway 1 with public information centers at either end of the coast, and planning for improved public access to the shoreline and to Los Padres National Forest and the Ventana Wilderness. This Monterey County supervisor, along with many residents, essentially pleaded the case for local management of a national treasure. Shipnuck stressed, however, that the board did not want to reject the possibility of obtaining federal funds for preservation. In the wake of Proposition 13, Shipnuck explained that diminishing revenues at the local level might necessitate the use of federal funds for several land-management goals outlined in the LCP: to purchase development rights for property that contained important wildlife and plants, or that fell within the viewshed; to acquire trail easements for increased public access; and to help coordinate the many agencies with management responsibilities along the coast.[70] It was a familiar western plea: federal assistance with no strings attached.

Meanwhile, the U.S. Forest Service provided weight to Shipnuck's case by testifying in favor of a locally crafted management plan. The forest service believed that the county's developing LCP had the potential to address many objectives of S.2551 without the cost of federal ownership. The agency's representative, the assistant secretary for natural resources and environment in the Department of Agriculture, emphasized that the forest service was committed to helping secure for Big Sur "adequate protection from overdevelopment and other uses that could forever destroy it" but was not yet willing to cast its support for S.2551. In a statement that must have cheered many residents, the assistant secretary remarked simply: "No one in this administration has yet said that we can zone [Big Sur] better from Washington."[71]

Individual Big Sur residents testifying at the capitol tackled head-on an issue close to their hearts and their property holdings. They strove to make legislators see this coastline as more than just a spectacular place to visit. In his testimony, Don McQueen of the Big Sur Chamber of Commerce reiterated the fact that Big Sur was a "sparsely populated rural community" and not just a "remote coastal wilderness," as many people in the East might believe.[72] Arguably, Monterey County and Big Sur residents themselves were at least partly responsible for this misconception. The Coast Master Plan's protection of open space and the fiercely guarded individualism of Big Sur residents obscured the presence of a community in Big Sur, while the viewshed proposal promised to perpetuate a parklike appearance for this coastline.

Locals likely understood that it was a reasonable question whether tourists or anyone outside Big Sur would actually notice if the third of the landscape held as private property changed hands and belonged to the federal government instead. Would the Big Sur experience be any different for the tourists if the federal government assumed management of this popular destination? Most residents certainly believed it would be, and they could envision a much-diminished experience for visitors. Whereas Adams considered the use of minibuses like those operating in Yosemite to take tourists through Big Sur, the *Big Sur Gazette* criticized the national-park experience as overly regimented and lacking a sense of history.[73] Moreover, most residents contended that federal ownership would degrade the land with more motels, restaurants, parking lots, "trailers to house additional government employees . . . obtrusive chainlink fences . . . new trails through the wilderness," and even "signs which tell you where to take a picture or redundantly point out that this is, indeed, a scenic area."[74] Most residents believed that federal ownership would cause Big Sur to lose its local flavor, to encourage conformity, to essentialize it, to make it into a place overrun by tourists and lacking the spontaneity of experience that tourists and locals apparently sought. They felt confident that Big Sur's appeal rested in its cultural heritage as well as in its beauty and therefore saw Big Sur as ill suited to federal management. A common refrain from residents, that "the coast has already been saved," indicated their confidence in the effectiveness of county and state planning measures.[75]

Residents argued that Big Sur was a better tourist destination and community because of its local autonomy. Keith Thompson of the Esalen Institute argued that Big Sur should be thought of as another country, with its "own language and customs, its own unique heritage, its own norms of social conduct, its own goals and values, its own pace of life" and that such conditions left this coastline "somewhat out of step with the rest of mainland America." Big Sur's exceptional qualities derived from and inspired creativity along this coast, so Thompson argued, and he challenged those who believed that Big Sur's unique essence could survive under federal ownership by asking, "How many artists are there in Yosemite?" Thompson, too, linked the debate to questions of personal autonomy and asserted that Big Sur offered a way of life based on individual freedom that he found missing in other parts of the country.[76] For Thompson and the Esalen Institute, and for others who derived meaning—and, not incidentally, a living—from the unusual blend of community and individuality along this coast, it was of the utmost importance that federal management did not come to define Big Sur.

The few residents testifying in favor of S.2551 were members of the Big Sur Foundation, a group that had formed several years earlier to explore long-term protection for this coastline. The foundation's board included Ansel Adams, former state senator Fred Farr, as well as several prominent landowners (some of them part-time residents) of Big Sur, and two full-time residents. Though the foundation itself was responsible for first advancing the idea of federal protection, its members wished to see a few modifications to S.2551. Namely their proposed amendments sought to provide greater peace of mind for current landowners by encouraging scenic easements over outright acquisition of private land; grandfathering in current land uses so as not to leave them subject to condemnation; and to treat the LCP as the primary land-use plan and regulatory program for Big Sur.[77] Such amendments, the foundation's members believed, would make the bill more palatable to residents and more equitable for landowners.

After reviewing numerous testimonies, statements, reports, and well over a hundred letters and other materials submitted by Senator Sam Hayakawa (R-CA) in opposition to the bill, the Senate subcommittee decided it was premature to call for increased federal authority prior to the completion of the state-certified Local Coastal Program. When the subcommittee shelved S.2551, Representative Phil Burton (D-CA), the chairman of the House Parks and Insular Affairs Subcommittee, expressed his support of a federal plan for Big Sur but deferred to Leon Panetta, the congressman representing Big Sur. Apparently seeing little other choice, Panetta penned "the best solution [he] could come up with" and in May 1980 introduced HR 7380, the Big Sur Coast Area Act.[78] Panetta developed an idea for a land-management council, in which the secretary of agriculture shared authority alongside a council of Big Sur residents. Together they were to draw up a regional master plan that included the LCP and would be binding on all landowners in the area, including Los Padres National Forest. Panetta explained his two overarching goals as ensuring the forest service's compliance with the LCP and providing financial compensation for landowners in the viewshed. Panetta estimated that it would cost thirty million dollars to support local land-management priorities, and he doubted that the county or even the state could successfully implement its own land-management plan without such federal funds.

The executive director of the California Coastal Commission, Michael Fischer, lent his support to Panetta's legislation. Fearing that Big Sur's LCP exceeded the capacity of the state's planning and regulatory program, Fischer argued that "a complementary backstop is needed to fully carry out our trust." It was important to Fischer that a federal initiative did not replace the LCP. Characterizing the local will to protect Big Sur as strong, Fischer reasoned that "local efforts should continue to be the principal thrust of a national program. But the nation has a responsibility to augment and buttress these local efforts." Because of what he saw as a federal responsibility for this prime tourist destination and the shortcomings of state preservation, Fischer felt federal legislation was appropriate for Big Sur. Moreover, he appreciated that Panetta's legislation, like Cranston's, "recognizes the importance of a real local-state-national partnership."[79] Such partnerships were rare, but becoming more politically viable in California as all levels of government faced constricted funds and as the Coastal Commission gained stature for its ambitious and well-developed coastal land-management strategies.[80]

Despite Panetta's efforts to craft a plan that incorporated residents' opinions and ideas, many residents questioned to what extent the federal agency would work in tandem with locals if given greater authority.[81] In the midst of an economic recession, these residents chose a prudent argument: that federal legislation for Big Sur would be unnecessarily costly. If the purpose of the Big Sur Coast Area Act was to protect the natural beauty of Big Sur, residents posited that the area needed no further protection than what they could offer through the nascent land-use plan. Why spend millions of taxpayer dollars, they argued, to preserve this largely undeveloped and restrictively zoned landscape? Yosemite cost the federal government millions in stewardship, whereas Big Sur's current ownership system cost the federal government only the maintenance of Los Padres National Forest, not the acquisition of private property within Big Sur or the ongoing costs related to recreational tourism along this coastline. This fiscal argument resonated in Washington, where a 1979 Government Accounting Office report concluded that federal agencies "overlooked viable alternative land protection strategies such as easements, zoning, and other Federal regulatory controls" and had instead paid to acquire as much land as possible without regard to need.[82]

The momentum that Ansel Adams and Senator Cranston had built for increased federal involvement in Big Sur convinced Representative Burton to provide guidance for Panetta's bill, and HR 7380 passed the House. Senator Cranston then pledged to see Panetta's bill to fruition during the fall legislative session. When it looked as if the Big Sur Coast Area Act would not reach a vote before the election recess, Representative Burton attached Panetta's bill as an amendment to a noncontroversial bill on funding city parks in Idaho that the Senate had already approved and that would not require any committee hearings.[83] This bill also passed the House, but when it was sent to the Senate a staffer for Sam Hayakawa noticed it, and the senator threatened to filibuster. Hayakawa disagreed with the premise that the federal government would provide the best protection for Big Sur. As a former lecturer at the Esalen Institute in Big Sur, Hayakawa drew on his knowledge of Big Sur's population to assert: "The people who live there are by nature, temperament, and training, conservationists" and "live a life which they hope to be individualistic and totally creative." Hayakawa's admiration for the Big Sur community derived at least in part from what he perceived as their rejection of conventional lifestyles, including "commercialism, development, condominiums and anything that reminds them of urban life."[84] He was drawn by the allure of Big Sur, believing that it possessed "a unique kind of subculture that belongs to Big Sur and nowhere else." Hayakawa's political convictions led him to assert that "Washington cannot provide and has never provided better protection than the local citizens themselves. . . . And that's why they say, 'Get the hell out of our lives, and don't try to barge in."[85] Senator Hayakawa effectively blocked passage of the bill before the legislative recess, earning him the title of conservationist of the year from the Friends of the Big Sur Coast, who feted him in honor of his efforts.[86]

Adams refused to be deterred in the face of the bill's defeat. He indicated to a national paper that federal management for Big Sur was important enough to warrant pushing against the political momentum and local resistance: "We'll just keep going. We may be opposing their wishes, but we're saving their skin and saving the countryside."[87] Adams's hopes for Alaska had been realized with the 1980 Alaska National Interest Lands Conservation Act, but the well-organized opposition to Cranston and Panetta's legislation, as well as the strength of the California Coastal Commission, led Washington legislators to hold off on federal investment in Big Sur. As Adams must have feared, large-scale federal preservation projects became even less viable after Republican Ronald Reagan won the 1980 presidential election. Reagan ran on a platform calling for a smaller federal government, and though he was a Californian who knew firsthand the beauty of the coast, Adams knew not to count on ideological support from someone who courted the sagebrush rebels. These western rebels were ranchers and miners who capitalized on resources found in federal lands and reacted to what they perceived as a federal bias for preservation by calling for a transfer of such lands to state control.[88] During a campaign stop in Utah, Reagan had proclaimed: "I happen to be one who cheers and supports the sagebrush rebellion. Count me in as a rebel."[89] Reagan went on to appoint James Watt as his secretary of the interior, thereby placing a person who self-identified as part of the sagebrush rebellion in charge of managing the nation's natural resources.[90]

Although on the face of it resistance in Big Sur to federal legislation shared something in common with the sagebrush rebels, those in Big Sur generally supported slow-growth and antidevelopment measures. And despite Reagan's rhetoric, and in contrast to the majority of Californians, voters in Big Sur registered a slim majority in favor of Democrat Jimmy Carter, who as president had in fact shifted from an initial opposition to Cranston's bill to support for Panetta's less-expensive proposal.[91] Panetta, too, took a majority of Big Sur votes, and Cranston lost by only a narrow margin.[92] In the midst of a fervent national debate about the value of wild lands and local autonomy, Big Sur residents' rising property values and opposition to federal land management may have prompted their critique of the Democrat-driven proposals to preserve Big Sur, but these conditions did not drive a majority of them into the Republican ranks. Over the coming years, residents again mobilized to shape local land management by way of the state-mandated land-use plan. Said one resident in regard to the work to be done per the Coastal Act: "We knew that if we didn't want others to do the planning for us, ours had better be a good plan."[93] The developing land-use plan provided locals and county and state officials the opportunity to try to reconcile the two political imperatives of property rights and environmentalism in order to preserve a prized landscape and culture.

SEVEN

Defining the Value of California's Coastline

The Big Sur coastline is, as you're keenly aware, one of the
nation's most majestic meetings of land and sea. The grandeur
of the Santa Lucia Mountains plunging into the Pacific, with
narrow, winding Highway One clinging to the heights above
crashing waves and offshore seastacks is known by millions
who have been there, and tens of millions more who have seen
stunning photographs. The awesome panoramas uncluttered
by man's structures ... make this ... stretch of the California
coast a national resource of inestimable value. Yet the decisions
which this generation will make for the Big Sur will determine
its future character—and significant degradation could be the
unfortunate result.

> MICHAEL L. FISCHER, *executive director, California Coastal
> Commission, to U.S. Representative Leon Panetta*

IN 1976 THE STATE LEGISLATURE made permanent the California
Coastal Commission and its companion agency the California State Coastal
Conservancy. Governor Jerry Brown lent his support to the effort by helping
to secure the necessary votes for the Coastal Act at the last hour. On the day
after the vote, Governor Brown and his staff member Bill Press traveled to
the Monterey Peninsula and stopped at the local Holiday Inn, a concrete box
of a hotel so intrusive on the beach landscape that its construction had helped
to galvanize local support for Proposition 20.[1] Admiring the bay from a bal-
cony, with his feet propped on the banister, Brown exclaimed, "This is what
we fought for yesterday!" Press, whose knowledge of the Coastal Act led him
to understand that the legislation would have prevented the construction of
such a hotel so close to the shoreline, responded unequivocally: "Jerry, no it
isn't! It isn't." Press presumably shared the story with the Coastal
Commission's executive director, Michael Fischer, who later recounted the
exchange and characterized Brown's sentiment as a "basic failure to grasp

the concept."[2] Even though Brown may not have been in close step with the conservation-minded authors of the bill, the governor probably spoke for many Californians who agreed with the commission's efforts to protect access to the coast and who could also overlook the sometimes ugly built environment to focus on the beauty beyond. Ultimately, there would be as many ways to interpret appropriate development, regulations, and preservation goals as there were Californians looking to enjoy the coast. The state's certification process for the Local Coastal Program would therefore be laborious and at times contentious. But more to the point, the negotiations reflected shifting ideas about preservation, private-property rights, and government responsibility in relationship to a coastline that Californians increasingly understood as a public commons.

When Californians passed Proposition 20, in 1972, voters across the country indicated their support for large-scale measures to address a deteriorating environment. But political conservatism was on the rise throughout the decade. By 1980, California held a national reputation for its strong environmental regulations and also stood as a leader in the conservative tax revolt.[3] As many Californians, and soon other Americans, became committed to reducing taxes, "saving the environment" became politically charged in a way it had never been before. By the early 1980s, an economic recession, a pro-business federal administration, a general aversion to big government, and a growing opposition to government-funded preservation fueled a broad retreat from the expansive pro-environment policies of the previous two decades.[4] Meanwhile, continually increasing coastal land values favored high-return development schemes over open space and rural land use. Voters and legislators had created the California Coastal Commission in advance of the conservative turn, and now in the 1980s the commission worked to implement the ideals of a different political era. It was therefore unsurprising that the agency needed support from other conservation-minded organizations that better reflected the current political possibilities.

Californians looking to prevent rapid coastal development in this era found success in creative partnerships that harnessed the regulatory power of the state with the flexibility, steadier financial resources, and greater political viability of private organizations. The California State Coastal Conservancy, a state agency established to implement Coastal Act policies, distributed state funds to local governments, public agencies, and nonprofits. Private land trusts in particular became an appealing and effective vehicle for securing preservation along the coast by negotiating conservation easements, which required less capital outlay and were more sensitive to property rights than was outright acquisition. The Coastal Act, born out of citizen activism, provided the infrastructure to support nongovernmental organizations looking to secure open space and habitat protection even when government coffers were low. This was not the form of preservation that Ansel Adams and others of his generation had fought for, but by the close of the twentieth century it proved more politically viable than traditional government acquisition and potentially as effective at halting development.

Not coincidentally, this collaborative public-private preservation became more prevalent in an era when Secretary of the Interior James Watt looked to maximize development of the nation's resources at the expense of the national parks and forests, and as Governor George Deukmejian did all in his power to reduce the authority and reach of the California Coastal Commission. Retreat from the momentum of the environmental movement produced its own backlash as membership in national environmental organizations grew rapidly in the 1980s and citizen volunteer groups tackled local restoration projects to compensate for diminishing government investment.[5] Deukmejian's efforts to defund the California Coastal Commission prompted even the development industry to call for sufficient funding for the agency in order for it to be able to adequately review construction permits.[6] As Americans grappled with just what it meant to care about the earth during a time when many argued that such concerns jeopardized jobs, Californians by and large accepted the idea that some level of regulation was necessary in order to preserve the value of the state's remarkable landscapes. Throughout the 1980s, California voters approved in every statewide election some proposition relating to parkland acquisition or environmental protection, with one specifically targeted at the coast.[7] A majority of Californians continued to support coastal preservation in the 1980s because they saw their well-being as directly related to the health and beauty of the coast, and they explored ways to protect it with or without the government's support.

Coastal protection was an uphill battle as the cumulative effects of rapid population growth and suburban and urban development were nearly everywhere apparent along California's coast. The state strained under a growing and increasingly wealthy population with a diverse set of ideas about the significance of the shoreline. This prized 1,072-mile-long coastal band—which housed 80 percent of the state's population; drove a multibillion-dollar tourist industry; served as the backdrop for countless films, television shows, advertisements, and literature; provided habitat for endemic and endangered species, and movie stars and the ultrawealthy—mattered culturally, economically, recreationally, or aesthetically, to every resident, in some way. And what happened in Big Sur, arguably the state's most striking coastal stretch, mattered a good deal.

NEGOTIATING A LOCAL COASTAL PROGRAM

As legislators, residents, and others discussed the federal proposals for Big Sur's land management in Washington and in newspapers and magazines throughout the country, the slow process of crafting the state-mandated land-use plan continued. It took five years of work by the Monterey County Planning Department, in collaboration with the Big Sur Citizens Advisory Committee (CAC), to complete the first iteration of Big Sur's state-mandated plan. Once paired with the necessary zoning regulations and additional ordinances, and approved by the California Coastal Commission, the land-use plan would eventually become Big Sur's Local Coastal Program. The plan submitted to the Monterey County Planning Commission in 1981 resulted from years of negotiations and considerable compromises designed to satisfy diverse stakeholders. Following the plan's submission, the Big Sur Citizens Advisory Committee reported to the Big Sur community that it endorsed the objectives and key policies of the county's plan, albeit with some questions, and believed any "differences will work out as the LCP develops further." In all, the CAC felt encouraged by the fact that the "county's draft clearly reflects the input of the CAC!"[8]

The draft plan quantified a total build-out for Big Sur by taking into account the number of buildable parcels and putting numerical limits on the amount of future development allowed: 950 housing sites, 200 hotel rooms, and 50 hostel spaces. The high numbers reflected the legal parcels in existence, but the plan included remarkable building restrictions to offset the developmental impact. Specifically, all property within view of the highway or major public viewing areas was to be off limits to new construction. The so-called viewshed plan was a creative means to accommodate residential growth within a renowned scenic landscape. To compensate affected property owners, the plan reintroduced the credit system first proposed in the 1962 Coast Master Plan, which would allow owners to build two structures outside the viewshed for each unbuildable parcel within view. Big Sur had few precedents to follow for a transfer of development credit system; county planners referenced only one California coastal area—the Santa Monica Mountains—but acknowledged that Big Sur's pricier real estate and its rural tradition made for a poor comparison.[9] The state supported Monterey County's novel concept and assigned a representative from the Coastal Conservancy to work with the county to develop the transfer credit system.[10] Big Sur's land-use plan worked off the long-standing premise that unusual measures were required to sustain Big Sur's land, people, and scenic reputation.

Compared with the Coast Master Plan or the aesthetic zoning measures established during the interwar period, this proposed plan was environmentally more ambitious and subject to greater legal challenge. The chairman of Monterey County's Planning Commission admitted of Big Sur's land-use plan: "This thing on the whole scares me to death. It's really a grand recreation plan. It treads on private property rights which I hold very dearly."[11] Despite the chairman's reservations, the transfer development credit system remained in the planning commission's approved plan. The planning commission, however, did revise other features of the plan in the interest of residents, including the omission of language that would have sought prescriptive rights for trails and access points through private property with a history of public use. Prescriptive rights were so controversial that one commissioner considered them "shooting words in Big Sur." A similar statement could be made of other residential areas of the California coast.[12] Legally speaking, the California coastline is public below the mean high-tide line, but it took a concerted effort based on the Coastal Act to establish these rights in places where private residents had nullified access. Monterey County may have leaned toward protecting residents' long-cherished ideas of property rights, but Big Sur's land-use plan had to satisfy the California Coastal Commission's requirement to increase, not restrict, access to the coast, and therefore the final draft approved by the California Coastal Commission would protect prescriptive rights along the Big Sur shoreline.[13] Balancing public and private interests in Big Sur's land-use plan caused continual friction because there was simply so much at stake for residents and visitors alike.

In 1981 the Monterey County Planning Commission approved Big Sur's land-use plan and sent it to the Monterey County Board of Supervisors for review. The board upheld the viewshed and the transfer development credit (TDC) system, along with a forty-acre minimum for residential development, and established a slope density that required up to 320 acres for a house built east of the highway on an incline of 30 percent or more.[14] The county developed a ratio system to determine future lodging units, allowing two units on a parcel that would have qualified for one residence.[15] Big Sur's developing land-use plan

FIGURE 17. Many an admirer of the Big Sur coast has strayed off public trails into private property. During the counterculture movement of the 1960s and 1970s, squatters often occupied private ranch land. Aside from their aversion to a loss of privacy, Big Sur landowners consider trespassers, and their possible campfires and cigarettes, as fire threats. (Historic photo from an anonymous source.)

struck at least one supervisor as a significant shift in society's approach to private property. Michal Moore, the supervisor who crafted the local TDC system, called the process the "death of an old land ethic. It's mine; I'm going to carve it up and plant something."[16] The Coastal Act required a rethinking of a generations-old approach to the California coast and, really, the American landscape. Although a majority of Americans had shown their support for stewarding certain public goods like air and water, regulating private property in the name of the common good struck many as a violation of their fundamental rights of citizenship.[17] Held in tension with this entrenched belief was the developing idea that California's shoreline was a public good that required protection from narrow local or corporate interests.

Monterey County was treading new regulation waters with the Big Sur land-use plan. Tasked by the Coastal Act to conform to new state policies regarding habitat protection and coastal access, the Monterey County Board of Supervisors approved a plan they believed struck the right balance of public and local priorities. The plan's requirement for a large minimum lot size, its viewshed policy, and its resource-protection measures had all been designed to comply with the Coastal Act and to honor besides Big Sur's slow-growth tradition. Michael Fischer, the Coastal Commission's first executive director, indicated that protecting Big Sur from overdevelopment was "clearly one of the highest priority efforts for the protection of the California coastline."[18] Mother Nature's extravagance along this coastline, coupled with decades of careful planning and a good deal of development restraint practiced by locals and Monterey County, had earned Big Sur a reputation that would bring close scrutiny to the procedures of its Local Coastal Program.

The California Coastal Commission rejected Monterey County's first draft of its land-use plan in late 1981, citing the need for closer adherence to Coastal Act priorities. The commission approved the viewshed and the TDC plan but sought additional protection for coastal access. With Highway 1 traffic already near capacity, the state wanted to see the plan restrict residential subdivisions until improvements along Highway 1 would guarantee sufficient room for visitor traffic. The state also recommended that Monterey County consider additional public-access points and create more overnight accommodations in lieu of residences. Two other provisions of the Coastal Act—the protection of agriculture as a preferred land use and low-income housing—compelled the Coastal Commission to call for greater protection of pastureland and affordable housing opportunities in Big Sur. The Coastal Commission largely agreed with the county's environmental-protection measures, but the commission did want to see a ban on surface mining in the Big Sur and Little Sur River watersheds, as well as other watersheds with steelhead trout.[19]

As Big Sur's Local Coastal Program passed back and forth between the county and the state, Big Sur became a key place to hash out developing ideas regarding the proper relationship between Californians and their prized coastal landscape. Some landowners in Big Sur (and in other tourist destinations) argued that their taxes and private property were subsidizing public recreation, a critique first leveled at the Coast Master Plan.[20] Others simply worried that public priorities would supersede those of the Big Sur community.[21] The question of who was to be the primary beneficiary of the state's coastal resources underlay every land-use debate, creating endless opportunities for disagreement about the rights and responsibilities of landowners along the coast. Not all Californians agreed that natural resources faced the greatest threat in this era; some argued instead that developing regulations posed a greater threat to the rights of property owners.[22] In 1987 the U.S. Supreme Court weighed in on a case brought against the California Coastal Commission by beachfront property owners James and Marilyn Nollan. The justices ruled that the Coastal Commission's requirement that the Nollans grant a public easement in order to receive a building permit to replace a bungalow with a three-bedroom house did indeed constitute a taking under the Fifth Amendment.[23] The Nollan case, along with two other cases of such takings decided in the 1980s, revealed that a majority of Supreme Court justices, like a significant number of citizens, were skeptical of the government's growing regulatory power.[24]

In Big Sur, the Coast Property Owners Association (CPOA) frequently voiced its concern about the impact of a land-use plan that placed such a high priority on coastal access and preservation. The Coastal Act required locals and county officials to codify relationships and arrangements in Big Sur that had thrived on informality. For two generations, Big Sur's loose culture had brought it popularity, and now this popularity ensured that new state regulations would be applied with care to this well-preserved coastal stretch. Understanding the stakes, members of the CPOA invested more than two thousand volunteer hours in creating proposed revisions to the draft land-use plan. Of primary concern was the viewshed's profound impact on property owners. The CPOA recommended implementing screening methods that would allow for residential development in view of the highway. The CPOA also stood firmly opposed to the use of the transfer development credits to achieve a near-wild look for Big Sur. That Big Sur should no longer appear a residential landscape struck many locals as excessive in order to achieve a scenic landscape. The Coast Master Plan, a locally generated plan designed first and foremost for residents, was based upon the idea that private stewardship was sufficient for preserving an appealing landscape. By law, Big Sur's Local Coastal Program would have to treat the perceived needs of visitors as on par with locals', and the CPOA disagreed with the viewshed's premise that residences spoiled the visual effect of Big Sur's public commons.

During revisions to Big Sur's Local Coastal Program in the coming years, when it became clear that the transfer development credit (TDC) system would go forward, the CPOA argued that in order to be fair, landowners should be able to choose between these credits or monetary compensation for their unbuildable parcels. County officials acknowledged the potential legal challenge to the TDC program that treated all Big Sur lots as if they were of equal value, which was "just not the case," as one planning commissioner admitted.[25] John Harlan had said as much when he wrote to the board of supervisors over concern for the system's "immense costs and legal implications," arguing that the program was still only a theory, yet unproven.[26] During one hearing on the land-use plan, another Big Sur resident presented each supervisor with a "TDC can of worms," full of strips of paper with questions about the feasibility of the program.[27] No one yet knew how the system might work—some thought it too risky—but the viewshed and TDC system remained central features of each draft of the plan. To those at the county and state level, at least, these policies appeared to be the most viable tools for sustaining Big Sur's status quo while meeting the demands of tourism.

The CPOA, seeking to protect the Big Sur community, found that simple economics, compounded by Coastal Act mandates, threatened the community's alternative reputation. Those who could afford to buy one of the large lots dictated by the land-use plan and cover the growing costs associated with planning and permits in the coastal zone were people of considerable means. In 1970, the average cost of construction for a single-family home in Big Sur was $36,000. By 1979 that price had risen to $107,000.[28] Inflation contributed to the growing value of coastal property, as did the increasing allure of a well-preserved coastline.[29] Concerned about the social implications, the CPOA argued with the Monterey County Board of Supervisors that viewshed regulations would exacerbate conditions that stunted the Big Sur community. Soon, the CPOA argued, Big Sur's community would be made up of only three types of residents: millionaires, a few older long-term residents, and single residents working public- or service-sector jobs and living in barracks or other employee housing.[30] An oft-repeated plea was to allow for less stringent development regulations lest Big Sur become a place "where the only ones living here will be millionaires."[31]

An important protection against this scenario, the CPOA argued, was to include language in the land-use plan to encourage additional caretakers' quarters that traditionally housed low- and moderate-income earners in Big Sur. A predominance of wealthy landowners was inevitably a part of Big Sur's future, but the CPOA hoped to secure one of the few accompanying benefits that these elite residents brought to the rest of the residents. The CPOA recommended doubling the allotted number of permitted caretakers' homes, and although this recommendation was rejected in the final draft, the land-use plan did encourage low-cost hand-built housing and alternative dwellings.[32]

The Monterey County Board of Supervisors ultimately failed to adopt the majority of the CPOA's recommendations for the land-use plan, eliciting frustration from many locals about the procedures by which the land-use plan was created.[33] The board found itself negotiating on the one side with residents who saw themselves as competent stewards of this prized landscape and on the other with the mandates of the Coastal Act. It is entirely possible that the Coastal Commission would have rejected certain of the CPOA's ideas, such as aiming to freeze visitorship at its current numbers, or the CPOA's removal of wording that described the Coastal Act as at odds with continued residential development and Highway 1 as primarily a recreational road. But other discarded CPOA recommendations were in keeping with the spirit of the overall plan, such as calling for protecting aesthetics by screening off parking lots and public restrooms. Writing in 1978, the Coastal Commission's executive director, Michael Fischer, already understood the controversies involved in implementing the Coastal Act. "Tough issues are tough to deal with," said Fischer. "Low-income housing, small-lot subdivision and lot splits, the intense emotional desire to live on the shoreline; no matter what decision we make, someone will be unhappy." He referenced the broader purpose of the Coastal Act to help reconcile the loss to coastal residents: "For every private cost we impose there should be at least an equivalent public benefit."[34] The CPOA tried to minimize these costs to the Big Sur community but found that the larger community of Californians now held a considerable claim on the state's coveted coastal landscapes.

SHIFTING TOPOGRAPHY

In the midst of the planning negotiations came a dramatic natural event that put the planning process on hold for over a year and served as a reminder of the intergovernmental collaboration necessary to keep Big Sur accessible to the public and livable for the residents. Heavy rainstorms in the winter of 1983 caused enormous landslides from mountains still compromised from the Marble-Cone Fire. The results were four major road washouts, resulting in a fourteen-month closure of portions of Highway 1. The road closure brought residents closer together as they pooled resources to sustain themselves while their local economy came to a standstill. Hotels, restaurants, and shops south of the slide experienced a 95-percent drop in business, and the Big Sur Chamber of Commerce estimated that 90 percent of the Big Sur workforce lost employment during this fourteen-month period. As a result, residents became acutely dependent on both the state and the federal government for services and goods ranging from emergency food stamps, to the Army and National Guard's helicopter delivery of essential food, fuel, and medicine, to the clearing of the highway. Community members filled in the gaps, with the Big Sur Volunteer Fire Brigade providing the leadership and coordination for local emergency measures.[35]

Residents' experiences during the road closure granted them a view of Big Sur that almost no one else knew, evoking in residents a feeling of belonging as they remained in their homes even when it may have brought more difficulties than pleasure. As one resident had recently argued in regard to Adams's federal proposal for Big Sur: "Real environmentalists aren't in the Wilderness Society, Sierra Club, the Big Sur Land Trust, or the Big Sur Foundation. They are the people that live on the land—not those that come for the weekend or summer, but those that come and stay through the disasters."[36] In early 2017, at the writing of this book, heavy rains prompted mudslides that led to the failure of the Pfeiffer Canyon Bridge and a one million ton landslide that buried Highway 1 under fifty feet of debris. Authorities estimate it will take nearly a year to reopen the entire stretch of highway, halting all north-south travel through Big Sur in the interim. Residents have always been well aware that in Big Sur nature's beauty and its disasters exist on a grand scale and that embracing both is simply part of living along this dynamic coastline.

Despite residents' resistance to the federal bills in 1980, the road closure of the early 1980s, like the wildfires, revealed the extent to which residents depended on government services. Fifty years after state crews blasted the mountainsides to forge a path for Highway 1, the 1983 landslides necessitated once again the use of dynamite and massive earth-moving efforts to try to reshape the shifting topography. Some residents remembered the days before the highway, and though they had largely approved of the road, they had predicted then that the steep Santa Lucia Mountains could only temporarily be tamed by bulldozers and pavement. The road closure was as much a human-induced disaster as one of nature, and the road's key beneficiaries— the residents—were deeply implicated.

A year into the effort to remove the debris and rebuild portions of the highway, the California Department of Transportation estimated that the project would constitute the "largest clearance of a public thoroughfare in California history."[37] An editorial in the *Los Angeles Times* suggested a surprising approach to the costly and dangerous highway repairs: permanently closing the highway through Big Sur. Big Sur certainly warranted a highway to its borders, opined the author. It was, after all, a "natural wonder of international repute . . . but does there need to be a highway *through* Big Sur?" The editor argued that the financial constraints caused by Proposition 13 should compel the state to reconsider its continual rebuilding of the highway.[38] Of course, this argument held little sway with tourists, residents, or the state legislature, which had already invested so much in Highway 1. The unlikelihood of the proposal underscored that even though many may have thought of Big Sur as wild, most did not wish for it to become a wilderness best experienced as a backcountry. Though some cherished the isolated stretches of the Santa Lucia Mountains, the majority of tourists craved easy access to the coast as well as contact with Big Sur's culture, a culture created by artistic residents, homesteader families, and affluent landowners who all relied upon the highway. Big Sur was too important to the state's tourist economy for one more road clearing to cause legislators to suddenly withdraw funding for highway repairs. Moreover, the Coastal Act provided additional justification for maintaining access to one of California's few remaining undeveloped coastlines.

The Coastal Act also compelled the county and state to examine a nineteenth-century federal statute that offended the modern sensibilities of many tourists and residents who cherished Big Sur's image as a unique coastal oasis. As the road clearing continued, Monterey County and the Coastal Commission challenged federal mining regulations within the Santa Lucia Mountains. The General Mining Act of 1872 gave citizens the right to prospect for minerals on federal land and to establish claims on economically feasible operations. Granite Rock, a mining company based in Santa Cruz County, held unpatented mining claims within Los Padres National Forest, where it obtained approval from the forest service to begin mining the chemical- and pharmaceutical-grade limestone on Pico Blanco in 1981. Monterey County subsequently instructed Granite Rock to apply for a coastal-development permit for any new work, believing that unregulated mining activity in Big Sur's sensitive habitat could undermine the protection intended by the state-mandated land-use plan.

Rising high within the Santa Lucia Range, with its distinctive white top, Pico Blanco holds aesthetic importance within the Big Sur landscape. But its significance extends beyond aesthetics alone. The peak sits within the Little Sur River watershed, part of the California Protected Waterways system, bringing heightened attention to the impact of mining on the larger ecosystem.[39] There is also reason to believe that Pico Blanco held special meaning to the Esselen Indians as the center of creation.[40] The protection of Pico Blanco stood for the county and state's ability to prioritize something less tangible than direct material benefit. In 1983 Ansel Adams wrote to the California Coastal Commission to urge them to assert all their authority to oppose the federal mining law. Adams attached high stakes to the situation,

FIGURE 18. Pico Blanco, rising 3,700 feet, held cultural significance for the Esselen people. In the twentieth century, the mountain was mined for its high-quality limestone. Today Pico Blanco sits within the California Protected Waterways system. (Photo: Edward Dickinson.)

arguing that "the fate of the Big Sur Coast depends largely on whether this mining can be arrested in the early stages of its development." Writing on Big Sur Foundation letterhead just three years after the defeat of his proposed federal legislation, Adams had ostensibly accepted the era's new parameters for preservation. At this point, Adams no doubt preferred working with an environmentally conscious state agency to engaging with a federal administration that he did not trust to protect the nation's resources. In closing his letter, Adams encouraged the Coastal Commission's director: "Keep up the good work and please let us know how we can help."[41] Nathaniel Owings also weighed in on the Pico Blanco debate with his fervent support for strict mining regulations. Owings asserted, only partly in jest, that the land-use plan should contain the prohibition THOU SHALT NOT MINE PICO BLANCO.[42]

Adams and Owings voiced what more and more Californians were coming to believe in the late twentieth century: that the potential financial rewards of extractive industries in the state's most scenic areas could not justify the potential risks incurred by the general public.[43] The Santa Barbara oil spill was a recent painful example that helped put Californians on an environmental policy course that did not always run parallel to the nation's as a whole, especially under President Reagan. Reagan's secretary of the interior, James Watt, encouraged offshore oil-tract leases in several of California's most scenic coastal regions, going so far as to recommend opening offshore drilling in Big Sur and Point Reyes, and in Mendocino County.[44] Watt's pro-development stance spurred the Coastal Commission to plead with him to slow down sales and "help industry finish exploring and developing those tracts already sold." Understanding that Watt was of no mind to halt the nation's energy production off California's continental shelf, the Coastal Commission counseled prudence: "Finish what you have started before attempting more."[45] The Coastal Commission went further with Pico Blanco, attempting to use its regulatory authority to bring Granite Rock into compliance with state regulations. But did the Coastal Commission's authority extend over federal property within the coastal zone? Granite Rock said no and brought suit against the Coastal Commission when told to apply for a state development permit in 1983. Granite Rock lost in the federal circuit court but won on appeal. The U.S. Supreme Court then granted the Coastal Commission a review of the case and delivered its opinion in 1987.

In *California Coastal Commission v. Granite Rock Co.,* the Coastal Commission maintained that its intention was not to prohibit mining but to regulate Granite Rock's mining activity in accordance with environmental standards established in the Coastal Act. Granite Rock argued that such regulations would conflict with federal law; that any state permit requirement, in effect, was preempted. The Supreme Court ruled in favor of the Coastal Commission on the grounds that federal statutes (including forest-service regulations, federal land-use statutes, and the Coastal Zone Management Act) did not preempt the Coastal Commission's imposition of a permit requirement on the operation of an unpatented mining claim in a national forest.[46] The state had pushed hard for this outcome, arguing against Granite Rock's unregulated mining "in the heart of the scenic, nationally renowned Big Sur coast ... one of the most sensitive and valued portions of California's coastline."[47] The court's decision bolstered the commission's ability to regulate development based on environmental concerns in order to protect the public commons that was the California coastline.

Of course, not everyone fell into step with the plan to prioritize environmental concerns or scenic views over production. James Hill had recently inherited a 7,100-acre property in Big Sur—El Sur Ranch, which lay adjacent to Pico Blanco. Hill spoke in favor of allowing Granite Rock to continue harvesting limestone, perhaps not wanting to see a precedent set that would deny such commercial endeavors. Many years after the debate, Margaret Owings recalled just how passionately her husband felt about protecting Pico Blanco from industrial pursuits. She shared a story of a planning meeting in which James Hill purportedly exclaimed: "I don't see what the big deal is, taking seven hundred feet off the top of the mountain!" To which Nat Owings replied: "Young man, I'll tell you! It would be like a man of distinction and integrity with his head cut off."[48] Whether or not Margaret Owings recalled the precise language, she did not mistake the passion with which people debated Big Sur's land management.[49] In what could have been a debate strictly over environmental quality or economic opportunities, the discussion on Pico Blanco ultimately extended beyond the material or ecological value of the land and its resources and encompassed the aesthetic value that many attached to the mountain. The discussion ultimately reflected the class privilege of those involved. Landowners in Big Sur were by definition people of distinction by the 1980s, and their ideas regarding land management reflected both their property values and Big Sur's perceived cultural value.

PRESERVATION COSTS

It was impossible to ignore the fact that Big Sur was increasingly becoming an exclusive residential area. By 1980 a home in Big Sur cost on average 2 1/2 times as much as a home in Monterey, nearly twice as much as a home in Carmel, and substantially more than homes in Pebble Beach, all prime California real estate.[50] Big Sur's Local Coastal Program, once finalized and adopted, would only perpetuate the conditions that had created such expensive properties. Meanwhile, Big Sur's protected landscape also increased its tourist appeal and bolstered the service-sector economy that created an underclass of workers. Service-sector employment was on the rise across the country as high-skilled blue-collar jobs began to disappear in the 1970s. Alongside this development were increasingly high corporate salaries. Big Sur's population began to reflect this polarity, where the average family earned seventy-five thousand dollars a year by 1990, but the median income was closer to forty-five thousand (which was 20% higher than the statewide median income) and renter-occupied homes began to dominate the housing pattern in the 1980s.[51] Big Sur, once a retreat from America's suburban and corporate influences, offered no escape from the two-tiered society taking shape throughout the country.

Rising land values and an increasingly wealthy upper class meant that the state's most beautiful stretches were gradually becoming the domain of the well-to-do. Cost-of-housing concerns expressed by the Coast Property Owners Association (CPOA) echoed up and down the California coast during these years. The paradox of the Coastal Act was that its preservation-oriented regulations contributed to this phenomenon even as its other mandate required equitable access to the coast. To compensate, the Coastal Act included a provision to support the construction of low- and moderate-income housing along the coast. Michael Fischer acknowledged that the very process of securing the Coastal Act's priorities threatened the affordability of the coast, averring that "we didn't want to be in the business of protecting the coast and its views and its development only for the very rich."[52] But the affordable-housing measure, idealistic in its conception, was not politically feasible by the 1980s.

Fischer lamented that exclusive coastal communities tended to view the low-income housing provision as sociologically and politically threatening and exerted considerable pressure on their local governments to resist these developments.[53] Those looking to discredit the provision used the same arguments once leveled against the liberal policies of the Great Society and President Lyndon Johnson's administration: that inserting low-income housing along the coast was social engineering, an example of the California Coastal Commission grabbing power and overreaching its limits of authority.[54] A *Monterey Peninsula Herald* editorial criticized the Coastal Commission for insisting that a developer in Monterey County set aside five lots at less than market value for low-income housing, a clear example of "a well-intentioned government power gone wild with its own inflated sense of power." The editorial left no doubt that the commission "should not become an instrument of low cost housing on the Peninsula."[55] Pushback from developers, realtors, local governments, and others who coveted the valuable coastal real estate or the tax revenue that it provided all helped prompt the state legislature to amend the Coastal Act in 1981 to remove the affordable-housing provision.[56]

Big Sur's developing Local Coastal Program employed a form of environmental protection that was becoming more common in California as a response to limited government funding and high property values. Creative measures such as the transfer development credit system and conservation easements were designed to serve the public good and protect private interests through the use of novel business transactions. In 1982, while helping develop Big Sur's Local Coastal Program, Monterey County Supervisor Robert Franco acknowledged the need for such measures to conform to the

Coastal Act and protect Big Sur in the wake of Proposition 13 and a national recession. The challenge, as he saw it, was that the "only entity left becomes the private sector itself. Thus, the system we propose, while publicly regulated, relies entirely in its essence on private involvement and participation."[57] Franco referred specifically to securing the viewshed, but his assessment also applied to the broader land-management issues of this era. Big Sur's vast open spaces were coming to reflect the tensions of an era in which increasing wealth disparity and growing support for property rights occurred alongside wide-reaching government regulations and environmental consciousness.[58]

Fifty years after John and Florence Pfeiffer decided to sell a portion of their property to create the first California State Park in Big Sur, land trusts were now the more likely arbiter for those wishing to preserve a portion of their land in conservation or scenic easements in exchange for property-tax relief. Not only the Big Sur Land Trust but national trusts, as well, had a growing stake in Big Sur property, and these groups, like their counterparts across California, found support from the state Coastal Conservancy.[59] In 1987 the Big Sur Land Trust was one of only forty-two land trusts in the state, but in the coming years land trusts in California grew at twice the national rate in response to the lack of government funds and the great desire among residents to prevent popular landscapes from overdevelopment.[60] A Monterey County supervisor acknowledged just how critical these groups were by labeling land trusts "an absolutely essential element" in the preservation matrix.[61] And in 1982 Leon Panetta described the Big Sur Land Trust as "better, frankly, than having government or . . . taxpayer money involved. It's also the kind of effort that the President has been encouraging these days."[62] In an era with increasingly expensive coastal property and waning support for expensive federal projects that encroached on private property, conservation easements and purchase by nonprofit conservancies became more economically and politically feasible preservation tools than government acquisition.

THE PLAN TAKES EFFECT

Before the Coastal Commission would certify Big Sur's Local Coastal Program, a decision needed to be made about one particular expanse of the coastline, a decision that brought into flux questions about private-property rights, Big Sur's aesthetic value, and Monterey County's environmental standards. These questions were brought to the fore by James Hill's development proposal for his El Sur Ranch, once part of a Mexican land grant that now encompassed six miles of shoreline and some of Big Sur's most dramatic public views. After inheriting the ranch from his grandfather, Hill looked for income-generating opportunities to offset taxes. Hill's initial proposal included a two-hundred-room hotel, a conference center, a restaurant, and a cabin complex that would in total cover just 2 percent of the property. The Coastal Conservancy worked with Hill to reduce the environmental impact and settled on a plan that included more than three thousand acres of conservation easements, a one-hundred-room hotel, a two-hundred-seat restaurant, and ninety-eight private home sites situated outside the viewshed. Monterey County approved of this revised plan, sending it along for review by the Coastal Commission.[63] Though everyone involved may have wished that Hill would not alter his thousands of acres of prime real estate, his property rights could not be denied simply because such large-scale development had yet to occur in Big Sur.

In 1984, fifty Big Sur residents traveled to the Coastal Commission proceedings to protest the development proposal for El Sur Ranch. They argued that the county granted Hill preferential treatment by allowing him rights to well beyond the thirty-room hotel limit. Moreover, residents saw the scale of the proposal for El Sur as out of character for Big Sur and opposed setting such a precedent for future visitor-serving centers. They found sympathetic commissioners who rejected the development plan for El Sur Ranch with a vote of ten to none. The commission disagreed with the concept of such a large complex, which would detract from the overall tranquility of Big Sur's landscape. Meanwhile, local elections in Monterey brought in two new supervisors committed to environmental protection. These supervisors opposed the deal for El Sur Ranch and helped revise the land-use plan in order to include greater protection against large development.[64] El Sur Ranch presented an unusual opportunity in the 1980s to regulate a portion of the California coast that still appeared largely as it did during the nineteenth century. The juxtaposition of the proposed modern complex situated within thousands of acres of pastureland highlighted as almost no other place could what California had once been and where wealth and a high tourist demand could lead. Neither the county nor the state could buy out Hill's property rights—had he even been looking to sell.[65] But the county could and did revise Big Sur's Local Coastal Program to encourage large ranches to remain pastoral through the use of easements secured by the state Coastal Conservancy, the Big Sur Land Trust, and the Trust for Public Land.[66]

A full decade of negotiations produced in 1986 a Local Coastal Program for Big Sur that addressed the interests of multiple stakeholders. As Monterey Supervisor Karin Strasser Kauffman described it, the plan was "not the county's" or "the government's," but "the plan of those people who value Big Sur.... It's a very strong environmental plan, and at the same time it respects private property rights."[67] Lee Otter, a planner for the Coastal Commission, commended Monterey County for its completed Local Coastal Program, calling it what the commission thinks "is really what the Legislature had in mind with the Coastal Act." Otter acknowledged that the act had in essence asked counties to make development decisions on behalf of all Californians, not just local constituents, and that Big Sur's plan reflected this dual responsibility.[68]

So what exactly did the Big Sur Coast Local Coastal Program (LCP) set out to do? The plan formalized Big Sur's "semiwilderness" character and identified the primary objective as minimizing development in order to protect the coast as a "scenic rural area where residents' individual lifestyles can flourish, traditional ranching uses can continue, and the public can come to enjoy nature and find refuge from the pace of urban life." What the LCP did not do was capitalize on Big Sur's tourist draw. Tourist amenities were kept to a minimum, with visual access taking precedence over more active recreational uses of the Big Sur coast.[69] The county, responding in part to residents, chose to protect this prized coastline from overdevelopment despite the fact that "large sums of money could be generated out of Big Sur," as Supervisor Kauffman explained. Quoted in a statewide journal, *California County,* and in the *Los Angeles Times,* Supervisor Kauffman emphasized: "We encourage people to pass through. We want them to have a stunning—but brief—experience. We want to protect what people value most about Big Sur—just to stand on the coast, make a full-circle turn and look at nature in every direction."[70]

The multiple priorities of open space, public access, and conservation all generated in Big Sur a Local Coastal Program that emphasized visual access by way of more scenic turnouts on the highway rather than additional hiking trails, and a limited number of campgrounds and lodging facilities. Such limitations reflected the plan's intent to provide public access without allowing "the beauty of the coast, its tranquility, and the health of its environment" to be "marred by public overuse or carelessness."[71] This approach stood in sharp contrast to that taken in Yosemite, where park authorities and concessionaires had long responded to similar tourist numbers with extensive amenities. A confidential internal report written by the National Park Service in 1986 identified twenty-four separate problems concerning

FIGURE 19. The Big Sur Local Coastal Program defines agriculture, and in particular grazing, as a preferred land use. Not incidentally, pastureland helps protect open space and the scenic views from Highway 1. (Photo: iShutterStock.)

Yosemite's water, air, wildlife, and vegetation that all resulted from overuse.[72] In hopes of preventing similar problems in Big Sur, the LCP stipulated: "Additional funding should be allocated by the State and Federal governments to manage and maintain existing public recreation areas before more public land is opened to recreational use by these same agencies."[73] The Big Sur LCP prioritized the region's rural heritage as a way to protect against excessive public and private development. As a result, the plan helped promote two seemingly contradictory purposes for this coastline: wildness and habitation.

The LCP regulated against commonplace activities associated with mass recreation, including golf, tennis, cinemas, mechanized recreation (including off-road vehicles), and boating facilities. Big Sur was to be off limits to industrial development, onshore or offshore energy facilities, large-scale mineral and oil extraction or mining, commercial timber harvesting, or manufacturing other than the cottage industry or art production. All commercial development had to "carry out the rustic character of Big Sur" whether in size, scale, activities, or design, and the LCP prohibited offsite advertising, exterior or interior neon, plastic, moving, or flashing signs.[74] Utility lines were to be buried wherever possible.[75] These regulations all sought to retain a certain look for Big Sur, revealing not only how locals envisioned their ideal home but also what visitors had come to expect along this coast.

Big Sur's image also encompassed its ranching heritage, and the LCP therefore classified agriculture, especially grazing, as a preferred use of coastal lands. It did so even as this practice ceased to be economically viable. Big Sur's LCP articulated the appeal of these open spaces, explaining, in short: "The presence of livestock enhances the rural western feeling of Big Sur and adds to visitor's enjoyment of the area."[76] Monterey County therefore sought all levels of government funding to purchase scenic easements and provide economic assistance to ranchers. The county also supported the work of nonprofit private and public conservancies (such as land trusts and the Coastal Conservancy) to "assist in the conservation of important natural and cultural values" represented in ranchland and other prime lands.[77] The scenic and cultural value of the pastoral landscape gave weight to its preservation—not just in Big Sur but throughout the state—and had done so for some time. The state's Williamson Act of 1965 gave a tax incentive to agricultural landowners who chose to keep their land in open space rather than realize its full development potential. A decade later, the Coastal Act also attempted to offset the rapid conversion of farmland taking place throughout the state. And in the 1980s the Big Sur LCP identified Big Sur's pastures as a bulwark against unwanted modern development.

Arguably, in many ways the Big Sur LCP did not actually resemble a land *use* plan. The creation of new residential lots was limited to one hundred additional parcels; and where new construction was allowed, it was severely restricted. Minimum lot sizes ranged from 40 to 320 acres, depending on the terrain.[78] Given the Coastal Act's mandate to increase access to the beaches and the coastline, it is significant that the Coastal Commission approved for Big Sur a plan that prioritized minimally invasive visitor access and emphasized the quality rather than the quantity of access to Big Sur.[79] For all its restrictions, the LCP protected residents' place in this exceptional landscape; and though the LCP was a circuitous route to preservation, supporters of increased federal control could appreciate the open-space planning and viewshed policy that protected the iconic image of Big Sur.[80] It was not a perfect plan, but its numerous contributors and careful review process brought it clout. Monterey County Planning Director Bob Slimmon could report just a few years after the plan took effect that it was difficult to "imagine anyone having the guts to amend the plan for development. A lot of people were involved in its preparation; there were compromises on both sides. Everyone is willing to give it a try for a long time."[81]

The LCP guided an already unique coastal landscape. The forest service owned just over half the land; the state (mostly in state parks) covered 8 percent; and privately owned land accounted for 39 percent of the acreage in the planning boundary, some of which was protected through scenic easements that prevented future development.[82] Monterey County now had the legal power to ensure compliance with the LCP, which was backed by the California Coastal Commission. In an era when the federal government called for reduced-cost preservation, and a growing number of Americans sought freedom from big government, Big Sur was a prime example of the collaborative effort among public and private entities to secure effective preservation. In the end, Big Sur's LCP was as noteworthy for what it did not do: it avoided defining Big Sur as entirely a preserve, or solely as a residential and commercial coastline. Two powerful strains of the time—environmental protection and private-property rights—combined to create a hybrid space in Big Sur that reflected Monterey County's and locals' belief that the land could be inhabited while still evoking popular ideas of the wild.

PIONEERING LAND MANAGEMENT, AGAIN

Two years before the California Coastal Commission approved Big Sur's Local Coastal Program, and four years after the failed federal legislation, Ansel Adams reached the final days of his long and fruitful life. On 22 April 1984, Adams passed away at the age of eighty-two from heart failure, aggravated by cancer. Even during his final year, Adams remained intensely involved with the national discussion on preservation. During a prominent interview in 1983 Adams called President Reagan's secretary of the interior, James Watt, "an incredibly slimy character" and viewed Watt's pro-development policies as indicative of his determination to undermine the integrity of the parks. Adams feared the next step would be for the federal government to back out of the initial purpose of the National Parks, an action Adams considered as bordering on the criminal for its violation of America's heritage.[83] Months before Adams passed away he had the satisfaction of seeing Watt tender his resignation in the face of extensive public opposition to his environmental policies and, to some extent, to his abrasive personality. But even without Watt in office, Adams's concerns remained relevant, for they revealed a truism about Americans and their relationship to nature: just as the land itself is dynamic, people's feelings about nature are not static. Nature's perceived value is ever shifting. Adams, and everyone involved in

Big Sur's planning, understood that these concepts could be negotiated, even after the creation of Big Sur's Local Coastal Program (LCP).

In the same year that the Coastal Commission certified Big Sur's LCP, California Republican Senator Pete Wilson introduced in 1986 a new federal bill for Big Sur's preservation. Senate Bill 2159, the Big Sur National Forest Scenic Area Act, proposed placing land-management authority with the National Forest Service. The act called for prohibiting commercial resource extraction throughout Big Sur, including oil drilling, but exempted mining claims like the one at Pico Blanco. A novel feature of the proposal included the establishment of a private foundation to raise funds, to be used by the secretary of agriculture, to buy out landowners in the Scenic Area. At the same time, Wilson's bill allowed for property condemnation in the event that Big Sur's LCP was significantly weakened by amendment or court action and a land parcel pending development ran contrary to the values of the Big Sur coast.[84]

A coalition consisting of nearly every group in Big Sur, from the Coast Property Owners Association to the Big Sur Land Trust, formed to oppose Wilson's bill. They found support from most county, state, and federal legislators.[85] Some critics of Wilson's bill believed that the senator was engaged in a political maneuver to paint the Republican Party as environmentally minded during the state's election year. When challenged on this point, Wilson argued that his interest in Big Sur's preservation was genuine. He explained that although he would generally "err on the side of the local government if we were talking about land that was to be developed . . . we're talking about Big Sur, which I regard as a natural treasure." It came down to making "California a place worth living in," argued Wilson.[86] The Republican senator (who had, ironically, filled the seat of Senator Sam Hayakawa, who had helped defeat the 1980 federal proposal) believed the most effective means to achieve protection would come through the federal, not state or local, government. In another political twist, Democrat Leon Panetta expressed skepticism of the federal proposal, explaining that events of the past six years had left him no longer "convinced . . . that handing an area like Big Sur to any federal entity is the way to protect it." Panetta queried whether "you need to inject a whole new entity" or if locals and the various government agencies involved in Big Sur could work together to preserve this coastline. Meanwhile, the Big Sur Foundation, the organization that had fought hardest for the passage of Cranston and Panetta's legislation in 1980, saw in Wilson's bill important preservation merits but nevertheless criticized Wilson's move as creating "suspicion and diversion" among locals and for being politically dumb.[87] By the late 1980s, almost everyone involved in Big Sur—regardless of political leaning—placed great faith in local planning. Congressman Panetta believed so firmly in the effectiveness and appropriateness of the LCP that he announced he would oppose the bill in Congress, where it did indeed die.[88]

Intent on making local preservation succeed, Panetta forged the Big Sur Multi-Agency Advisory Council (BSMAAC) to coordinate all levels of government involved in Big Sur. The group managed to bring together the many agencies that held land-management authority in Big Sur—from Los Padres National Forest to the Big Sur Land Trust to the Monterey County Regional Parks District—and to secure their compliance with the goals laid out in the LCP. Most notably, Los Padres National Forest officials agreed to honor the LCP by supporting the withdrawal of all land in the Monterey District from mineral, oil, and gas leases. The forest service, in hopes of protecting against major wildfires, also agreed to a fourfold increase in the acreage subject to prescribed burning.[89] The BSMAAC provided a single forum for residents to voice concerns and receive feedback from the various agencies along the coast. Of critical concern was securing sufficient funding for the policies laid out in the LCP, specifically the viewshed. The BSMAAC successfully sought solutions that included state-bond money earmarked for preservation.[90] The passage of Proposition 70 in 1988 provided $776 million for wildlife, coastal, and parkland conservation. Of this, $25 million went to Monterey County to conserve viewshed properties in Big Sur. Of the twenty-five properties purchased with these funds, the Big Sur Land Trust facilitated seventeen.[91] The collaborative efforts of the various members of the BSMAAC led Panetta to feel confident about the area's future protection. He argued that local government was capable of protecting "a national treasure like Big Sur if there is a firm commitment by local government and the community to do so and there is adequate support from, and coordination with, state and federal government."[92]

The BSMAAC stood as a prime example of the increasingly common intergovernmental and private collaboration in this era, and it achieved effectiveness by respecting the role of each, as well as the role of private citizens. Big Sur residents held five seats on the council, and additional seats went to local organizations such as the Coast Property Owners Association, the Friends of the Big Sur Coast, the Big Sur Land Trust, and the Big Sur Chamber of Commerce.[93] The BSMAAC gained legitimacy and support among most locals for its inclusiveness. Everyone recognized that the LCP's success would determine whether the county could maintain primary land-management authority. Events of the previous decade made it entirely clear that legislators and nature-advocacy organizations cared very much what happened in Big Sur and would likely act again if they deemed local preservation efforts unsuccessful.

A few years before the close of the twentieth century, Michael Fischer (who no longer worked for the California Coastal Commission but instead led the Coastal Conservancy) contributed to a report entitled *Coastal Agenda 2000: Protecting and Managing California's Coast in the 21st Century*. The report began from the premise that California's coast was a public good, for which all were responsible and from which all could benefit. Having argued that point for decades, Fischer highlighted the growing need for a comprehensive approach to coastal preservation: "We must connect the economy to the environment; local agencies to the state and federal; general interests to the neighborhood; the neighborhood to the watershed; the future to the present."[94] To a significant extent, Monterey County, Big Sur locals, and the state had already worked to connect these dots for Big Sur, creating what has been labeled "one of the strongest local environmental programs in the country."[95]

The Big Sur Local Coastal Program protects not only the prized Big Sur landscape but also the residents who are fortunate enough to live within it. With the benefit of hindsight, it became evident that neither fear expressed at the 1980 Senate hearings on Big Sur came to pass: residents never faced the reality of a federal landlord, and the landscape did not deteriorate under private hands. Instead, intergovernmental collaboration, private initiatives, compromise, and creative planning defined an unusual path in which the late-twentieth-century politics of property, privilege, and preservation rendered a place at once wild and inhabited, used and protected, appreciated and productive. As in any landscape, including federal parks, Big Sur's borders and preservation-oriented management are not permanent; shifting economic realities and perceptions of nature's worth can alter the place. However, if the integrity of the LCP is maintained, including the protection of Highway 1 as a two-lane road, minimal change will come to Big Sur's built environment. But it is less the physical boundaries (though these are formidable) that prevent overdevelopment in Big Sur than the social boundaries erected to preserve something unique along the California coast. Considerable momentum backs the commitment to Big Sur's wild and storied land, and the status of both these elements will continue to reveal a good deal about Californians' relationship to their beloved coast.

Epilogue

MILLIONAIRES AND BEACHES: THE SOCIOPOLITICAL ECONOMICS OF CALIFORNIA COASTAL PRESERVATION IN THE TWENTY-FIRST CENTURY

> The California coast is world famous for its wildness—notwith-standing population growth and development pressures. People wouldn't come to Big Sur or the North Coast if a lot of hotels and private homes were there, spoiling the views and sense of wilderness.
>
> PETER DOUGLAS, *executive director,*
> *California Coastal Commission*

MORE THAN A CENTURY after Robinson Jeffers first encountered Big Sur, a fellow admirer could have a surprisingly similar experience traveling through this region. Eschewing the highway, an adventurous traveler could today walk south for seventy-five miles through the Santa Lucia Mountains and cross over only a single paved road.[1] Like Jeffers, this contemporary traveler would see the expansive Pacific, the towering mountains, the inviting redwood canyons, the dense chaparral-covered hillsides, and likely observe more than a few native animals. The southern sea otter, a creature that Jeffers in 1914 would have considered extinct, is today an established member of the local marine ecosystem. And the California condor, nearly extinct by the late twentieth century, now populates the Santa Lucia Mountains in encouraging numbers. Today's visitor would observe only a slightly larger human population than Jeffers did, despite the fact that the state's population has increased fifteenfold since 1915.[2] By such measures, Big Sur appears to have been left behind as some outpost of a bygone era. But the thin corridor of high-end real estate and tourist amenities along Highway 1 reveals that the highway did indeed bring the advanced civilization that Jeffers dreaded. But was it a harbinger of doom, as he feared? And would a traveler today have any less reason to be in awe of the Big Sur coast?

Though the march of civilization undoubtedly reached Big Sur, it took an unexpected detour when it arrived. When society discovered Big Sur, on the eve of World War II, there were those who could envision a path forward that eschewed modern developments for this arresting landscape. Conservation-minded and quality of life–minded residents and county officials kept Big Sur protected during the midcentury boom so that the place still remained largely undeveloped by the time California voters became committed to statewide coastal protection. Big Sur did indeed become folded into modern life, but under the guidance of many layers of government and private stewardship intended to protect a timeless look and feel for this region. The effort was so successful that in 2003, when Monterey County and the Coastal Commission reviewed the Big Sur Local Coastal Program, their report declared the implementation of the viewshed as "one of California's great regulatory success stories."[3] The executive director of the Coastal Commission echoed this praise when he highlighted the sense of wilderness to be experienced in Big Sur.[4] Indeed, with the additional wilderness acres added in 2002 to the Monterey County portion of Los Padres National Forest, Big Sur now encompasses roughly 80 percent of the state's coastal wilderness.[5] This prized coastal stretch may appear unique within the state (and beyond), but it is very much a product of a broader land-use ethic that also guides such places as Malibu and the port of Long Beach.

Today, California's coast reflects residents' dual desire to protect a remarkable environment and a high quality of life. The world-famous coastline is integral to the state's economy, to residents' sense of well-being, and to the California Dream. But not until the 1960s did a groundswell of support emerge to protect that dream, and that prized resource, from spoliation. Alarm over rapid change along the coast, including its deterioration through residential and commercial development, disappearing wetlands, new marinas, and proposed freeways and nuclear plants, began to overwhelm and catalyze the people who had come to know the coast as the geographic soul of California.[6] Voter support for the Coastal Initiative flowed out of these concerns and sustained the movement to create a permanent statewide agency to regulate coastal development. Once in operation, the California Coastal Commission, the Coastal Conservancy, and the numerous guiding local coastal programs have prompted support and appreciation from many

Californians, as well as emulation from coastal governments around the country and the world.[7] But there has also been pushback and resistance from California industries, government officials, and private citizens who believe the Coastal Act gave the state agency too much power to regulate private property. It has therefore been the aim of the Coastal Commission and Coastal Conservancy to cultivate in Californians a sustained commitment to the coast as a fragile, irreplaceable, and common resource for which regulation is appropriate and necessary.[8]

Perhaps the individual best associated with this initiative is the late executive director of the Coastal Commission, Peter Douglas. Until his death in 2012, Douglas was a central figure in California's coastal protection for over four decades.[9] As a new graduate of the UCLA School of Law in the early 1970s, Douglas served as an aide in State Assemblyman Alan Sieroty's office, where he worked to establish legislation for coastal preservation. Douglas and an attorney involved with the Coastal Alliance wrote the text for Proposition 20, which embodied much of the idealism that Douglas had developed in his years as an activist. Well before he had identified the environment as a cause worth fighting for, Douglas had sought change in the realm of civil rights, including fair housing, Native American rights, and prison reform. To Douglas, the Coastal Act became the "people's law" for its protection of the coast for everyone. He was particularly committed to the affordable-housing component, and decades later remained, quite frankly, angry about the scrapping of that feature in 1981.[10] He would not entirely escape defeat and compromise after this, but Douglas also knew how to apply similar resistance to those looking to dismantle the Coastal Act.

Douglas began working for the Coastal Commission in 1977 and spent eight years as deputy director before succeeding Michael Fischer as head of the commission. Fischer later characterized Douglas's determination in the face of Governor Deukmejian's hostility as a decision to "take this thing [the Coastal Commission] and carry it across the desert so that it can bloom again," and he praised Douglas for maintaining the agency through the troubled Deukmejian years.[11] The governor had run on a platform that included abolishing the Coastal Commission but once in office could not sway the majority of the legislature to undo the Coastal Act and so chose instead to reduce the agency's funding. In response, Douglas felt compelled to close the North Coast Coastal Commission office, but flatly refused to do worse when the governor continued to threaten cuts and called for additional closures. The burden became too great on the residents, Douglas argued, by requiring lengthy travel to engage with the commission. Douglas, who had the backing of the majority of the Coastal Commissioners, won this particular battle with Deukmejian and kept open the remaining offices.[12]

The Coastal Commission faced additional challenges from Californians who were accustomed to a weak state land-use regulatory system prior to the Coastal Act and chafed against the restrictions placed on private property and commercial development under the new local coastal programs.[13] One of the better-known showdowns occurred in Malibu, along Carbon Beach (aka Billionaire's Beach), where the ultrarich beachfront homeowners applied creative measures to restrict public beach access. Advocates of the Coastal Act repeatedly challenged the fake no-parking signs and the falsified red curbs, the locked access gates, the hired security guards patrolling the beach, and the general hostility of some Carbon Beach homeowners toward the public.[14] These offenses were so blatant that the City of Malibu acknowledged the problem of blocked access in its Local Coastal Program, and the Coastal Commission pursued legal action.[15] Numerous court cases and many decades later, after two homeowners had originally agreed to provide access in exchange for building permits, two permanent paths were finally opened in 2007 and 2015 to connect the Pacific Coast Highway to the popular beach. The executive director of the Coastal Commission spoke before reporters and eager beachgoers on the day when the second path opened, proclaiming, "The access is now open. It is your coast. It's a coast for everybody."[16] Coastal Commissioner Mary Shallenberger interpreted the opening of Carbon Beach as a fulfillment of the Coastal Act's public-access mandate in an era when income inequality threatened this earlier ideal, and she highlighted the commission's ability to "stand its ground to the 1 percent" by persistently enforcing state law.[17]

Acting in the name of the people, the Coastal Commission has challenged homeowners seeking to claim exclusive rights to a slice of the California coastline, while some of these homeowners, in turn, have maintained that they are fighting to protect the individual from a powerful government agency. Privilege undergirds both sides of this ongoing land-management debate, with distinct principles guiding each position. Douglas was known to call himself a radical pagan heretic, an activist who stood in wonder and reverence of nature.[18] Like many a proponent of the Coastal Act, Douglas operated from a belief system that prioritized open landscapes over lucrative developments, whereas opponents of the Coastal Commission often see preservation as designed to benefit nonlocals at the expense of the taxpaying landowner. One UCLA law professor has called the California Coastal Commission the "single most powerful land use authority in the United

States," and his assessment came before the 2014 amendment to the Coastal Act that grants the Coastal Commission the authority to levy fines of up to $11,250 per day against those who violate the Coastal Act's public-access policies.[19] Although some Californians have long believed that the Coastal Commission is able to force too much private property into compliance with a far-reaching Coastal Act, people in support of the act regret the many lost opportunities to preserve natural resources and bemoan the slow process of extending coastal access.[20] Carbon Beach, with its enormous show of wealth and prime sand beaches, became a battleground of sorts between the diverse sociopolitical concepts that guide Californians' interactions with their coast.

The Coastal Commission and Coastal Conservancy have clearly created some adversaries in their efforts to preserve access and mitigate development impacts, but these efforts have also engendered gratitude among many Californians. Support for their mission is in evidence during the Coastal Commission's annual beach-cleanup day, when tens of thousands of Californians collect litter from beaches, roadsides, and rivers. It was with great satisfaction that Peter Douglas could say two decades after the passage of the Coastal Act: "The notion that we share a stewardship responsibility toward the coast is now widely accepted. . . . Many individuals are willing to do their share, and there is strong public support for coastal management at the state level."[21] Public surveys conducted by the nonpartisan Public Policy Institute of California (PPIC) corroborate Douglas's assessment. Beginning in 2000, the PPIC initiated a statewide survey series on the environment; its periodic surveys on coastal and marine issues suggest that Californians' appreciation for their coast has only grown with time. Of adults surveyed in 2003, 88 percent reported that that the condition of the ocean and beaches is important to them personally, with three-quarters of respondents characterizing these conditions as "very" important.[22] These numbers grew to over 90 percent in the coming years.[23] Perhaps most striking was a 2006 PPIC survey in which 44 percent of those surveyed reported that the Coastal Commission was not strict enough in controlling coastal development, with only 10 percent believing the commission's regulations were too strict.[24]

But voter support for coastal protection has not continued on a consistently upward trajectory. Californians appear to gauge to what extent their personal contributions are necessary to maintain a healthy coast. During the 1980s, when Governor George Deukmejian worked to abolish the Coastal Commission while also exhibiting a general disregard for the environment, voters passed nine measures intended to protect the state's natural resources (while rejecting only three).[25] The end of the Cold War, however, caused a deep recession in defense-heavy California that challenged voters' and the legislature's commitment to sustained funding for the environment. Beginning in 1990 and throughout the decade, voters rejected seven environmental propositions, passing only two in support of wildlife.[26] At the same time, the state legislature failed to provide any new funding for the Coastal Conservancy for the first time in its fourteen-year history. As voter and legislative support floundered, local efforts were already helping to fill in the gaps. Speaking in late 1990, the head of the state's Coastal Conservancy, Peter Grenell, found reason to be optimistic:[27]

> In some cases, local bond acts have been proposed to help fund these [environmental and related growth-management] activities. Regional river park groups are now active in several coastal and other locations. Broader geographic and functional viewpoints are also reflected in the increasing interest in identification and management of wildlife corridors and regional ecosystems.... These efforts suggest a basis for positive state government action on a host of critical environmental concerns, including coastal ones, in concert with local government and nonprofit groups. They offer the promise of cooperation, rather than contention; performance rather than paralysis.

In a period when state funding was so low that California State Parks began to entertain corporate sponsorship, local and private efforts became necessary to sustain the preservation momentum begun in more flush times.[28]

In recognition of the continued development pressures facing the coast, especially as the economy began to rebound, voters in 1997 elected Governor Gray Davis on a platform that included saving the coast, and within a few years voters again felt confident about investing in environmental bond measures. Throughout the first decade of the twenty-first century, Californians approved four measures that prioritized coastal preservation, rejecting no such measures. But the injection of government funds into coastal protection would not alone do the job. Private efforts were so critical that in 1996 Coastal Conservancy Director Michael Fischer could say of land trusts that they represented "the strongest arm of the conservation movement."[29] In the San Francisco Bay Area about half of all new land protected around the turn of the century occurred on private property with the use of conservation easements negotiated by land trusts and public agencies. As the Coastal Conservancy acknowledged, "government simply can't own and manage enough land to achieve today's conservation needs."[30] There were of course those in Big Sur and elsewhere who would argue that government ownership of scenic and environmentally sensitive coastal land was never the ideal anyhow. With that belief in mind, residents of Big Sur and local officials pioneered creative preservation measures in the 1960s that would become increasingly common throughout the state. Open-space planning, conservation easements, land trusts, and intergovernmental collaboration and citizen activism all addressed preservation in an age of increasingly high land values, erratic voter support, and unpredictable government funding.[31]

Californians, as private individuals and entities, and together with their local and state governments, have built over the past five decades a fairly durable commitment to preserving the coast's ecological integrity and public access. Such support makes sense in a state where the majority of the population lives within the coastal zone and three-quarters of residents visit an ocean beach at least several times per year.[32] But widespread buy-in for coastal regulations also reflects Californians' understanding of the coast's economic significance.[33] The San Francisco Bay Conservation and Development Commission (BCDC) has long operated on the premise that suitable development projects must go hand-in-hand with the preservation and restoration of the bay. Since its formation in 1965, the BCDC has helped guide over twenty billion dollars' worth of waterfront development while restoring approximately thirty square miles of bay habitat and increasing public access.[34] In the mid-1990s, the Coastal Conservancy's quarterly newsletter summed up in one sentence the coast's great value: "The coast not only symbolizes California to the world, it is the state's most important recreational resource and the magnet that attracts a $44 billion–a-year tourist industry, the state's largest employer."[35] In a state that relies heavily upon tourism and houses more than a tenth of the nation's population (densely settled along the coast), it comes as little surprise that Californians express greater support for land-use regulations and the use of public funds to preserve open space as compared with the average American.[36] Common resources are carefully regulated in densely populated California, where the majority of residents link the quality of their environment to their quality of life.[37]

Tourists, recreationists, and those who cater to these groups all benefit from an appealing coastline, but arguably coastal homeowners are the primary beneficiaries of coastal regulation, even when taking into account the considerable private-property restrictions that accompany such regulation. Big Sur's aesthetic zoning in the 1930s and its Coast Master Plan in 1962 were early examples of applying the brakes to coastal development in order to protect scenery, property values, and the good life for its residents. Such slow-growth measures generally work well in the places where wealth is already established and people are looking to protect what they have already acquired. In those circumstances, growth becomes counterproductive, as it diminishes the privilege associated with own-ing a piece of desirable property. California's rapid development after World War II eventually engendered a strong interest among nearly all residents for land-use regulations, but it is still the well-to-do who lend the most support to local slow-growth initiatives. Approval for such measures rises in accordance with a resident's age, income, and education. And unlike environmental priori-ties that are often partisan issues, slow-growth initiatives are equally popular among Democrats, Republicans, and independent voters.[38] In part, slow growth is politically viable along portions of California's coast because certain places, like the port of Long Beach and other stretches of the southern California coast, along with much of the densely settled Bay Area, have already been given over to production and development. Though natural resources benefit when Californians link the health of the coast to their financial and overall well-being, there is an obvious social cost associated with coastal preservation.

Those involved with the creation of the Coastal Act understood that the regulations designed to protect the coast from overdevelopment would also contribute to an increase in the cost of coastal homeownership.[39] Part of the public-access component, then, included the low- and moderate-income hous-ing provision that was scrapped after only five years. Though the Coastal Commission's mandate as originally conceived in 1972 was decidedly liberal, the effects of Proposition 13, passed just six years later, made it politically and financially untenable to continue the affordable-housing mandate. Homeownership along California's coast was indeed going to be for the afflu-ent, and increasingly so, as local coastal programs guided development, the population grew (and grew wealthier), and the coastline all the while remained the same size. Land-use regulations and the economics of supply and demand contributed to the high cost of coastal real estate while the impact of Proposition 13 meant that the Coastal Commission and the Coastal Conservancy had to work within the parameters of tight government budgets and a constituency that wanted access to its coast, wanted it kept beautiful, and did not want to have to pay very much for any of these services.[40] Land trusts and collaborative public-private efforts have in many areas picked up the slack for reduced gov-ernment funding, especially in high-income regions like the Bay Area, because of residents' ability and willingness to fund these organizations.

Despite their different ideological origins, the effects of Proposition 20 and Proposition 13 have been surprisingly similar. Most obviously, each measure led to a transfer of authority from the local to the state level. The tax revolt meant that counties lost revenue and turned to the state for necessary funding, and the Coastal Act created a structure by which the state had the final word on coastal land-use regulations. Arguably, in both instances the wealthiest Californians stood to gain the most. Companies with large landholdings enjoyed a tax benefit from Proposition 13 that dwarfed the tax relief experienced by private homeowners, and owners of high-value real estate enjoyed greater tax relief than owners of more modest homes. Not dissimilar is the advantage the real-estate developer holds over the homeowner hoping to build along the coast. A company generally possesses a greater ability to allot time and expertise to the logistics of presenting a case to the Coastal Commission (from paperwork to research to attending meetings), and developers own greater expanses of land on which to dedicate the open space sometimes required. Companies aside, wealthier Californians fare better than their poorer neighbors in these same regards. Perhaps it is not surprising, therefore, that each initiative created the potential for contentious relationships between neighbors. Longtime property owners pay significantly less property tax than their new neighbors in sometimes identical homes.[41] And in Coastal Commission hearings, it is not uncommon for a resident to present material in opposition to a neighbor's proposed development plan out of a distaste for the changes it would bring.[42] During the 1970s both initiatives were promoted as populist measures, but their implementation has helped to increase the good life for residents who already possessed a measure of wealth. Social stratification in California and in the nation is the result of many factors, including even developments ostensibly intended to benefit a wide swath of the population.[43]

As California's coast gentrified, Peter Douglas identified the tall challenge of working to retain community character and cultural resources in this region.[44] Ironically, Douglas not only lamented the changing demographics but contributed firsthand to this phenomenon as the owner of two homes along California's beautiful coastal stretches.[45] Many locals in Big Sur possess the same social advantage as Douglas did and would also agree with his concern for community. Residents of Big Sur have argued for decades that ongoing public-land acquisition, rising land and housing prices, restrictive land-use policies, and gentrification all challenge the community's viability.[46] The economic realities associated with coastal preservation in Big Sur are stark: the cost of a one-bedroom home can easily soar above a million dollars; estates are often worth tens of millions.[47] Big Sur is an uberexample of California's increasingly elite coastal housing conditions. And yet, to this day, the Grange, an adult softball league, a volunteer fire brigade, a local arts initiative, and several small schools all reveal that Big Sur contains not just wealthy second-home owners, but also year-round residents and families who contribute their time and energy to sustaining the community. It is, however, a community that reflects the socioeconomic realities of an increasingly coveted landscape. The population, on the whole, is older than the national and county averages, contributing to declining school enrollments in the South Coast of Big Sur. The area's primary industry—tourism—generates a service-sector labor force that must seek creative housing arrangements or commute long distances from less expensive parts of Monterey County.[48] Long gone are the days of a struggling artists' community that sustained the likes of Henry Miller. Writers, poets, painters, and craftsmen still live in Big Sur, but living comfortably requires an income not usually associated with the arts.

A brief look at the history of the Big Sur Softball League reveals some of the changes occurring in Big Sur over the past several decades. The Nepenthe Outlaws, the league's dominant team in the 1970s, were an all-Caucasian team with a name reminiscent of Big Sur's original Old West image. The Rebel Wreckers, also all-white, took the trophy in 1985, displaying a Confederate battle flag in their championship photo. They very well may have been invoking the antifederalist sentiment of the 1980 national seashore debate. In 2005, the Post Ranch Burritos claimed victory. Sponsored by the local Post Ranch Inn (a cattle ranch turned high-end luxury resort), the team lineup reflected the steady increase in the number of Latino residents, or commuters, many of whom help run the local service economy. The Big Sur softball games are played inside Pfeiffer Big Sur State Park, where the community has brokered a deal with California State Parks to allow players to enter the park without paying the entrance fee. All games take place on Monday, Tuesday, and Wednesday evenings, when the fewest tourists are likely to be in the park. The Big Sur community has at times led the changes unfolding along this prized coastline—the Coast Master Plan being a case in point—but the community has more often adapted to the economic and social realities of California's ever more expensive and more popular coast.

Certain tourism-related challenges continue to foil residents and local officials looking to perpetuate Big Sur's hybrid landscape. Despite planning successes (and in some cases because of them) several enduring issues plague the community and the landscape intended for preservation. Today, locals and county leaders voice decades-old concerns, including dangerously congested traffic conditions, degradation of campgrounds, illegal fires (such as the one that ignited the 2016 Soberanes Fire), litter (including human waste because of insufficient restrooms), short-term rentals and housing shortages, trespassing on pri-

FIGURE 20. The Big Sur Softball League holds its games in Pfeiffer Big Sur State Park, one of the few public spaces with enough flat ground for a field. Even so, a portion of the outfield is stopped many feet short by trees, with league rules dictating bases earned for hits to right field. (Photo: author.)

vate property, and a lack of law enforcement.[49] The pressures of tourism in the past several decades have changed only in scale, not in form. But even as some bemoan the impact of Big Sur's popularity, its reputation continues to grow.

Big Sur highlights the thrill of California to many people around the world, despite the chronic problems facing its community and landscape. This single coastal stretch encompasses a good deal of what is notable about the state, including arresting scenery, stunning homes, famous residents past and present, left-leaning and alternative lifestyles, and a collaborative public-private commitment to the environment. *National Geographic Traveler* took such features into account when, in 1999, it bestowed upon Big Sur the label of one of the fifty greatest destinations in the world. Unlike the magazine's feature at midcentury, which omitted any mention of inhabitants along the stunning coastal stretch, the magazine now acknowledged Big Sur's cultural richness in addition to its nature. Altogether this amounted to a fine example of "civilization and nature in harmony," opined the magazine.[50] This iconic stretch of California has a way of drawing out such praise. A 2001 PBS/*NATURE* film entitled "Living Edens: Big Sur—California's Wild Coast" proclaimed its natural wonders, and a 2009 *Los Angeles Times* obituary cast Big Sur as at once exotic, alluring, elite, and environmentally sound.[51] As California's population grows and development pressures increase along the coast, the essence as well as the very existence of Big Sur becomes ever more culturally important.

In 2009 the *Los Angeles Times* ran a story on the passing of Joseph William "Bill" Post III, an 88-year-old Big Sur native with a direct link to the region's early homestead families. "In the patch of paradise called Big Sur," the obituary opened, "Post was the last cowboy." Bill Post represented continuity from Big Sur's pioneering days to its status in the early twenty-first century as a world-class destination. His great-grandmother, Anselma Onesimo, part Rumsien Indian, married Connecticut native William Brainard Post in Carmel Valley. They moved to Big Sur in 1858. William Post was a strong advocate for bringing the first dirt road from Monterey down past the Big Sur River and worked with the county to ensure its construction. Three generations later, Bill Post grew up on the family's expansive ranch, joined the military during World War II, and later worked as an electrician for Caltrans, the state's transportation agency. After his retirement in 1979, a neighbor and friend asked Post to consider a new project, a resort, on a portion of his ranch. Post purportedly agreed to sell nearly one hundred acres for the construction of the Post Ranch Inn under two conditions: that he would excavate and grade the land himself and that the resort's design would be environmentally sensitive.[52]

Post tapped into a long family tradition of catering to tourists when he developed his inn. Even before the highway, his family had led hunting parties and other visitors on horseback through the Santa Lucia Mountains.[53] During the interwar period Bill's parents opened a small resort on the Post family property.[55] A second-generation Post, Frank, became a fixture at the family resort, sharing stories of the old Sur country. His reputation earned him a feature in *Westways,* a statewide magazine, in which the journalist praised both Frank and his beloved landscape. The 1952 article painted Frank as the John Wayne

FIGURE 21. The Big Sur River Inn encourages visitors to enjoy the beauty and tranquility of the region while offering amenities such as food, lodging, and community space. Perhaps this inn helped prompt *National Geographic Traveler* in 1999 to label Big Sur a fine example of "civilization and nature in harmony." (Photo: author.)

of Big Sur: "[Frank] is a big man, as big as the country around him."[55] Frank and Bill Post became icons to a society continuously enamored with the Old West. At the close of the twentieth century, Bill could think on a grander scale than his parents had done by tapping into Big Sur's international reputation and a growing demand for deluxe accommodations. Closing in on his seventieth birthday, Bill Post spent the better part of a year clearing the land for the first thirty rooms and necessary roads. In all, he decided only one tree had to be removed. After the inn opened, in 1992, Bill became the resident historian and nature guide, delighting guests with his stories of Big Sur's early days. The resort's name and logo—the ranch's cattle brand—were meant to evoke Big Sur's heritage while capitalizing on the much more lucrative tourist industry. When interviewed some years after the inn opened, Post articulated the changes to the Big Sur country that his long life encompassed. "In many ways, I'm still a rancher," he opined, "only now I'm cultivating a crop of vacationers."[56]

These vacationers were of the most elite variety, who could afford to pay up to $1,000 per night, and no less than $750; in short, they were not the crowd that Coastal Act proponents had in mind when including the public-access component. But this high-end resort also displayed unusually low-impact development. What the *Los Angeles Times* described as "organic architecture" includes "sod roofs, avant-garde treehouses and guest rooms

FIGURE 22. Post Ranch Inn, a luxury resort built by Bill Post, a member of an original homesteading family. (Photo: Nicki Dugan Pogue, https://commons.wikimedia.org/wiki/File:Our_Hobbit_House_at_Post_Ranch_Inn.jpg.)

built into the oceanfront bluffs" designed to leave old-growth trees standing and to achieve an artistic and natural feel that visitors have come to expect in Big Sur. The Post Ranch Inn proudly proclaims its environmentally friendly attributes, such as solar panels, an endangered-species habitat, and drought-resistant landscaping, and includes its fleet of hybrid Lexus SUVs as evidence of its commitment to the environment.[57] During a period of road closures in 2017, the inn launched its "Escape through the Skies" package to deliver its guests to the cut-off coastline by helicopter.[58] The Post Ranch Inn's clientele can revel in the features that have become a hallmark of Big Sur: scenery, well-designed land use, and luxury; all key touchpoints of the *Los Angeles Times* obituary. In case the cultural weight assigned to Bill Post and his inn was unclear, the obituary also included a short epitaph from Thomas Steinbeck, son of the novelist John Steinbeck. The two families had known each other for the past century, leading Thomas to say of Bill that he was not only "a piece of history" but also "a great steward of the land."[59]

That stewardship of the California coast is now a widely praised attribute reveals the extent to which the Coastal Commission and Coastal Conservancy, the Bay Conservation and Development Commission, numerous land trusts and citizen environmental groups, and some local governments have all successfully garnered support for California's coastal resources. Nevertheless, in 2011, the year before he passed away, Peter Douglas bemoaned what he described as a "politically myopic era," when residents seemed unwilling to grapple with the problems on the horizon, and when corporations could use their influence to advance development. Douglas, like others in the Coastal Commission, felt certain that the Coastal Act would have failed to come to fruition in a more recent political climate. With the money behind development dwarfing that of conservation, and without a group such as the Coastal Alliance to galvanize the vote, Douglas reasoned that any initiative similar to Proposition 20, or even an amendment to strengthen the Coastal Act, would be doomed to failure.[60] Indeed, few environmentally focused statewide propositions have appeared on the ballot since 2006 (and even fewer have passed), during the same time when a California recession also hurt government funding for coastal conservation.[61] Again, though, the absence of a group like the Coastal Alliance speaks to the success of the public and private efforts that have become fixtures in coastal conservation. These regulations have given voters confidence that preservation is already under way, while the various conservation organizations have provided outlets for citizen engagement.

As Peter Douglas was well aware, the shape and substance of coastal preservation is ever evolving in response to demographic, political, and ecosystem-level changes in the state. Today, California's population is almost exactly double what it was when voters passed Proposition 20 in 1972. Adding to the environmental and economic challenges of a growing population is the issue of climate change and what rising sea levels will mean for California's beloved coastline. Charles Lester, a former staff member of the Coastal Commission who succeeded Douglas as executive director in late 2011, took stock of the agency and the tasks set before it. He committed his staff to crafting an updated strategic plan and a Sea Level Rise guide for statewide planning, while also succeeding in securing increased funding to support robust local coastal programs.[62] But politics seems to have derailed Lester, and in January 2016 Coastal Commissioners called for a hearing to consider his removal on grounds that he had failed to adequately communicate with commissioners concerning the agency's work.

In response to the proposed dismissal hearing, fourteen thousand letters of support for Lester poured into the Coastal Commission's office, praising his commitment to coastal preservation. Hundreds of concerned residents gathered at the hearing, providing hours of impassioned testimony in favor of the director's work. When commissioners retreated for a private vote, a slim majority voted against him. In addition to the charges of poor communication, the vote reflected concern among certain commissioners that Lester's office had been overly critical of legitimate development projects while also failing to secure sufficient access to low-cost coastal accommodations.[63] In what seemed a telling divide, the five commissioners who voted to keep Lester in place were the same five commissioners who had most consistently voted in favor of conservation in 2015 commission hearings.[64] The overwhelming public response to the dismissal was that commissioners had kowtowed to development interests. But the chair of the Coastal Commission, Steve Kinsey (who did not vote in favor of the dismissal), announced after the hearing that the debate "revolved around leadership and not around an issue of greater flexibility for development."[65] Few were placated by his remarks. Assembly Speaker Toni Atkins, the legislator responsible for appointing several of the Coastal Commissioners, expressed disappointment following Lester's removal: "Let me apologize to the public. I truly thought my appointees would be better stewards of the coast."[66]

It remains to be seen what effect this event will have on the public's relationship to coastal regulation. Will it help to galvanize a concerned public to pursue conservation through additional local and private methods? Is Lester's dismissal indicative of a downswing in support for the commission's tradition of favoring conservation, and if so, how widespread is this opinion? While it is too soon to tell what direction the Coastal Commission will take under the leadership of the new executive director, John Ainsworth, Lester's removal and the decline in commissioners' votes in favor of coastal conservation since 2014 may both suggest a tilt toward treating property rights and development at least on par with coastal preservation.[67] Though well aware of these conditions, Lester interpreted this trend not as simply a scenario pitting development versus the environment but rather as something "more nuanced."[68] For more than forty years California's coastal regulation has reflected the political, economic, and ideological considerations that maintain the state's dual image of natural splendor and fine coastal living. It is in the tension between these two defining features that all coastal regulation must navigate. Political vagaries may temporarily tip regulation in one direction or the other, but the fundamental question of how to accommodate a growing number of residents and admirers within an exceptionally beautiful coastal landscape requires that property rights, public access, and scenery all receive serious and lasting attention.

In Big Sur, this tension between gracious living and coastal preservation appears close to seamless, an exemplar of coastal regulation to which Peter Douglas and others from the Coastal Commission could point proudly.[69] Recent events in the Point Reyes National Seashore bring into relief just how difficult it is to maintain this scenic and residential balance. The National Park Service retains this seashore for the millions who admire its stunning coastline and idyllic pastoral landscape. Written into the 1962 charter for the Point Reyes National Seashore was protection for the area's ranching heritage. Today, fifteen ranches operate on land leased from the park service. Lacking the economies of scale that their highly efficient valley counterparts enjoy, the ranches in Point Reyes find financial viability by establishing creameries that supply local markets and the organic food markets of the San Francisco Bay Area. To some degree, this land-management structure reflects the same appreciation for the ranching tradition that the Coastal Commission supports in Big Sur, but the lack of private ownership in Point Reyes makes a considerable difference.

Three environmental groups brought forward a lawsuit against the Point Reyes National Seashore in 2016, arguing that cattle grazing is causing erosion, harming endangered species (such as salmon and tule elk), and polluting waterways. Moreover, given the park's public mandate, these groups are concerned that the ranches in some cases block public access with no-trespassing signs. The suit asks the National Park Service to suspend the renewal of twenty-year ranch leases until an environmental impact study is completed, as part of an updated General Management Plan.[70] Meanwhile, ranchers have at times felt stymied by park policies that conflict with ranching priorities, such as the protection of the tule elk population.[71] In the early 1960s, residents of both West Marin and Big Sur had anticipated the sorts of challenges that locals might experience under federal ownership and had argued in favor of protecting private property. After heading down divergent paths, both areas serve tourists, but it is only in Big Sur that community heritage and historic land use find approbation and protection from the state and, ostensibly, an admiring public.[72]

Built into the parameters of Big Sur's well-preserved scenery is an unusual blending of the preservation and property-rights strands that guide land use along the California coast. A long-held belief in Big Sur maintains that the land is enhanced by the culture of its inhabitants whereas residents and visitors, in turn, are enriched by the area's unmarred beauty. The state-approved Local Coastal Program is premised upon this idea, that preservation and habitation can be mutually supportive endeavors. Big Sur's unconventional land ethic reflects Jeffers's beloved verse: "Man dissevered from the earth and stars and his history . . . often appears atrociously ugly. Integrity is wholeness, the greatest beauty is organic wholeness, the wholeness of life and things. . . . Love that, not man apart from that."[73] Today, Big Sur is arguably every bit as beautiful as it was when Robinson Jeffers first immortalized it, in part because his verse helped engender a powerful commitment to preservation from multiple generations of locals and nonresidents who cherish this coastline.

Big Sur has long been a privileged perch from which to critique contemporary developments, but as in all wild places, Big Sur reflects, albeit through a mask, many current political, economic, and social realities. The Esalen Institute, perhaps the single most recognizable destination in Big Sur, is itself a vivid example of this reflection. During the heady 1960s the institute forged new paths for California's (and the nation's) counterculture. Floundering somewhat in defining its purpose in the 1970s, Esalen then made its mark with hot-tub diplomacy in the 1980s. The institute hosted many Russians, including the Washington ambassador, for culture-bridging activities. Increasingly in the decades to come, Esalen catered to the wealthy with self-reflective seminars and golf trips to the Monterey Peninsula. The institute and its setting have made a deep impression on many of its visitors. A Russian economist reflected in the early 1980s, "the word 'Esalen' is magic to me. It is a symbol of people who, like myself, understand the value of things other than material wealth."[74] This quote and its context go a long way in explaining the essence of this coastline.

The name Big Sur conjures up images of a place uniquely Californian, carved out of the geologic and cultural forces of which the state has a disproportionate share, but also of a place that is not dependent on the trappings of society, a place of personal freedom. In many ways and for many people, Big Sur is all these things, but it is also undeniably a place that has been carefully cultivated by and for some of society's most prosperous members. Even with most homes hidden from view, residents' material wealth is nonetheless part of what defines Big Sur to the broader public. The series finale of the popular television program *Mad Men,* which aired in 2015, neatly encapsulated Big Sur's contemporary resonance in American society. The episode, set in 1970, depicted the lead character finding rejuvenation at the Esalen Institute, meditating alongside the Pacific, and then hitting upon a brilliant advertising campaign for Coca-Cola. Big Sur, and California more broadly, hold immense cultural weight for the potential they have long represented to a nation that reveres both natural beauty and personal wealth. Big Sur captures the collective imagination because it is such a fine example of the entrenched American belief that these two ideals can be reconciled.

ABBREVIATIONS

The following abbreviations are used throughout the notes for the archives, reports, and periodicals appearing in this list.

Big Sur Lib.	Big Sur Library, Local History Collection, Big Sur, California
BSGD	*Big Sur Guide*
BSGZ	*The Big Sur Gazette*
BSRU	*Big Sur Round-Up*
CA Arch._ CCC	California State Archives, California Coastal Commission Records, Sacramento, California
CA Arch._PW	California State Archives, Public Works Records, Sacramento, California.
CA C&O	*California Coast & Ocean/California Waterfront Age*
CA HistRm_ Big Sur	California History Room, Big Sur File. Monterey Public Library, Monterey, California
CA HistRm_ Coastal Reg.	California History Room, Coastal Regulation File. Monterey Public Library, Monterey, California
CA Hist. Room_ Hwy 1	California History Room, Highway 1 Clipping File. Monterey Public Library, Monterey, California
CCC_SntaCrz	Central Coast California Coastal Commission Office, Santa Cruz.
CMP	Monterey County Coast Master Plan

CMP_SOM	Monterey Coast Master Plan, Skidmore, Owings & Merrill
CPC	*The Carmel Pine Cone*
LAT	*Los Angeles Times*
LCP	Big Sur Coast Local Coastal Program
MoCo Board of Sup.	Monterey County Board of Supervisors, Clerk of the Board Office
MPH	*Monterey Peninsula Herald*
NARA	National Archives and Records Administration, Laguna Niguel
NYT	*New York Times*
Panetta Inst. Arch.	Leon and Sylvia Panetta Institute Archives, California State University, Monterey Bay
SFC	*San Francisco Chronicle*
SPECOLDAV	Shields Library, Special Collections, University of California, Davis
USDA	United States Department of Agriculture

NOTES

INTRODUCTION

The epigraph to this chapter cites a statement from William A. Turnage, executive director, The Wilderness Society, quoting Ansel Adams. United States Congress. Senate. Committee on Energy and Natural Resources. Subcommittee on Parks, Recreation, and Renewable Resources. *Hearing before the Subcommittee on Parks, Recreation, and Renewable Resources.* 96th Cong., 2nd sess., 24 Apr. 1980: *A Bill to Establish the Big Sur Coast National Scenic Area in the State of California,* S.2551. Publication no. 96–125, p. 189.

1. This description of Big Sur is informed by the work of Paul Henson and Donald J. Usner, *Natural History of Big Sur* (Berkeley and Los Angeles: University of California Press, 1993).

2. In May 2017 a million-ton landslide piled some fifty feet of debris on Highway 1, adding thirteen acres to the coastline along the southern stretch of Big Sur.

3. Robinson Jeffers lived in Carmel-by-the-Sea from 1914 until his death, in 1962. So much of his poetry was set in Big Sur that his name became synonymous with this coastal stretch. Henry Miller lived in Big Sur from 1944 until the early 1960s; these years inspired his memoir *Big Sur and the Orange of Hieronymus Bosch.* Jack Kerouac lived in Big Sur for only part of one summer in 1960, an experience that led him to publish a memoir, *Big Sur.* Ansel Adams moved to Carmel Highlands in 1962 and remained until his death, in 1984. His home afforded him a view of the northern coast of Big Sur and proximity to inspiring locations for his work.

4. James J. Rawls and Walton Bean, *California: An Interpretive History,* 8th ed. (Boston: McGraw Hill, 2003), 340–42.

5. Robinson Jeffers, "The Coast-Road," *The Selected Poetry of Robinson Jeffers* (New York: Random House, 1959), 581.

6. Robinson Jeffers, "Storm as Deliverer," *The Collected Poetry of Robinson Jeffers,* ed. Tim Hunt, vol. 4, Poetry, 1903–1920, Prose, and Unpublished Writings (Stanford, CA: Stanford University Press, 2000), 262.

7. Fred Storm, "Unchanged by Years: Big Sur Country—A Timeless Eden" *SFC,* 24 Oct. 1965. CA HistRm_Big Sur.

8. Richard J. Orsi, Alfred Runte, and Marlene Smith-Baranzini, eds., *Yosemite and Sequoia: A Century of California National Parks* (Berkeley and Los Angeles: University of California Press, 1993), 124.

9. Median price for a three-bedroom house in Big Sur Sept. 1978–Mar. 1979: $228,000. (Data compiled by Monterey Peninsula Board of Realtors.) U.S. median home price Jan. 1979: $60,300. The median price of an owner-occupied home in California in 1980: $84,500. (1980 Census of Housing, California, 6–7.)

10. Big Sur Coast Local Coastal Program, certified by the California Coastal Commission 1986, 7, 14.

11. Gary Breschini and Trudy Haversat, *The Esselen Indians of the Big Sur Country: The Land and the People* (Salinas, CA: Coyote Press, 2004), 191–94.

12. Lillian Bos Ross, *The Stranger: A Novel of the Big Sur* (New York: W. Morrow and Company, 1942).

13. Jeff Norman and the Big Sur Historical Society, *Images of America: Big Sur* (Charleston, SC: Arcadia Publishing, 2004). Anthony Godfrey, *The Ever-Changing View: A History of the National Forests in California, 1891–1987* (Vallejo, CA: USDA Forest Service, 2005), 70.

14. Connie Chiang, *Shaping the Shoreline: Fisheries and Tourism on the Monterey Coast* (Seattle: University of Washington Press, 2008).

15. Hal K. Rothman, *Devil's Bargains: Tourism in the Twentieth-Century American West* (Lawrence, KS: University of Kansas Press, 1998), 15–16. Rothman identifies three types of western relationships to tourism: the urban and rural model notable in Nevada and Hawaii, where tourism trumps all other economic strategies; the rural model where tourism is a "by-product" or "shadow economy" that occurs in the background of agriculture, ranching, or other forms of production; and the urban, cosmopolitan model of which Monterey County is a part, where tourism is an integral part of a diverse economy, but not dominant.

16. William Cronon, "The Trouble with Wilderness; or, Getting Back to the Wrong Nature," *Uncommon Ground: Rethinking the Human Place in Nature,* ed. William Cronon (New York: W. W. Norton & Co., 1996), 69–90. There was an extensive, and passionate, response to Cronon's essay, debated in a roundtable in the first issue of *Environmental History,* in *The Great New Wilderness Debate,* ed. J. Baird Callicott and Michael P. Nelson (Athens: University of Georgia Press, 1998), and *The Wilderness Debate Rages On: Continuing the Great New Wilderness Debate* (Athens: University of Georgia Press, 2008), and in Tom Butler, ed., *Wild Earth: Wild Ideas for a World Out of Balance* (Minneapolis: Milkweed Editions, 2002).

17. Donald Thomas Clark, *Monterey County Place Names: A Geographical Dictionary* (Carmel Valley: Kestrel Press, 1991). Norman and Big Sur Historical Society, *Images of America,* 7.

CHAPTER 1. JEFFERS'S COUNTRY

The epigraph to this chapter: Robinson Jeffers, "The Coast-Road," *The Collected Poetry of Robinson Jeffers,* ed. Tim Hunt, vol. 2, *1928–1938* (Stanford, CA: Stanford University Press, 1989), 523.

   1. Horace Lyon, ed., *Jeffers Country: The Seed Plots of Robinson Jeffers' Poetry* (San Francisco: Scrimshaw Press, 1971).

   2. Ibid.

   3. At some point the term "Jeffers Country" entered common usage, and in 1971 a collection of Jeffers's work was published under the title *Jeffers Country.*

   4. *TIME Magazine* 15, no. 14 (1932).

   5. James J. Rawls and Walton Bean, *California: An Interpretive History,* 8th ed. (Boston: McGraw Hill, 2003), 340–42.

   6. Richard Hughey and Boon Hughey, *Jeffers Country Revisited: Beauty without Price,* 1. SPECOLDAV. Quotation from Robert Brophy, ed., *The Robinson Jeffers Newsletter, A Jubilee Gathering, 1962–1988* (Los Angeles: Occidental College, 1988), 10. Jeffers's wife, Una, recounted the numerous locations along the Big Sur coast that served as place settings for Robinson's poems and how local history and lore inspired parts of his stories. She explained that "Woven all through his poems are scattered bits of old legends of the country": Ann N. Ridgeway, *The Selected Letters of Robinson Jeffers* (Baltimore: The Johns Hopkins University Press, 1968), Una Jeffers to Lawrence Clark Powell, 15 Apr. 1932.

   7. In 1999, thirty-seven years after Jeffers's death, *Smithsonian Magazine* depicted Jeffers as the "harbinger and the bard for the still-continuing wave of runaways to hit Big Sur": Robert Wernick, "Big Sur," *Smithsonian Magazine* 30, no. 8 (Nov. 1999), 101–2. Local and state sources ascribed similar influence to Jeffers. Fred Storm, "Unchanged by Years: Big Sur Country—A Timeless Eden" *SFC,* 24 Oct. 1965. CA HistRm_Big Sur. Rosalind Sharpe Wall, *A Wild Coast and Lonely: Big Sur Pioneers* (San Carlos: Wide World Pub./Tetra, 1989).

   8. 1910 Monterey County Population Census; 1910 Tax Assessor Rolls. In 1910, for the first time, a handful of residents of Big Sur made a living through the arts, choosing Big Sur as their home for its scenic qualities without working the land in any way. Big Sur also began to house a number of professionals not directly reliant upon the land. The coast had a diverse set of laborers: from hired hands toiling at odd jobs, to the blacksmiths, carpenters, wood choppers, and other skilled laborers, to those who rented farms and ranches, those who owned their farms and ranches free of mortgages, to the handful of property owners with over a few thousand acres of land and hundreds of dollars' worth of cattle, horses, and hogs. And although those at the very top were few, there existed a solid group of large landowners, as well as a good number of homesteaders who owned their own farms. Over thirty families owned a ranch or farm, which was a greater number than those who worked in any single extractive industry at the time.

9. "Should Have the Telephone," *Monterey New Era,* 12 Oct. 1904. CA HistRm_Big Sur. The newspaper editorialized that a telephone line in Big Sur would boost its tourist appeal and estimated that Big Sur saw hundreds of summer campers and visitors each year.

10. William Brown, *History of Los Padres National Forest, 1898–1945* (San Francisco, 1945), 164.

11. James Karman, ed., *The Collected Letters of Robinson Jeffers: With Selected Letters of Una Jeffers,* vol. 1, *1890–1930* (Stanford, CA: Stanford University Press, 2009), 412.

12. 1910 Monterey County Population Census. Of the 204 working adults listed in the census for the Big Sur coast, 112 were involved in agriculture or ranching. In addition, one-quarter of laborers worked in an extractive industry, either a limekiln or lumber business, with a handful of supporting jobs, such as a stage teamster. The remaining employed residents worked as teachers, merchants, nurses, artists, a preacher, federal employees (working for Point Sur Light Station and for the Bureau of Indian Services), or odd-job laborers. One family had independent income and lived in Big Sur without employment. These numbers do not take into account the children and wives who did not earn wages, nearly all of whom lived on owned or rented farms or ranches.

13. Jeff Norman and the Big Sur Historical Society, *Images of America: Big Sur* (Charleston, SC: Arcadia Publishing, 2004), 87–89.

14. 1920s Idlewild Brochure, W. T. Mitchell, Proprietor. CA HistRm_Big Sur.

15. Norman and Big Sur Historical Society, *Images of America,* 78.

16. Karman, ed., *Collected Letters,* 539.

17. John Woolfenden, "Modernism Creeping into Once Isolated Big Sur Life," *MPH,* May 1967. CA HistRm_Big Sur.

18. Karman, ed., *Collected Letters,* 412.

19. Kathleen Davis, "Cultural Resource Inventory of Pfeiffer Big Sur State Park," Preliminary Draft: Cultural Resource Inventory Unit, Resource Protection Division, California Department of Parks and Recreation, 9 Feb. 1990. Norman and Big Sur Historical Society, *Images of America,* 80–81.

20. "Road Problems, Sur, 1916," *Noticias del Puerto de Monterey* 21, no. 2 (1977).

21. John Walton, "The Poet as Ethnographer: Robinson Jeffers in Big Sur," *California History* 87, no. 2 (2010), 22.

22. Ben Blow, *California Highways: A Descriptive Record of Road Development by the State and by Such Counties as Have Paved Highways* (San Francisco: H. S. Crocker Co., 1920), 185.

23. Monterey County Administrative Offices, Salinas, Planning Department Records: CA Arch._PW.

24. Karman, ed., *Collected Letters,* 411.

25. Christy Borth, *Mankind on the Move: The Story of Highways* (Washington, D.C.: Automotive Safety Foundation, 1969), 177.

26. John Woolfenden, *Big Sur: A Battle for the Wilderness, 1869–1981* (Pacific Grove: Boxwood Press, 1981), 99–107.

27. Blow, *California Highways,* 181.

28. California State Senator Elmer S. Rigdon to Highway Commission, Western Union Telegram, 11 Sept. 1921: CA Arch._PW.

29. Borth, *Mankind,* 190.

30. Blow, *California Highways*, dedication.

31. Marguerite S. Shaffer, *See America First: Tourism and National Identity* (Washington, D.C.: Smithsonian Institution Press, 2001), 138.

32. Borth, *Mankind,* 177–85.

33. "California Taxpayer's Association: Financial History of California State Highways, 1909–1934," SPECOLDAV. Blow, *California Highways,* 1.

34. Ibid., 185.

35. "California Taxpayer's Association: Financial History of California State Highways, 1909–1934," SPECOLDAV: Federal aid supplied more than 17 percent of total money spent on state system since 1920 (when published in 1934).

36. Preliminary Report with Plans on Proposed Highway, 3 Oct. 1918. CA Arch._PW.

37. State Senator Elmer S. Rigdon to A. B. Fletcher, Western Union Telegram, 24 May 1921. CA Arch._PW.

38. L. H. Gibson, "Partington Canyon Bridged by Blast Making a 25,000 Cubic Yard Rockfill," *California Highways and Public Works,* Aug. 1935, 28.

39. *California Highways and Public Works,* July–Aug. 1945, 8. In one section alone, 70,000 cubic feet of earth ended up in the ocean below: *California Highways and Public Works,* July 1937, 15.

40. Personal communication with Tim Thomas, Historian, Monterey History and Art Association and Maritime Museum, Aug. 2008.

41. Norman and Big Sur Historical Society, *Images of America,* 98.

42. *California Highways and Public Works,* July–Aug. 1945, 8.

43. Norman and Big Sur Historical Society, *Images of America,* 95.

44. Works Progress Administration, "A Guide to the Monterey Peninsula, Tour 3: Big Sur" (Berkeley, CA: Press of the Courier, 1941), 175.

45. F. W. Panhorst, "Big Creek Bridge Is Unique," *California Highways and Public Works,* July 1938, 28.

46. "20 Mile Section of San-Simeon–Carmel Highway Not Open," *California Highways and Public Works,* Oct. 1935, 7.

47. Philip Johnston, "Our Unknown Seacoast," *Touring Topics,* May 1930, 18.

48. Tim Hunt, "A Voice in Nature: Jeffers' Tamar and Other Poems,' *American Literature* 61, no. 2 (1989), 232–34.

49. Jeffers, "The Coast-Road," *The Collected Poetry of Robinson Jeffers,* 523.

50. Paul Sutter, *Driven Wild: How the Fight against Automobiles Launched the Modern Wilderness Movement* (Seattle: University of Washington Press, 2002), 15.

51. Karman, ed., *Collected Letters* (above, note 12), 408.

52. Works Progress Administration, "Guide," 185.

53. Norman and Big Sur Historical Society, *Images of America,* 21.

54. Ibid., 99.

55. Rosalind Sharp Wall, memoir, Monterey County Historical Society, Salinas.

56. Blow, *California Highways,* 86. Frederic Paxson, "The Highway Movement: 1916–1935," *American Historical Review* 51, no. 2 (1946), 127.

57. Earl Pomeroy, *In Search of the Golden West: The Tourist in Western America* (New York: Knopf, 1957), 140. Patricia Limerick "Seeing and Being Seen," in *Seeing and Being Seen: Tourism in the American West,* ed. David M. Wrobel and Patrick T. Long (Lawrence: University of Kansas Press, 2001), 46. Hal K. Rothman, *Devil's Bargains: Tourism in the Twentieth-Century American West* (Lawrence, KS: University of Kansas Press, 1998), 14–15.

58. *MPH* article with interview of homesteader/rancher Alejandro Boronda on the encroachment of the highway, CA Hist. Room_Hwy 1. The romantic image of the cowboy as an individual laborer in touch with nature and somehow separate from and superior to modern capitalist ventures echoed in other areas of labor. Matthew McKenzie examines the popular portrayals of artisanal fishermen in turn-of-the-century New England as traditional workers of moral virtue who served as a counterpoint to the modern industrialization of the fisheries: "Iconic Fishermen and the Fates of New England Fisheries Regulations, 1883–1912," *Environmental History* 17 (Jan. 2012): 3–28.

59. Evelyn Gail Gardiner, "Seventy Miles of Yesterday," *Travel,* Dec. 1935. CA Hist. Room_Big Sur.

60. Irene Harlan, "Big Sur Pioneers: Harlans of Lucia," 1988, local history collection, King City Branch, Monterey County Free Libraries. Works Progress Administration, "Guide," 185.

61. Quoted in Pomeroy, *In Search of the Golden West,* 115, 146.

62. Neil Maher, *Nature's New Deal: The Civilian Conservation Corps and the Roots of the American Environmental Movement* (Oxford: Oxford University Press, 2008), 67. Warren Belasco, *Americans on the Road: From Autocamp to Motel, 1910–1945* (Cambridge, MA: MIT Press, 1979), 72.

63. Alexander Wilson, "The View from the Road: Recreation and Tourism," in *Discovered Country: Tourism and Survival in the American West,* ed. Scott Norris (Albuquerque: Stone Ladder Press, 1994), 5–20.

64. Johnston, "Our Unknown Seacoast," 56.

65. Stanford E. Demars, *The Tourist in Yosemite, 1855–1985* (Salt Lake City: University of Utah Press, 1991), 68.

66. John Jakle, *The Tourist: Travel in Twentieth-Century North America* (Lincoln: University of Nebraska Press, 1985), 139.

67. *California Highways and Public Works,* July 1937, 4.

68. David Louter, *Windshield Wilderness: Cars, Roads, and Nature in Washington's National Parks* (Seattle: University of Washington Press, 2006), 4.

69. Sutter, *Driven Wild,* 16.

70. Shaffer, *See America First,* 127.

71. Louter, *Windshield Wilderness,* 14.

72. David Rogers, "A Brief Land Status History of the Monterey Ranger District, Los Padres National Forest, Monterey County, California," *Double Cone*

Quarterly 5, no. 3 (2002): http://www.ventanawild.org/news/fe02/mrdmaps.html (accessed 11 May 2017).

73. U.S. Forest Service History, 1929: Forest Service L-20 Regulation for Primitive Areas. http://www.foresthistory.org/ASPNET/policy/Wilderness/1929_L-Reg .aspx (accessed 28 Aug. 2016.)

74. Brown, *History of Los Padres National Forest,* 167.

75. Norman and Big Sur Historical Society, *Images of America,* 68–73. Brown, *History of Los Padres National Forest,* 53.

76. Ibid., 70, 111.

77. "Caia's New Scenic Road," *Baltimore Sun,* 27 June 1937. "Monterey Coastal Road: Modern Highway Makes Primitive Region in Central California More Accessible," *New York Times,* 28 June 1937. Newspaper clippings, Mayo Hayes O'Donnell Library, Monterey, California.

78. Karman, ed., *Collected Letters,* 731.

79. J.J. Shinabarger, *The Grove at High Tide,* 1 Mar. 1929. CA Hist. Room_ Big Sur.

80. Central Records, General Correspondence 1928–48, Report of R.E. Roach, 15 Dec. 1924, quoted in Davis, "Cultural Resource Inventory," 79.

81. Florence Pfeiffer, "Some Facts of John Pfeiffer's Life." CA Hist. Room_Big Sur.

82. William E. Colby, "Highway and Park Departments Join in Saving Coast Areas for Public Use," *California Highways and Public Works,* Jan.–Feb. 1933, 13.

83. Davis, "Cultural Resource Inventory," 79.

84. Ibid., 83.

85. Ibid., 67–71.

86. There was precedent for such invasive measures. In the early decades of the U.S. National Park System, administrators encouraged or allowed the systematic removal of predator species and sought to increase visitor contact with popular species through such measures as feeding bears from trash cans or even installing petting zoos. Dwight T. Piteaithley, "A Dignified Exploitation: The Growth of Tourism in the National Parks," in *Seeing and Being Seen: Tourism in the American West,* ed. David M. Wrobel and Patrick T. Long (Lawrence: University of Kansas Press, 2001), 304.

87. Brown, *History of Los Padres National Forest,* 110.

88. Robinson Jeffers, "Storm as Deliverer," *The Collected Poetry of Robinson Jeffers,* ed. Tim Hunt, vol. 4, *Poetry, 1903–1920, Prose, and Unpublished Writings* (Stanford, CA: Stanford University Press, 2000), 262.

89. Robinson Jeffers, *The Double Axe and Other Poems, Including Eleven Suppressed Poems* (New York: Liveright, 1977), "Author's Original Preface," 171.

90. Karman, ed., *Collected Letters,* 487.

91. Sutter, *Driven Wild,* 14–15, 237.

92. *Motorland Magazine,* July 1937. CA Hist. Room_Big Sur.

93. Valentine Porter, "Coast Country," *CPC,* 22 July 1938. CA Hist. Room_Big Sur.

94. Jeffers, "The Coast-Road," 523.

The epigraph to this chapter: Henry Miller, *Big Sur and the Oranges of Hieronymus Bosch* (New York: New Directions, 1957), 6.

1. "New Road on Coast Popular," *Oakland Tribune*, 7 July 1937. Newspaper clippings, Mayo Hayes O'Donnell Library, Monterey, California.

2. Taylor Coffman, *Building for Hearst and Morgan: Voices from the George Loorz Papers* (Berkeley: Berkeley Hills Books, 2003), 334, 337.

3. Bulletin, California Mission Trails Association, June 1937. "Great Scenic Highway," *Oakland Tribune*, 25 June 1937. *New York Herald Tribune*, June 1937, newspaper clipping. CA Hist. Room_Hwy 1.

4. James Herrera, "Life of a Scenic Highway," *Monterey County Herald*, 25 Apr. 1997. CA Hist. Room_Hwy 1.

5. Rolf L. Bolin, "Reappearance of the Southern Sea Otter along the California Coast," *Journal of Mammalogy* 19, no. 3 (1938): 301–3.

6. Anthony Godfrey, *The Ever-Changing View: A History of the National Forests in California, 1891–1987* (Washington, D.C.: U.S. Government Printing Office, 2005), 287. There was a period in which a condor egg could fetch up to $1,000.

7. Works Progress Administration, "A Guide to the Monterey Peninsula, Tour 3: Big Sur" (Berkeley: CA, Press of the Courier, 1941), 178–79.

8. Albert S. Bard, "Highway Zoning Sustained by California Court: Design in Community Planning Upheld for Monterey County," *National Civic Review*, 26 Dec. 1938, 619.

9. *Euclid v. Ambler Realty* 272 U.S. 365 (1926), 395. https://www.law.cornell.edu/supremecourt/text/272/365 (accessed 3 Sept. 2016).

10. Carol M. Rose, "Property Rights, Regulatory Regimes and the New Takings Jurisprudence—An Evolutionary Approach" (1990), Faculty Scholarship Series, Paper 1821. http://digitalcommons.law.yale.edu/fss_papers/1821 (accessed 3 Sept. 2016).

11. *Euclid v. Ambler Realty*, 394.

12. Bard, "Highway Zoning," 619.

13. Mel Scott, *American City Planning since 1890: A History Commemorating the Fiftieth Anniversary of the American Institute of Planners* (Berkeley and Los Angeles: University of California Press, 1969), 350.

14. Bard, "Highway Zoning," 619.

15. Lee Cooper, "Would Preserve Roadside Beauty: Many States Act to Guard Land along Highways from Blight," *NYT*, 27 Dec. 1938. CA Hist. Room_Hwy 1. Richard Babcock, *The Zoning Game: Municipal Practices and Policies* (Madison: University of Wisconsin Press, 1966), 12.

16. "New Highway Opened for Travel, San Simeon Area," *Inglewood Daily News*, 28 June 1937. CA Hist. Room_Hwy 1.

17. "A Frontier Passes," *San Jose Mercury-Herald*, 22 June 1937. CA Hist. Room_Hwy 1.

18. Paul Sutter, *Driven Wild: How the Fight against Automobiles Launched the Modern Wilderness Movement* (Seattle: University of Washington Press, 2002), 41–42.

19. David M. Kennedy, *Freedom from Fear: The American People in Depression and War, 1929–1945* (Oxford: Oxford University Press, 1999), 618.

20. G-Permits–Los Padres: found in Record Group No. 95, Box 1, 1954–59, NARA.

21. "History of Fires in Los Padres National Forest," Los Padres National Forest, Fire Records, 1911–1929, unfiled, NARA. William Brown, *History of Los Padres National Forest, 1898–1945* (San Francisco: n.p., 1945), 125–27.

22. Allan J. West, "A Decision Maker's Point of View on Fire in Chaparral," undated talk delivered by Forest Supervisor, Los Padres National Forest, Goleta, California, found in Record Group No. 95, Box 16, NARA.

23. Neil G. Sugihara et al., *Fire in California's Ecosystems* (Berkeley and Los Angeles: University of California Press, 2006), 333.

24. Works Progress Administration, "Guide," 185.

25. Ibid.

26. Kennedy, *Freedom from Fear*, 615–17. As Joseph Stalin famously remarked: "The United States . . . is a country of machines."

27. Howard Thompson, review of *Zandy's Bride*, written by Lillian Bos Ross and Marc Norman, directed by Jan Troell, *NYT*, 20 May 1974. CA HistRm_Big Sur.

28. Lillian Bos Ross, *The Stranger: A Novel of the Big Sur* (New York: W. Morrow and Co., 1942), "Note."

29. California Cultural Studies, Sonoma State University, http://www.sonoma.edu/users/c/cannon/steinbeckmaptowns.html (accessed 10 Oct. 2015).

30. John Steinbeck, *Flight*, 1. SPECOLDAV.

31. Anthony Brandt, "The Fight to Save Big Sur," *The Atlantic Monthly* 248, no. 3 (Sept. 1981), 70.

32. Henry Miller, *The Air-Conditioned Nightmare* (New York: New Directions, 1945), 20.

33. Henry Miller, *Big Sur*, 33.

34. Anais Nin, *Diary of Anais Nin*, vol. 3 (New York: Harcourt, Brace & World, Inc., 1969), 310.

35. Henry Miller, *Air-Conditioned Nightmare*, 24, 41.

36. Ibid., 20.

37. Quoted in Elaine Fitzpatrick, "The Raconteur and the Poet," *Jeffers Studies*, winter 1999, 19.

38. Henry Miller, *Air-Conditioned Nightmare*, 24.

39. Henry Miller "Big Sur," *BSGD*, 1954. CA HistRm_Big Sur.

40. Nin, *Diary*, vol. 3, 310.

41. Jeff Norman and the Big Sur Historical Society, *Images of America: Big Sur* (Charleston, SC: Arcadia Publishing, 2004), 59–77.

42. Quoted in "The Big Sur: Yesterday, Today and Tomorrow," *A Guide to Highway 1 from Monterey to Morro Bay*, ed. Emil White and Patricia Roberts (published by *Big Sur Guide*, Big Sur, 1954), 28–29. CA HistRm_Big Sur.

43. Anais Nin, *Diary of Anais Nin*, vol. 4 (New York: Harcourt, Brace & World, Inc., 1971), 102.

44. Henry Miller, *Big Sur*, 26, 14.

45. Elaine Fitzpatrick, "The Spirits of Nepenthe," 19. CA HistRm_Big Sur. Miller's son, Tony, recounts some of his favorite childhood memories of living in Big Sur with his father, suggesting that it felt like a paradise for more than just his father: "One of Dad's favorite things to do was take my sister and [me] and the dogs on long walks into the Partington Ridge forest area.... And then, coming home the dogs exhausted from chasing everything, we would contemplate the unreal sunsets.... Our house and patio overlooked the Pacific with views unobstructed out in front and able to see clearly Nepenthe to the North. Great friends, food, books, people.... That is and was community for us.... We never forget our years there.... We don't use photos or paintings or books to remind us.... It is within our family." Tony Miller, personal communication, 28 Jan. 2010.

46. Norman and Big Sur Historical Society, *Images of America*, 54–55. Jean Hersey, "Big Sur: Utopia, U.S.A.?" *Family Circle*, Dec. 1951. CA HistRm_Big Sur.

47. For an in-depth study of an artists' colony in the early twentieth century and its place within the larger tradition of artists' retreats, see Flannery Burke, *From Greenwich Village to Taos: Primitivism and Place at Mabel Dodge Luhan's* (Lawrence: University of Kansas Press, 2008).

48. "Coast Wonderland," *Game and Gossip*, 6, no. 1 (1952). CA HistRm_Big Sur.

49. "This is Big Sur," *Carmel Pacific Spectator Journal*, 1955. Hersey, "Big Sur." CA HistRm_Big Sur. Henry Miller, *Big Sur*.

50. Ibid., 404.

51. Ibid., 402–3.

52. Ibid., 349.

53. Samuel T. Dana and Myron E. Krueger, *California Lands: Ownership, Use, and Management* (Narberth, PA: Livingston Publishing Co., 1958), 6.

54. George W. Long, "New Rush to Golden California" *National Geographic* 105, no. 6 (June 1954): 768. Los Angeles swelled with new residential construction as early as World War II and continued to attract new residents after the war as the G.I. Bill made buying a home an economic reality for millions of veterans.

55. Henry Miller, *Big Sur*, 26.

56. Miller's son, Tony, remarked about his father's ability to love his family while still giving himself to his work, his art. As Tony wrote of his father in an e-mail interview: "Nature grabbed him and allowed him to channel energies into writing and painting.... All of his major works published in Europe were still banned here.... He wasn't making any money.... There was nowhere else for him to go with two kids and a wife. He was a very loyal father and he constantly strived to do the right thing." Tony Miller, personal communication, 20 Jan. 2010.

57. Tony Miller, personal communication, 28 Jan. 2010. Henry Miller, "Beyond Good and Evil," *New Yorker* 74, no. 25 (24 Aug. 1998): 106.

58. Tony Miller, personal communication, 28 Jan. 2010.

59. Henry Miller, *Big Sur*, 37.

60. Robinson Jeffers, *The Double Axe and Other Poems, Including Eleven Suppressed Poems* (New York: Liveright, 1977), 173.

61. James M. Shebl, *In This Wild Water: The Suppressed Poems of Robinson Jeffers* (Pasadena: Ward Ritchie Press, 1976), 82.

62. Jeffers, *Double Axe,* foreword (by William Everson), x.

63. Ibid., "So Many Blood-Lakes," 132.

64. Robinson Jeffers, *Stones of the Sur: Poetry by Robinson Jeffers; Photographs by Morley Baer; Selected and Introduced by James Karman* (Stanford: Stanford University Press, 2001), 5.

65. "Henry Miller, The Art of Fiction No. 28," interview by George Wickes, *The Paris Review* 28 (1962). http://www.theparisreview.org/interviews/4597/the-art-of-fiction-no-28-henry-miller (accessed 20 Sept. 2016).

66. James Karman, ed., *The Collected Letters of Robinson Jeffers: With Selected Letters of Una Jeffers,* vol. 1 (Stanford, CA: Stanford University Press, 2009), 914. Henry Miller, *Big Sur,* 403.

67. Charles Mohler, "The Unconquered Valley," *Westways,* Sept. 1948, 13. Found in the archive of the Automobile Club of Southern California.

CHAPTER 3. BIG SUR: UTOPIA, U.S.A.?

The epigraph to this chapter: Henry Miller, *Big Sur and the Oranges of Hieronymus Bosch* (New York: New Directions, 1957), 403.

1. "This Is Big Sur," *Carmel Pacific Spectator Journal,* 1955. CA HistRm_Big Sur.

2. Monterey Coast Master Plan, County of Monterey, Oct. 1960 (Skidmore, Owings, Merrill, Planning Consultants), Section 1, 23. Calculation based on a 150,000-acre boundary.

3. Leo Trombatore, "From the Corner Office: Highway 1; A Destination in Itself," *Going Places,* May–June 1987, vol. 1.

4. Henry Miller, *Big Sur,* 6.

5. George W. Long, "New Rush to Golden California," *National Geographic* 105, no. 6 (June 1954), 763, 768.

6. Hunter S. Thompson, "Big Sur: The Tropic of Henry Miller," *Rogue Magazine* 6, no. 10 (1961): 35.

7. Roderick Nash, *Wilderness and the American Mind,* 3rd ed. (New Haven: Yale University Press, 1982), 215–17.

8. John Wills, "'Welcome to the Atomic Park': American Nuclear Landscapes and the 'Unnaturally Natural'" *Environment and History* 7, no. 4 (2001): 449–72. Mark Fiege, "The Atomic Scientists, the Sense of Wonder, and the Bomb," *Environmental History* 12, no. 3 (2007), 578–613. Rebecca Solnit, *Savage Dreams: A Journey into the Landscape Wars of the American West* (New York: Vintage Books, 1994).

9. Elaine Tyler May, *Homeward Bound: American Families in the Cold War Era* (New York: Basic Books, 1988), 1. May argues that "the self-contained home held out the promise of security in an insecure world."

10. Long, "New Rush," 803.

11. "This Is Big Sur," *Carmel Pacific Spectator Journal.*

12. Works Progress Administration, "A Guide to the Monterey Peninsula, Tour 3: Big Sur" (Berkeley, CA: Press of the Courier, 1941), 182–83.

13. "This Is Big Sur," *Carmel Pacific Spectator Journal.*

14. Emil White, "What Is Big Sur, and Where?" *Circle of Enchantment,* 1964, 50. CA HistRm_Big Sur.

15. Jean Hersey, "Big Sur: Utopia, U.S.A.?" *BSGD,* 1954, 53–55. Emil White, "What Is Big Sur, and Where?" *BSGD,* 1960, 22.

16. Ibid, 23.

17. "Big Sur 1955," *Carmel Pacific Spectator Journal,* Sept. 1955. CA HistRm_Big Sur.

18. Henry Miller, *Big Sur,* 45–46.

19. Mildred Edie Brady, "The New Cult of Sex and Anarchy," *Harper's Magazine* 194, (Jan.–June 1947): 312.

20. Edward Halsey Foster, *Understanding the Beats* (Columbia, S.C.: University of South Carolina Press, 1992), xii; Kostas Myrsiades, ed., *The Beat Generation: Critical Essays,* (New York: Peter Lang, 2002), 2.

21. Ibid., 2, 77.

22. *People of the State of California, Plaintiff, v. Lawrence Ferlinghetti, Defendant,* Hon. Clayton W. Horn, presiding. http://mason.gmu.edu/~kthomps4/363-s02 /horn-howl.htm (accessed 3 Feb. 2016).

23. Myrsiades, ed., *Beat Generation,* 1.

24. Nash, *Wilderness,* 44.

25. For an analysis of authenticity, see Miles Orvell, *The Real Thing: Imitation and Authenticity in American Culture, 1880–1940* (Chapel Hill: University of North Carolina Press, 1989).

26. Jack Kerouac, *Big Sur* (New York: Penguin Books, 1962), 3.

27. Ibid., 46, 44.

28. Mary V. Dearborn, *The Happiest Man Alive: A Biography of Henry Miller* (New York: Simon & Schuster, 1991), 281, 286–87.

29. *Big Sur: The Way It Was,* produced and directed by Robert Blaisdell, Big Sur Film Company, 1995 (footage from 1960s). CA HistRm_Big Sur.

30. James Conaway, "Destination America: At Home in Big Sur," *Smithsonian Magazine* 40, no. 2 (May 2009): 65.

31. Sister Tanya Zeitfuchs and Sister Monila Meyrose, "Big Sur Grange Song" (1948). Big Sur Lib. Local History Collection, Monterey County Free Libraries, Big Sur, California.

32. Patrons of Husbandry, *California State Grange, Journal of Proceedings,* 1945, 8, 71–73. In 1944 and 1945 the Grange added more than six thousand members in California.

33. Ibid., 11–12.

34. "Big Sur Potluck Revue," *Circle of Enchantment,* 1956. CA HistRm_Big Sur.

35. *BSRU,* Apr. 1957. Big Sur Lib. Local History Collection, Monterey County Free Libraries, Big Sur, California.

36. "Big Sur 1955," *Carmel Pacific Spectator Journal.*

37. Henry Miller, *Big Sur,* 264.

38. Henry Miller, "Big Sur" (written 1948), *BSGD,* 1954. CA HistRm_Big Sur.

39. Dorothy Stevenson, "'Down-the-Coast' Residents Worry over Building Boom: Big Sur Area Is Called 'Crowded,'" *MPH,* 30 Sept. 1948. CA HistRm_Big Sur.

40. Ibid.

41. "In Partington Canyon Beauty Is Spectacular," *MPH,* 26 June 1937. CA HistRm_Big Sur.

42. "Interesting Locale South of Big Sur: No Hate Cult—But Intriguing Homes; One with an Elevator," *MPH,* 14 Oct. 1947. CA HistRm_Big Sur.

43. Ibid.

44. "Orson Welles Buys Trails Club Cabin Just South of Big Sur," *MPH,* 3 May 1944. CA HistRm_Big Sur.

45. "This Is Big Sur," *Carmel Pacific Spectator Journal.*

46. "LIFE Visits a Lovely Star's Home on the Ocean Cliffs of the Big Sur Country: Kim Novak in Her Hideaway by the Sea," photographed by Eliot Elisofon, *LIFE Magazine* 56, no. 16 (17 Apr. 1964): 109.

47. "Big Sur Potluck Revue," *Circle of Enchantment.*

48. "Rugged, Romantic, World Apart: Creative Colony Finds a Haven in California's Big Sur," photographs by J. R. Eyerman, *LIFE Magazine* 47, no. 1 (6 July 1959): 65.

49. Fred Storm, "Unchanged by Years: Big Sur Country—A Timeless Eden," *SFC,* 24 Oct. 1965. CA HistRm_Big Sur.

50. Big Sur Coastal Planning Unit, Draft Environmental Statement, Los Padres National Forest, 1976. The 1970 U.S. Census indicated that only two people listed themselves as farm laborers.

51. White, "What Is Big Sur, and Where?" 23.

52. Henry Miller, *Big Sur,* 6.

53. Adam Rome, *The Bulldozer in the Countryside: Suburban Sprawl and the Rise of American Environmentalism* (Cambridge: Cambridge University Press, 2001), 121. By 1945, machinery developed during the war enabled builders to transform areas like wetlands and hillsides that had previously been off-limits. Over the next three decades nearly a million acres of wetlands were destroyed by urban development.

54. NARA, Record Group 95, Box No. 46, Blohm Land Exchange.

55. Utah had the second-highest number of visitors, with 4,970,800 for the year 1958. NARA, Record Group 95, Box No. 4, U-Statistics, Reports—General.

56. Letter to regional forester from Los Padres supervisor, 2/3/56. NARA, Record Group 95, Box 2, L-Cooperation, State Division of Recreation and Parks.

57. William Brown, *The History of Los Padres National Forest, 1898–1945* (San Francisco, 1945), 161. In a 1962 report to the regional forester, a Monterey district forester explained that two land exchanges were up for consideration: "Both parties offer land in Wilderness Primitive Areas. This makes both applications of equal

desirability." NARA, Record Group 95, Box No. 47, Norman & Clement Exchange Completed 11/9/65.

58. Paul Hirt, *A Conspiracy of Optimism: Management of the National Forests since World War Two* (Lincoln: University of Nebraska Press, 1994). Hirt identifies "a conspiracy of optimism"—a cultural practice of disregarding natural limitations and instead believing that people can control nature in a way beneficial to those who rely on its resources. Hirt highlights the U.S. Forest Service's decision to allow a fourfold increase in timber removal to meet the nation's construction demand while building sixty-five thousand miles of roads through the forests to reach the trees.

59. NARA, Record Group 95, Box No. 3, S-Plans-Report, 25 Mar. 1959.

60. Ibid.

61. Mark Harvey, *Wilderness Forever: Howard Zahniser and the Path to the Wilderness Act* (Seattle: University of Washington Press, 2005), 73–77.

62. Nicholas Roosevelt, editorial, *MPH,* 20 Oct. 1959. CA HistRm_Big Sur.

63. Earl Hofeldt, "Brown to Preserve Highway 1 Scenery," *MPH,* 14 Jan. 1960. Idem, "Big Crowd at Hearing," *MPH,* 16 Aug. 1961. CA HistRm_Big Sur.

64. Margaret Wentworth Owings, *Voice from the Sea and Other Reflections on Wildlife & Wilderness* (Monterey: Monterey Bay Aquarium Press, 1998), 84, 143.

65. "Big Sur Group in Opposition to Super Highway through Area," *MPH,* 29 July 1959. CA HistRm_Big Sur.

66. U.S. Congress, Senate, Committee on Interior and Insular Affairs, *Hearing before the Committee on Interior and Insular Affairs on S. 846, A Bill for the Establishment of a National Outdoor Recreation Resources Review Commission,* 85th Cong., 1st Sess., 15 May 1957, p. 1.

67. Luther Gulick, spokesman for the Social, Economic, and Political Change Discussion Group at the Outdoor Recreation Resources Review Commission, Proceedings of the Second Joint Meeting with the Advisory Council, 25–26 Jan. 1960.

68. "Conservation of Aesthetic Qualities of Route 1 Urged," *MPH,* 24 Apr. 1959. CA HistRm_Big Sur.

CHAPTER 4. OPEN SPACE AT CONTINENT'S END

The epigraph to this chapter: Robinson Jeffers to Sister May James Power, 1 Oct. 1934, in Ann N. Ridgeway, ed., *The Selected Letters of Robinson Jeffers* (Baltimore: The Johns Hopkins University Press, 1968), 221.

1. The United States government lifted its ban on Henry Miller's novels in 1961, but several of them were still labeled "obscene" by the Citizens for Decent Literature: Henry Miller, "Big Sur in Retrospect," *Circle of Enchantment,* 1964, 47.

2. Jennifer Audrey Stevens, "Feminizing the Urban West: Green Cities and Open Space in the Postwar Era, 1950–2000" (Ph.D. dissertation, University of California, Davis, 2008), 127.

3. Amy Meyer, with Randolph Delehanty, *New Guardians for the Golden Gate: How America Got a Great National Park* (Berkeley and Los Angeles: University of

California Press, 2006), 18. Mike Davis, *City of Quartz: Excavating the Future in Los Angeles* (New York: Verso, 2006), 158.

4. This is based on the 1960 census data of 600 residents within a 150,000 acre boundary.

5. CMP_SOM, 13.

6. Ray Dasmann, for one, questioned the desirability of California's growth in his book *The Destruction of California* (New York: Macmillan, 1965). Warren quoted in http://bancroft.berkeley.edu/Exhibits/Looking/comingofage.html (accessed 20 Oct. 2016).

7. George Leonard, "California: A Promised Land for Millions of Migrating Americans," *LOOK Magazine* 26, no. 20 (25 Sept. 1962), 31.

8. Dasmann, *Destruction*, 202.

9. "The Tract Way of Life," *LOOK Magazine* 26, no. 20 (25 Sept. 1962), 32.

10. Linda Sargent Wood, "Contact, Encounter, and Exchange at Esalen: A Window onto Late Twentieth-Century American Spirituality," *Pacific Historical Review* 77, no. 3 (2008), 458.

11. Marion S. Goldman, *The American Soul Rush: Esalen and the Rise of Spiritual Privilege* (New York: New York University Press, 2012), 6. Walter Truett Anderson, *The Upstart Spring: Esalen and the American Awakening* (Reading, MA: Addison-Wesley, 1983), 145–65.

12. Goldman, *American Soul Rush,* 1.

13. Jeffrey Kripal and Glenn W. Shuck, eds., *On the Edge of the Future: Esalen and the Evolution of American Culture* (Bloomington: Indiana University Press, 2005), 4.

14. Goldman, *American Soul Rush,* 25.

15. "Where 'California' Bubbled Up," *The Economist* 385, no. 8560 (19 Dec. 2007), 75–76.

16. Sara Fingal, "Designing Conservation at the Sea Ranch," *Environmental History* 18 (Jan. 2013): 185–90.

17. As Halprin later reflected: "If we could link buildings and nature into an organic whole ... then we could feel that we had created something worthwhile which did not destroy, but rather enhanced the natural beauty we had been given." Quoted in Donlyn Lyndon and Jim Alinder, *The Sea Ranch* (Hudson, NY: Princeton Architectural Press, 2004), 19.

18. CMP_SOM.

19. William Whyte, "Open Space Action," Report to the Outdoor Recreation Resources Review Commission, No. 15 (Washington, D.C.: U.S. Government Printing Office, 1962), 3. Whyte described the legislative history of open-space planning, arguing: "In enabling legislation a good place to start is California. Back in 1959, citizens in Monterey County were trying to get an open space program underway. Fortuitously, the State senator from Monterey County, Fred Farr, had been one of the leaders in California conservation. To give a hand to the Monterey effort, he went to work with State planner William Lipman on an enabling act." The bill that passed authorized counties to acquire land or conservation easements to preserve open space.

20. "Owings Wants Highway 1 to Be Most Scenic Highway in United States," *MPH,* 12 Aug. 1961, A5.

21. Adam Rome, *The Bulldozer in the Countryside: Suburban Sprawl and the Rise of American Environmentalism* (Cambridge: Cambridge University Press, 2001), 123. Hundley Norris, Jr., *The Great Thirst: Californians and Water, A History,* rev. ed. (Berkeley and Los Angeles: University of California Press, 2001), 575.

22. Minutes of Meeting—Coast Highway Master Plan Committee, 29 Mar. 1956. Monterey County Planning Department, Salinas, California.

23. "Modern Living: To Cherish Rather Than Destroy," *TIME Magazine* 92, no. 2 (2 Aug. 1968), 41–42.

24. U.S. Congress, Senate, *Congressional Record,* Proceedings and Debates of the 87th Congress, 1st Session, 7 Feb. 1961, vol. 107, part 3, no. 24, 1872.

25. Ibid., 1873.

26. Ibid., 1874–75.

27. Ibid., 1874, 1876.

28. Bruce J. Schulman, *Lyndon B. Johnson and American Liberalism: A Brief Biography with Documents* (Boston: Bedford Books of St. Martin's Press, 1995), 99.

29. *Wilderness Act* (16 *U.S.C.* 1131), passed 3 Sept. 1964.

30. Stewart Udall, *The Quiet Crisis* (New York: Holt, Rinehart and Winston, 1963), 172.

31. Ibid., 167.

32. Quoted by William Duddleson, "Protecting the Big Sur," *American Land Forum* 7, no. 2 (Mar.–Apr. 1987), 29.

33. "Modern Living: Conservation; The Big Sur Saved," *TIME Magazine* 80, no. 26 (28 Dec. 1962), 42.

34. Suzanne Riess, "Margaret Wentworth Owings: Artist, and Wildlife and Environmental Defender," interviews 1986–88, published by the Regents of the University of California, Regional Oral History Office, Bancroft Library, 1991.

35. "Owings Wants Highway 1 to Be Most Scenic Highway in United States," *MPH.*

36. "Coast Plan under Study by Planners" *MPH,* 12 Oct. 1960. CA HistRm_ Big Sur.

37. CMP_SOM, 8.

38. CMP_SOM, 14–16. Whyte, "Open Space Action," 93.

39. CMP_SOM, 11–15. This was known as a viewshed proposal.

40. Nicholas Roosevelt, "Laymen and Experts Draw Master Plan to Save Beauty for Those to Come," *MPH,* 12 Aug. 1961, A3.

41. CMP_SOM, 7.

42. "Owings Wants Highway 1 to Be Most Scenic Highway in United States," *MPH.*

43. Ibid.

44. CMP_SOM, 16–17.

45. California State Archives, State Government Oral History Program, Regional Oral History Office, University of California, Berkeley: Ann Lage, interview with Frederick S. Farr, California State Senator 1955–67, 9 Oct. 1987, Carmel, California, 33.

46. Roosevelt, "Laymen," A1. In 1963 California did adopt the category of scenic highway for certain highways.

47. Lage, interview with Frederick S. Farr, 42.

48. "Coast Residents Comment on Master Plan—Give It Strong Support" and "Old Timers Feel Master Plan Necessary: Bill Post, Ross Back Controls," *MPH*, 12 Aug. 1961, A7, A5.

49. "Park Expansion Plan Is Protested," *MPH*, 12 Aug. 1961, A2.

50. *BSRU,* Sept. 1961. Big Sur Lib.

51. John Harlan to Monterey County Board of Supervisors, personal correspondence, filed 28 Sept. 1962. MoCo Board of Sup.

52. Fred Sorri, "110 in Protest of Coast Master Plan" *MPH*, 1 Sept. 1961. CA HistRm_Big Sur.

53. Mr. and Mrs. Kobus to Monterey County Board of Supervisors, personal correspondence, filed 2 July 1962. MoCo Board of Sup.

54. Katherine and John Brazil to Monterey County Board of Supervisors, personal correspondence, filed 2 Nov. 1962. MoCo Board of Sup.

55. W. C. Boggess to Monterey County Board of Supervisors, personal correspondence, filed 29 Oct. 1962. MoCo Board of Sup.

56. Anonymous personal correspondence to Monterey County Board of Supervisors, filed 5 Nov. 1962. MoCo Board of Sup.

57. William F. Buckley, Jr., and his *National Review,* the John Birch Society, and Christian anticommunist societies, all founded in the wake of Joseph McCarthy's censure in 1954, mobilized tens of thousands of Americans from diverse economic and social backgrounds against a communist threat while encouraging these Americans to resist liberalism in American politics and society. See Richard Hofstadter, *The Paranoid Style in American Politics,* (Cambridge, MA: Harvard University Press, 1965), 69; and Godfrey Hodgson, *The World Turned Right Side Up: A History of the Conservative Ascendancy in America* (Boston: Houghton Mifflin Company, 1996), 83–90.

58. Monterey County Planning Commission, Meeting Minutes, 10 Apr. 1962. Monterey County Planning Department, Salinas, California.

59. "Californians Fight Each Other to Save Big Sur," *Life Magazine,* 22 Dec. 1961, 130. CA HistRm_Big Sur.

60. Riess, "Margaret Wentworth Owings," 151.

61. "An Editorial: Soaring Hills and Surging Waters" *MPH*, 12 Aug. 1961, A1, A3.

62. "Park Expansion Plan Is Protested," *MPH.*

63. Stevens, "Feminizing the Urban West," 123.

64. Earl Hofeldt, "Big Crowd at Hearing," *MPH*, 16 Aug. 1961. CA HistRm_ Big Sur. In this same era in which Big Sur residents began to carve out a special status for themselves along this coastline, their counterparts throughout the country were also claiming rights to increasingly valuable coastal property. In some areas of the American South, this meant a loss of coastal landownership for African Americans who had enjoyed it over the previous century. According to Andrew Kahrl, these African American landowners lost out as a coastal capitalism commodified the

beaches and privatized the coast into the domain of the wealthy. The minimum lot sizes secured in the Coast Master Plan helped ensure that Big Sur would also become a place for the well-to-do. See Andrew Kahrl, *The Land Was Ours: African American Beaches from Jim Crow to the Sunbelt South* (Cambridge, MA: Harvard University Press, 2012).

65. Nathaniel Owings, *The Places in Between: An Architect's Journey* (Boston: Houghton Mifflin Company, 1973), 204–7.

66. Dani and Plaskett to Monterey County Board of Supervisors, personal correspondence, filed 30 Sept. 1962. MoCo Board of Sup.

67. John Walton, "The Land of Big Sur: Conservation on the California Coast," *California History* 85, no. 1 (2007), 52.

68. Hans Ewoldsen stated at a planning commission meeting that he used to believe he would benefit economically from maximum development possibilities but now he recognized that "it would have ruined the land and was not economically profitable." Instead, Hans favored large lot sales to minimize housing development. Monterey County Planning Commission, Meeting Minutes, 10 Apr. 1962. Monterey County Planning Department, Salinas, California.

69. "Coast Residents Comment on Master Plan," *MPH*, A7.

70. "Old Timers Feel Master Plan Necessary," *MPH*, A5.

71. "Mabel Plaskett Laid to Rest Monday," *King City Rustler*, 22 Oct. 1964. King City Branch Library, Monterey County Free Libraries.

72. Mabel Plaskett, "Naciemiento Homestead," *King City Rustler, The Land,* Jan. 1961. King City Branch Library, Monterey County Free Libraries.

73. Mabel Plaskett, *King City Rustler, The Land,* Sept. 1964. King City Branch Library, Monterey County Free Libraries.

74. Hans Ewoldsen to Monterey County Board of Supervisors, personal correspondence, filed 25 July 1962. MoCo Board of Sup.

75. "Coast Residents Comment on Master Plan," *MPH*, A7.

76. Michael Murphy to Monterey County Board of Supervisors, personal correspondence, filed 27 July 1962. MoCo Board of Sup.

77. A local historian, Jeff Norman, explained that Sam Hopkins is who Henry Miller called the perfect resident of Big Sur: interview with Jeff Norman, Nov. 2005.

78. Samuel Hopkins to Monterey County Board of Supervisors, personal correspondence, filed 25 July 1962. MoCo Board of Sup.

79. "Coast Residents Comment on Master Plan," *MPH*, A7.

80. William Colby to Monterey County Board of Supervisors, personal correspondence, filed 30 Oct. 1962. MoCo Board of Sup.

81. Ansel Adams to Monterey County Board of Supervisors, personal correspondence, filed 24 July 1962. MoCo Board of Sup.

82. George Leonard, "California: What It Means," *LOOK Magazine* 26, no. 20 (25 Sept. 1962), 96.

83. Coast Property Owners Association, "CPOA Mission." www.cpoabigsur.org (accessed 11 Oct. 2015).

84. See Carol M. Rose, "Property Rights, Regulatory Regimes and the New Takings Jurisprudence—An Evolutionary Approach" (1990), Faculty Scholarship Series, Paper 1821. http://digitalcommons.law.yale.edu/fss_papers/1821 (accessed 3 Sept. 2016.

85. CMP, 7–12; "Compromise Coast Master Plan Bared," *MPH,* 15 Feb. 1962. CA HistRm_Big Sur.

86. CMP, 7–11.

87. Ibid., 6. The planning director, Ed DeMars, explained that the planning commission "wants to protect the strip between the ocean and the highway, but also wants to keep the plan general enough so that it does not prevent construction in that area." Monterey County Planning Commission, Meeting Minutes, 8 May 1962. Monterey County Planning Department, Salinas, California.

88. CMP, 4.

89. CMP_SOM, 5.

90. Udall, *Quiet Crisis,* 167.

91. Whyte, "Open Space Action," 93, 3.

92. Big Sur's early, locally driven preservation does not entirely conform to theories about self-governing associations of common-pool resources, most specifically because Big Sur was not facing a clear and present threat of deterioration or scarcity of its rich natural resources when residents and the county moved forward with the Coast Master Plan. Some commonalities with these social theories do exist, however, including the Big Sur community's largely shared vision for the future of Big Sur's scenic, undeveloped landscape; the recognition that residents across the economic spectrum would be similarly impacted by the potential deterioration of their landscape; and a certain amount of professional organizational experience among locals that helped guide local planning efforts. See Elinor Ostrum, "Self-Governance and Forest Resources," Center for International Forestry Research, Feb. 1999.

93. Meyer, *New Guardians,* 27.

94. Point Reyes National Seashore, "Ranching at Point Reyes." http://www.nps.gov/pore/historyculture/people_ranching.htm (accessed 18 June 2017).

95. Harlan Trott, "Point Reyes Seashore—More Room for Californians," *Christian Science Monitor,* 16 Sept. 1960. CA HistRm_Big Sur

96. For a history of land use and ownership in Point Reyes, see Laura A. Watt, *The Paradox of Preservation: Wilderness and Working Landscapes at Point Reyes National Seashore* (Oakland: University of California Press, 2017).

97. U.S. Senate, Committee on Interior and Insular Affairs, before the Subcommittee on Public Lands, *Hearings on S.476, A Bill to Establish the Point Reyes National Seashore,* 87th Cong., 1st sess., 28–31 Mar. 1961.

98. Meyer, *New Guardians,* 31–32.

99. Douglas Hillman Strong, *Tahoe: An Environmental History* (Lincoln: University of Nebraska Press, 1984), xiv.

100. Dewey Anderson, "Tahoe: Then and Now," *National Parks Magazine* 44, no. 271 (1970), 4.

101. Strong, *Tahoe,* 42–50.

102. Anderson, "Tahoe," 6.

103. Strong, *Tahoe,* 52.

104. Ibid., 123.

105. Ibid., 111–44. Michael J. Makley, *Saving Lake Tahoe: An Environmental History of a National Treasure* (Reno: University of Nevada Press, 2014), 38–56.

106. Dewey Anderson, "Where the Forest Meets the Sea," *National Parks Magazine* 43, no. 265 (1969), 5–12; idem, "Tahoe," 4.

107. "The Plan in Brief," *Monterey Peninsula Herald,* 12 Aug. 1961, A1.

108. "Owings Wants Highway 1 to Be Most Scenic Highway in United States," *MPH.*

109. CMP_SOM, 7. From Rachel Carson's *The Sea around Us* (Oxford: Oxford University Press, 1951).

110. Leonard, "California," 31.

111. Dasmann, *Destruction,* 20–21.

112. CMP_SOM, 7. From Robinson Jeffers, "The Continent's End," *The Collected Poetry of Robinson Jeffers,* ed. Tim Hunt, vol. 1, *1920–28* (Stanford, CA: Stanford University Press, 1988), 16–17.

113. Joan Didion, "Notes from a Native Daughter," in *Slouching towards Bethlehem* (New York: Farrar, Straus, and Giroux, 1968), 172.

CHAPTER 5. THE INFLUENCE OF THE
COUNTERCULTURE, COMMUNITY, AND STATE

This chapter's epigraph is quoted from Jack Kerouac, *Big Sur* (New York: Penguin Books, 1962), 15.

1. "A Utopia Turning into Paradise Lost: What Are They Doing to Big Sur?" *Saturday Evening Post,* 237, no. 6 (15 Feb. 1964): 24.

2. "Big Sur—Its Challenge to Adventure," *SFC,* 31 Oct. 1965. CA HistRm_Big Sur.

3. William Mathewson, "The Changing Character of Big Sur," *Game and Gossip* 14, no. 10 (10 June 1966): 15.

4. John Woolfenden, "Riding Herd on Big Sur," *MPH,* 7 Sept. 1971. CA HistRm_Big Sur.

5. Kevin Howe, "Two Views on 'Hippie' Invasion of Big Sur: Nomads Worried about Controls," *MPH,* 28 July 1970. CA HistRm_Big Sur.

6. Woolfenden, "Riding Herd," *MPH.*

7. Kathleen Davis, "Cultural Resource Inventory of Pfeiffer Big Sur State Park," Preliminary Draft. Cultural Resource Inventory Unit, Resource Protection Division, California Department of Parks and Recreation, 9 Feb. 1990, 144.

8. Roy Nickerson, "New Beatnik Breed Confuses Big Sur: Invasion by S.F. 'Cats' Alarming to Old Timers" *MPH,* 6 July 1965. CA HistRm_Big Sur.

9. Roy Nickerson, "Hippies Frustrate Big Sur" and "On Hippie Invasion: Sur Residents Meet Lawmen," *MPH,* 8 June 1968. CA HistRm_Big Sur. Mathewson, "Changing Character," 15.

10. Tom Wieder, "Curb on Transients Proposed," *MPH,* 28 July 1970. CA HistRm_Big Sur.

11. Howe, "Two Views," *MPH.*

12. Ibid.

13. Theodore Roszak, *The Making of the Counter Culture: Reflections on the Technocratic Society and Its Youthful Opposition* (Garden City, N.Y.: Doubleday & Company, Inc., 1969), 160–63.

14. Linda Sargent Wood, "Contact, Encounter, and Exchange at Esalen: A Window onto Late Twentieth-Century American Spirituality," *Pacific Historical Review* 77, no. 3 (2008): 460.

15. Howe, "Two Views." Nickerson, "On Hippie Invasion" and "New Beatnik Breed," *MPH.*

16. John Woolfenden, *Big Sur: A Battle for the Wilderness, 1869–1981* (Pacific Grove: Boxwood Press, 1981), 119.

17. Anthony Godfrey, *The Ever-Changing View: A History of the National Forests in California, 1891–1987* (Vallejo, CA: USDA Forest Service, 2005), 446.

18. Woolfenden, "Riding Herd.," *MPH.*

19. Woolfenden, *Big Sur,* 120–21.

20. Cheryl J. Hapke and Krystal R. Green, "Rates of Landsliding and Cliff Retreat along the Big Sur Coast, California—Measuring a Crucial Baseline." U.S. Geological Survey Fact Sheet 2004–3099–2005. http://pubs.usgs.gov/fs/2004 /3099/ (accessed 20 Apr. 2016).

21. Woolfenden, *Big Sur,* 121.

22. USDA, Forest Service, "Environmental Statement: Big Sur Coastal Land Management Plan," 28. CA HistRm_Big Sur. From 1963 to 1976 an average of two thousand acres per year burned in the Monterey District of Los Padres National Forest. Three-quarters of the fires were caused by campfires.

23. "Lack of Financial Aid Riles Big Sur Residents," *MPH,* 20 Nov. 1972; and "Owners Lose Big Sur Slide Trial to State," *MPH,* 12 July 1975. Both CA HistRm_Big Sur.

24. "Juan Mann's Opinion," *BSRU,* Sept. 1972. Big Sur Lib.

25. Rebecca Kneale Gould, *At Home in Nature: Modern Homesteading and Spiritual Practice in America* (Berkeley and Los Angeles: University of California Press, 2005), 139–70.

26. Richard Patrick Norris, "Back to the Land: The Post-Industrial Agrarianism of Ralph Borsodi and Austin Tappan Wright" (Ph.D. dissertation, University of Minnesota, 1977), 4–15; M. G. Kains, *Five Acres and Independence* (Scarborough: New American Library, 1948); idem, *Five Acres and Independence: A Handbook for Small Farm Management* (New York: Dover Publications, 1973); Helen and Scott Nearing, *Living the Good Life: How to Live Sanely and Simply in a Troubled World* (New York: Schocken Books, 1954; reprint, 1970).

27. William Poole, "Conservation and Patriotism: A Conversation with William Cronon," *Land & People Magazine* 18, no. 2 (Fall 2006): 46–50. Eric T. Freyfogle, ed.,

The New Agrarianism: Land, Culture, and the Community of Life (Washington, D.C.: Island Press, 2001).

28. James Bohlen, *The New Pioneers Handbook: Getting Back to the Land in an Energy-Scarce World* (New York: Schocken Books, 1975); Roszak, *The Making of the Counter Culture,* 1–8.

29. Scott Barr, "American Agrarianism and the Back-to-the-Land Movement" (M.A. thesis, Ohio State University, 1975), 2–3.

30. Wendell Berry, "Discipline and Hope," *A Continuous Harmony* (New York: Harcourt Brace Jovanovich, 1970), 121–22, 87.

31. Wendell Berry, *The Gift of Good Land: Further Essays, Cultural and Agricultural* (San Francisco: North Point Press, 1981), xiii.

32. *The New Yorker* 39, no. 13 (18 May 1963), 152. "Median and Average Sales Prices of New Homes Sold in United States," 1. http://www.census.gov/const/uspricemon.pdf (accessed 4 May 2016).

33. Serena Embree, "A Good Life in Big Sur Country," *Game and Gossip* 15, no. 4 (1967). CA HistRm_Big Sur.

34. Gould, *At Home in Nature* (above, note 26), 218.

35. Hilton Als, "Queen Jane, Approximately: How Jane Fonda Found Her Way Back to Acting," *The New Yorker* 87, no. 12 (9 May 2011), 58.

36. Vivien Ellen Rose, "Homesteading as Social Protest: Gender and Continuity in the Back-to-the-Land Movement in the United States, 1890–1980" (Ph.D. dissertation, Binghamton University, 1997), 267–95.

37. Roszak, *The Making of the Counter Culture,* 34.

38. USDA, Forest Service, "Environmental Statement," 38.

39. 1970 U.S. Population Census, California Tract 115. Tract 115 does not encompass the entire area considered as Big Sur, so these statistics reflect the bulk, but not the entirety, of the community.

40. USDA, Forest Service, "Environmental Statement," 37–44.

41. Ibid., 19.

42. Dewey Anderson, "Where the Forest Meets the Sea," *National Parks Magazine* 43, no. 265 (1969): 12.

43. The number of licensed commercial abalone fishermen had increased from just eleven in 1928 to more than five hundred in 1963, whereas the sea otter population hovered around five hundred in the early 1960s: Shawn E. Larson, ed., *Sea Otter Conservation* (San Diego: Elsevier Academic Press, 2015), 337.

44. Ibid., 341–48. A five-year review conducted by the U.S. Fish and Wildlife Service placed the southern sea otter population at 2,944 in 2014. https://www.fws.gov/ventura/docs/species/sso/Southern%20Sea%20Otter%205%20Year%20Review.pdf (accessed 18 Feb. 2017).

45. For her many efforts, Owings won the National Audubon Society's Medal, the United Nations Environmental Program's Gold Medal Award, and the U.S. Department of the Interior's Conservation Service Award.

46. Margaret Wentworth Owings, *Voice from the Sea and Other Reflections on Wildlife & Wilderness* (Monterey: Monterey Bay Aquarium Press, 1998), 99–101.

47. Ibid., 135.

48. President Lyndon B. Johnson's remarks at the signing of the Highway Beautification Act of 1965, 22 Oct. 1965.

49. USDA, Forest Service, "Environmental Statement," 3.

50. Margaret Owings, *Voice from the Sea,* 143.

51. Ibid.

52. Hal K. Rothman, *Saving the Planet: The American Response to the Environment in the Twentieth Century* (Chicago: Ivan R. Dee, 2000), 126.

53. USDA, Forest Service, "Environmental Statement," 3.

54. Godfrey Hodgson, *The World Turned Right Side Up: A History of the Conservative Ascendancy in America* (Boston: Houghton Mifflin Company, 1996); Lisa McGirr, *Suburban Warriors: The Origins of the New American Right* (Princeton: Princeton University Press, 2001); Thomas and Mary Edsall, *Chain Reaction: The Impact of Race, Rights, and Taxes on American Politics* (New York: W. W. Norton & Company, 1991).

55. Ronald Reagan, "A Time for Choosing," Address on behalf of Senator Barry Goldwater, 27 Oct. 1964. http://cdn.constitutionreader.com/files/pdf/constitution /ch123.pdf (accessed 14 June 2017).

56. Ibid.

57. McGirr, *Suburban Warriors,* 149. As McGirr explains in regard to the ultraconservative Orange County residents, the right stood opposed to "the liberal Leviathan state, that was, in their eyes, the postwar federal government. The expansion of the scale and scope of the federal government, they believed, reduced civic autonomy and thwarted individual initiative and self-reliance, running counter to older Republican belief in the primacy of the locality and the state in determining the shape of public life."

58. Bill Boyarsky, *The Rise of Ronald Reagan* (New York: Random House, 1968), 227–28.

59. Lou Cannon, *Governor Reagan: His Rise to Power* (New York: Public Affairs, 2003), 308.

60. Rothman, *Saving the Planet,* 133–34.

61. Boyarsky, *The Rise of Ronald Reagan,* 216, 227.

62. Cannon, *Governor Reagan,* 301, 300.

63. Jared Orsi, "Restoring the Common to the Goose: Citizen Activism and the Protection of the California Coastline, 1969–1972," *Southern California Quarterly* 78, no. 3 (1996): 258.

64. Boyarsky, *The Rise of Ronald Reagan,* 219.

65. Julie Sze, *Noxious New York: The Racial Politics of Urban Health and Environmental History* (Cambridge, MA: MIT Press, 2007), 1–6, 128.

66. J. Brooks Flippen, "Richard Nixon and the Triumph of Environmentalism," in Louis Warren, ed., *American Environmental History* (Malden, MA: Blackwell Publishing, 2003), 270–85.

67. Janet Bridges of Earth Alert! interview with Ellen Stern Harris, 11 Aug. 2004, Adelphia Public Access Studios, Santa Monica, DVD.

68. Carl Lutrin and Allen Settle, "The Public and Ecology: The Role of Initiatives in California's Environmental Politics," *The Western Political Quarterly* 28, no. 2 (1975): 369.

69. Orsi, "Restoring the Common to the Goose," 258.

70. See Earth Alert! *Heroes of the Coast*, a DVD collection of interviews recorded between 2004 and 2012 with coastal activists and California Coastal Commission staff.

71. "Peninsula Breakdown of Vote Listed," *MPH*, 8 Nov. 1972. Of the Sur's residents, 309 voted in favor of Proposition 20 and 90 against it. CA HistRm_Big Sur.

72. John Walton, "The Land of Big Sur: Conservation on the California Coast," *California History* 85, no. 1 (2007): 54.

73. Daniel Press, *Saving Open Space: The Politics of Local Preservation in California* (Berkeley and Los Angeles: University of California Press, 2002), 6. By 2000, California had 600 nonprofit environmental groups and 125 land trusts.

74. Office for Coastal Management, National Oceanic and Atmospheric Administration. http://coast.noaa.gov/czm/act/?redirect=301ocm (accessed 20 Jan. 2016).

75. The San Francisco Bay Area coastal regulation is governed not by the California Coastal Commission but by the San Francisco Bay Conservation and Development Commission (BCDC), a temporary state agency created by legislation in 1965 and made permanent by the legislature in 1969.

76. California Coastal Act, Section 30241a.

77. Orsi, "Restoring the Common to the Goose," 266.

78. Author conversation with staff member of the California Coastal Commission, Santa Cruz Office, 6 Feb. 2008.

79. These nineteen residents included two members of the Friends of the Big Sur Coast, two trustees of the Big Sur Foundation, three trustees of the BSLT, members of the CPOA, Grange, Big Sur Chamber of Commerce, Volunteer Fire Brigade and Volunteer Ambulance, and members of the Sierra Club, Wilderness Society, Friends of the Earth, and the Audubon Society. "Citizens' Advisory Committee News Release," *BSRU,* July 1980, 10. Big Sur Lib.

80. Resolution by the Monterey County Board of Supervisors to Create the Citizen Advisory Committee states, "in offering its special insight [the CAC] should not feel constrained or limited to only those planning considerations set forth in the County's Work Program, but should present any ideas it feels are worthy of discussion in preparing a revised plan for the coast," 10 Apr. 1979. Panetta Inst. Arch.

81. Author conversation with staff member of the California Coastal Commission, Santa Cruz Office, 6 Feb. 2008.

82. Coordinating Committee for Big Sur Area Planning, Review of Consultant Gordon Hall's Report no. 4, 7 Nov. 1977. CCC_SntaCrz.

83. The Coast Property Owners Association (CPOA) feared the loss of community to the extent that they called for including in the Big Sur Land Use Plan: "to prevent an increase in federal land ownership management or control in Big Sur."

CPOA to Board of Supervisors in testimony for Big Sur Land Use Plan hearing, 9 July 1985. CCC_SntaCrz.

84. Six-member letter from the Citizens Advisory Committee to the Monterey County Board of Supervisors and Planning Commission, Re: Proposed Master Plan Revisions, 2 Sept. 1976. CCC_SntaCrz.

85. Emil White, *BSGD*, 1964. White described the community in 1964 as containing the Grange for social functions and a property owners' association. Aside from that, he believed that "everyone keeps pretty much to himself." Henry Miller, *Big Sur and the Oranges of Hieronymus Bosch* (New York: New Directions, 1957), 264. Miller wrote during the 1950s that in Big Sur "there is no common purpose, no common effort. There is remarkable neighborliness, but no community spirit."

86. Coordinating Committee for Big Sur Area Planning, Review of Consultant Gordon Hall's Report no. 4, 7 Nov. 1977.

87. No single census tract encompasses the area considered as Big Sur, and the census-tract boundaries have changed over time, making comparisons from one decade to the next inexact. There may have been more than 800 residents in 1970, close to 1,200 residents in 1980, and more than 1,300 residents in 1990. See Martha V. Diehl, "Land Use in Big Sur: In Search of Sustainable Balance between Community Needs and Resource Protection" (M.A. thesis, California State University Monterey Bay, 2006), 45. Diehl, a member of the Big Sur community, uses census data, as well as housing and occupancy data for the entirety of Big Sur, including the South Coast, in her population statistics and estimates.

88. John B. Wright, *Rocky Mountain Divide: Selling and Saving the West* (Austin: University of Texas Press, 1993), 15. By 1981 there were 431 land trusts throughout the country.

89. *BSRU*, Mar. 1979, 10. Big Sur Lib. In its first nine months, the BSLT received $31,500 in cash gifts, $7,500 of that from individuals, most of whom owned land or lived in Big Sur.

90. Wendy Grissam Brokaw, "Homegrown Preservation: The Big Sur Land Trust," *Monterey Life*, Apr. 1982, 32.

91. Author interview with staff member of the Big Sur Land Trust, Nov. 2005. BSLT letter to the editor, *BSRU*, Aug. 1980, 3 (Big Sur Lib.): a "landowner who donates a conservation restriction in perpetuity is permitted to deduct for income tax purposes the value of the restriction. This value is determined by subtracting the value of the property subject to the restriction from the fair market value of the property. . . . The deduction for income tax purposes will occur only once . . . but the saving in real estate taxes will occur each successive year forever."

92. "Incorporation of Big Sur Held Financially Feasible by Study," *MPH*, 16 Feb. 1978. CA HistRm_Big Sur.

93. "Meeting Set to Discuss Big Sur Incorporation," *MPH*, 14 Nov. 1978. CA HistRm_Big Sur.

94. Mary Barnett, "Who Will Save the Big Sur?" *BSGZ* 2, no. 10 (Oct. 1979): 26.

95. One resident wrote a letter to the editor of the *Los Angeles Times* after the paper ran an article on marijuana growers in Big Sur. This Big Sur resident explained:

"We resent such representation. If you feel compelled to publicize this place . . . then at least give equal time to the cultural events, the ordinary people and the gifted ones, the people who work with their hands and minds at something other than growing marijuana." *BSRU,* Dec. 1979, 8. Big Sur Lib.

96. Walter Truett Anderson, *The Upstart Spring: Esalen and the American Awakening* (Reading, MA: Addison-Wesley, 1983), 315, 317.

97. Brad Parker, "Residents Feel Area Will Survive: Big Sur on SatEvPost," *MPH,* date unknown. CA HistRm_Big Sur.

CHAPTER 6. THE BATTLE FOR BIG SUR; OR, DEBATING
THE NATIONAL ENVIRONMENTAL ETHIC

The two epigraphs to this chapter are quoted from Ansel Adams to Leon Panetta, personal correspondence, 22 Apr. 1979, Panetta Inst. Arch.; and from Ehud Yonay, "Big Sur: The Politics of Preservation," *New West,* 22 Dec. 1980, 43.

1. Alisa Fineman, "Where Extremes Meet: Local Perspectives on Preservation for Big Sur" (Senior thesis, Environmental Studies, University of California, Santa Cruz, 1984), 31–40.

2. On any given summer day in the early 1980s, 8,300 vehicles traveled along Big Sur's Highway 1 (95% of them recreational trips). Ed Brown, district director, California Coastal Commission, Central Coast to state commissioners and interested persons, Subject: Big Sur Coast Local Coastal Program, Sept. 1981. LCP, 63. CCC_ SntaCrz. Richard J. Orsi, Alfred Runte, and Marlene Smith-Baranzini, *Yosemite and Sequoia: A Century of California National Parks* (Berkeley and Los Angeles: University of California Press, 1993), 124.

3. USDA, Forest Service, Final Narrative, Marble-Cone Fire, 1–2. Statistics established by the Riverside Fire Laboratory. NARA.

4. Big Sur Coast Local Coastal Program (LCP). Certified by the California Coastal Commission, 1986. Monterey County Planning Department. 40.

5. Ehud Yonay, "Big Sur Revisited: Notes from the Fire" *New West,* 29 Aug. 1977. NARA.

6. Ibid.

7. Total cost $18 million, 6,000 firefighters: box 2, folder L-Statistics, Annual Statistics Report, NARA.

8. Ken Schultz, "Environmentalist Says: 'Make Big Sur a Park,'" *Salinas Californian,* 1 Dec. 1977. John Steinbeck Library, Local History Collection, Salinas, California. Census data, though not consistent in the area of coverage, indicated that the population grew by a quarter from 1970 to 1980 (from approximately 900 residents to 1,270), with over a hundred new residential parcel lots designated in this decade. Martha V. Diehl, "Land Use in Big Sur: In Search of Sustainable Balance between Community Needs and Resource Protection" (M.A. thesis, California State University, Monterey Bay, 2006)," 22, 43–45.

9. Jonathan Spaulding, *Ansel Adams and the American Landscape: A Biography* (Berkeley and Los Angeles: University of California Press, 1995), 321, 355.

10. *BSRU,* Mar. 1980. Big Sur Lib.

11. "Report on the Inability of Monterey County and the California Coastal Commission to Implement the Agricultural and Visual Resource Policies of the Big Sur Coast Local Coastal Program," The Big Sur Foundation, 10 Apr. 1980, 5. CA Arch._CCC.

12. Mary Barnett, "Who Will Save the Big Sur?" *BSGZ* 2, no. 10 (Oct. 1979): 26.

13. Ansel Adams, "My Camera in the National Parks," *The Living Wilderness* 43, no. 148 (1980): 15.

14. Yonay, "Big Sur," 37.

15. "Big Sur Committee Charges Conservationist Group with Campaigning for Park Plan," *Monterey Peninsula Herald,* 30 Nov. 1977. CA HistRm_Coastal Reg.

16. Adams to Panetta, 22 Apr. 1979.

17. Ansel Adams to Leon Panetta, personal correspondence, 16 July 1979. Panetta Inst. Arch.

18. Yonay, "Big Sur," 39.

19. Orsi, Runte, and Smith-Baranzini, *Yosemite and Sequoia,* 124–30. Fineman, "Where Extremes Meet," 53, 70.

20. Quoted in Simon Schama, *Landscape and Memory* (New York: Alfred A. Knopf, 1995), 9.

21. Peter Schrag, *Paradise Lost: California's Experience, America's Future* (New York: The New Press, 1998), 12.

22. Statement of the Vote, 6 June 1978. Proposition 13 vote in Sur precinct: 123 in favor, 39 opposed. Gorda precinct: 50 in favor, 16 opposed. Palo Colorado precinct: 66 in favor, 18 opposed. Monterey County Elections Office, Salinas, California.

23. Ibid., 82 registered Democrats voting for governor in primary election; 49 registered Republicans. Monterey County Elections Office, Salinas, California.

24. *Salinas Californian,* 27 Feb. 1980. CA HistRm_Coastal Reg.

25. "Big Sur Coast Planning Process Generates Passionate Debate: Verbal Cross-Fire Traded over Ultimate Density, Ownership of Land, Potential as National Seashore," *MPH,* 22 Jan. 1978. CA HistRm_Coastal Reg.

26. "Report," Big Sur Foundation, 22. CA Arch._CCC.

27. California Coastal Commission Executive Director Michael Fischer to Nathaniel Owings, 16 Oct. 1981. CCC_SntaCrz.

28. Yonay, "Big Sur," 42.

29. For analysis of the New Right and conservatism in the late twentieth century, see Godfrey Hodgson, *The World Turned Right Side Up: A History of the Conservative Ascendancy in America* (Boston: Houghton Mifflin Company, 1996). Michael Lienesch, *Redeeming America: Piety and Politics in the New Christian Right* (Chapel Hill: University of North Carolina Press, 1993). Michael Kazin, *The Populist Persuasion: An American History* (New York: Basic Books, 1995). David Bennett, *The Party of Fear: From Nativist Movements to the New Right in American History* (Chapel Hill: University of North Carolina Press, 1988). Thomas and Mary Edsall,

Chain Reaction: The Impact of Race, Rights, and Taxes on American Politics (New York: W. W. Norton & Company, 1991).

30. Spaulding, *Ansel Adams and the American Landscape,* 313–15.

31. Robert Turnage, "Ansel Adams: The Role of the Artist in the Environmental Movement," *The Living Wilderness,* 43, no. 148 (1980), 12. In this memo, Adams called the national parks to task for allowing commercial exploitation within their borders, believing that poor management threatened the long-term protection of these national treasures.

32. Mary Street Alinder and Andrea Gray Stillman, eds., *Ansel Adams: Letters, 1916–1984* (Boston: Little, Brown and Company, 1988), 367.

33. "Wilderness Society Priorities," *The Living Wilderness* 43, no. 148 (1980), 34–35.

34. The Democratic Party Platform of 1980 acknowledged: "We recognize the need for fiscal restraint.... As long as inflationary pressures remain strong, fiscal prudence is essential to avoid destroying the progress made to date in reducing the inflation rate."

35. U.S. Congress, Senate, Committee on Energy and Natural Resources, Subcommittee on Parks, Recreation, and Renewable Resources, *Hearings on S.2551, A Bill to Establish the Big Sur Coast National Scenic Area in the State of California,* 96th Cong., 2nd sess., 24 Apr. 1980, publication no. 96–125, 2–12. This 5% was based on the amount of private land held in 1980.

36. Statement of Keith Thompson, Esalen Institute, Big Sur, California, *Hearings on S.2551,* 199. Fineman, "Where Extremes Meet," 52–67.

37. Statement of James M. Josoff, general chairman, Friends of the Big Sur Coast, *Hearings on S.2551,* 203.

38. David Helvarg, *The War against the Greens: The "Wise-Use" Movement, The New Right, and Anti-Environmental Violence* (San Francisco: Sierra Club Books, 1994); Jacqueline Vaughn Switzer, *Green Backlash: The History and Politics of Environmental Opposition in the U.S.* (Boulder: Lynne Rienner Publishers, 1997); James Morton Turner, "'The Specter of Environmentalism': Wilderness, Environmental Politics, and the Evolution of the New Right," *The Journal of American History* 96, no. 1 (2009): 140; Robert Jones, "Big Sur Faces Cloudy Future, Identity Crisis," *LAT,* 30 Mar. 1980. CA HistRm_Coastal Reg.

39. Statement of Charles Cushman, executive director, National Inholders Association, Washington, D.C., *Hearings on S.2551,* 216–18.

40. Anthony Brandt, "The Fight to Save Big Sur," *The Atlantic Monthly,* Sept. 1981, 75. Statement by James M. Josoff, general chairman, Friends of the Big Sur Coast: MoCo Board of Sup., *Hearing on the Big Sur Land Use Plan,* 4 Jan. 1982.

41. "Residents Want Big Sur to Stay 'The Way It Is,'" *MPH,* 9 Mar. 1980, 2A. CA HistRm_Coastal Reg.

42. Switzer, *Green Backlash,* 252, and Helvarg, *The War against the Greens,* 198.

43. Switzer, *Green Backlash,* 254.

44. Hal K. Rothman, *Saving the Planet: The American Response to the Environment in the Twentieth Century* (Chicago: Ivan R. Dee, 2000), 178.

45. R. C. Horse, "Coastal Council Demands Federal Investigation if Big Sur Bill Has No Senate Subcommittee Hearings," *BSGZ* 3, no. 11 (Nov. 1980): 1.

46. Ibid., 27.

47. "Big Sur Coast Planning Process Generates Passionate Debate," *MPH.*

48. William Poole, "Conservation and Patriotism: A Conversation with William Cronon," *Land & People Magazine,* 18, no. 2 (Fall 2006): 46–50. According to Cronon: "Americans' suspicion of state power goes back to the Revolution. The conservative reaction against environmentalism arose not from a failure to love the land but rather from fear that environmental laws and regulations represented a potential new form of state tyranny. The collapse of bipartisan support for environmentalism was primarily a reaction, not against nature or the American land, but rather against centralized government power and its feared abuse."

49. Statement of the Vote, Monterey County: Gorda, Palo Colorado, and Sur precincts, 2 Nov. 1976 and 7 Nov. 1978 elections. Monterey County Elections Office, Salinas, California.

50. Fineman, "Where Extremes Meet," 63.

51. *BSGZ* 3, no. 9 (Sept. 1980): 30.

52. Big Sur Coast Recreation and Visitor-Serving Facilities Background Report, Prepared by the Monterey County Planning Dept., Jan. 1980: "In total, the Department of Parks and Recreation has current funding to purchase 6,332 acres, specific proposals to purchase 216 acres, and general long-range proposals to purchase an additional 27,085 acres." William Duddleson, "Protecting the Big Sur," *American Land Forum* 7, no. 2 (Mar.–Apr. 1987): 29.

53. Statement of James M. Josoff, *Hearings on S.2551,* 205. Close to 90 percent of residents and property owners signed a petition circulated by Friends of the Big Sur Coast stating that they opposed "any increase in the level of federal involvement or intervention" in Big Sur.

54. "Residents Want Big Sur to Stay 'The Way It Is,'" *MPH.*

55. Ibid. Doug Foster, "A War of Wills to 'Save' Big Sur Coast," *Salinas Californian,* 7 July 1980, 6D.

56. "Residents Want Big Sur to Stay 'The Way It Is,'" *MPH.*

57. Thomas Dunlap, "Communing with Nature," *History Today* 52, no. 3 (Mar. 2002): 37. Dunlap describes environmentalism and conservationism as "religions in the Jamesian sense: they give people an explanation of the world and how human life fits into it and so guide them as to how they should live." See also idem, *Faith in Nature: Environmentalism as Religious Quest* (Seattle: University of Washington Press, 2004).

58. Switzer, *Green Backlash,* 252.

59. Helvarg, *The War against the Greens,* 204.

60. Fineman, "Where Extremes Meet," 44.

61. Ibid., 123.

62. Jones, "Big Sur Faces Cloudy Future, Identity Crisis," *LAT.* CA HistRm_ Coastal Reg. In 1969 Nat Owings argued: "Private enterprise hears only what it wants to hear, and it listens for the promise of profit. Only national controls may be

strong enough to curb their spendthrift policies": Nathaniel Owings, *The American Aesthetic* (New York: Harper & Row, 1969), 144. He was not in principle opposed to federal intervention but was specifically in the case of Big Sur.

63. Turnage, "Ansel Adams," 6.

64. Robinson Jeffers to Albert Bender, 17 Oct. 1928, in Ann N. Ridgeway, ed., *The Selected Letters of Robinson Jeffers* (Baltimore: The Johns Hopkins University Press, 1968), 134.

65. Robinson Jeffers, *Stones of the Sur: Poetry by Robinson Jeffers; Photographs by Morley Baer; Selected and Introduced by James Karman* (Stanford: Stanford University Press, 2001), 6.

66. Spaulding, *Ansel Adams and the American Landscape*, 359: Adams's "pristine landscapes were intended to serve much the same purpose as the national parks themselves—precious fragments, beautiful and inspiring in their distinct opposition to the destruction around them. . . . Adams's contribution to public awareness of nature and its vital role in human life and culture could not be denied."

67. Schama, *Landscape and Memory*, 9. Adams acknowledged the spiritual dimension of his land ethic, which he described in a personal letter to Congressman Panetta as a "form of religion, or religious experience. You might term it a quasi-religion as it does not include Saints and Miracles (except for the constant miracle of nature itself)": Adams to Panetta, 22 Apr. 1979. Panetta Inst. Arch.

68. Hal K. Rothman, *Devil's Bargains: Tourism in the Twentieth-Century American West* (Lawrence: University of Kansas Press, 1998); William Cronon, "The Trouble with Wilderness; or, Getting Back to the Wrong Nature," in *Uncommon Ground: Rethinking the Human Place in Nature,* ed. William Cronon (New York: W. W. Norton & Co., 1996), 69–90; Mark David Spence, *Dispossessing the Wilderness: Indian Removal and the Making of the National Parks* (Oxford: Oxford University Press, 1999).

69. Statement of Barbara Shipnuck, supervisor, Monterey County Board of Supervisors, *Hearings on S.2551,* 37–41.

70. Ibid.

71. Statement of Hon. Rupert Cutler, assistant secretary for natural resources and environment, U.S. Department of Agriculture, *Hearings on S.2551,* 49.

72. Statement of Don McQueen, president, Big Sur, California, Chamber of Commerce, *Hearings on S.2551,* 194.

73. Barnett, "Who Will Save the Big Sur?" 26. Bill Bates, "Welcome to 117 Mile Drive," *BSGZ* 3, no. 8 (Aug. 1980): 16.

74. Statement of Keith Thompson *Hearings on S.2551,* 202.

75. Fineman, "Where Extremes Meet," 31–34.

76. Statement of Keith Thompson *Hearings on S.2551,* 201.

77. Statement of Saunders Hillyer, executive director, Big Sur Foundation, Monterey, California, *Hearings on S.2551,* 175.

78. Yonay, "Big Sur," 41.

79. Statement of Michael L. Fischer, executive director, California Coastal Commission: U.S. House of Representatives, Subcommittee on Ports and Insular Affairs, Field Hearing, Monterey, California, 21 June 1980. CA Arch._CCC.

80. Peter Douglas, executive director of the California Coastal Commission, recalled in 2011 how World Bank officials had met with coastal states around the world to examine coastal protection efforts and praised Douglas for what the officials called the strongest coastal program in the world (recounted in an interview by Janet Bridges of Earth Alert! with Peter Douglas at the California Coastal Commission's offices in San Francisco, 29 July 2011: Earth Alert! *Heroes of the Coast,* interviews recorded 2004–12 [DVD]).

81. Fineman, "Where Extremes Meet," 53–56.

82. "Big Sur Coast Planning Process Generates Passionate Debate," *MPH.* "Federal Drive to Acquire Private Lands Should Be Reassessed," U.S. Government Accounting Office, CED-80-14, 14 Dec. 1979, "Digest" and p. v. http://www.gao .gov/assets/130/128531.pdf (accessed 3 June 2017).

83. Norman Miller, *Environmental Politics: Interest Groups, the Media, and the Making of Policy* (Boca Raton: Lewis Publishers, 2002), 22.

84. Senator S. I. Hayakawa, "Report to Constituents," Apr. 1980, 2. CA Arch._CCC.

85. Fineman, "Where Extremes Meet," 32.

86. Photo caption and copy of Hayakawa's award, *BSGZ* 4, no. 3 (Mar. 1981): 14.

87. Cecilia Herron, "Ansel Adams; Protecting the Environment with a Camera," *Christian Science Monitor,* 6 Aug. 1981. http://www.csmonitor.com/1981 /0806/080660.html (accessed 14 Jan. 2015).

88. R. McGreggor Cawley, *Federal Land, Western Anger: The Sagebrush Rebellion and Environmental Politics* (Lawrence: University of Kansas Press, 1993), 9.

89. David F. Salisbury, "Sagebrush Rebels See Open Range in Ronald Reagan's Election Victory," *Christian Science Monitor,* reprinted in *BSGZ* 3, no. 12 (Dec. 1980): 36.

90. Elizabeth Drew, "A Reporter at Large: Secretary Watt," *The New Yorker* 57, no. 11 (4 May 1981), 104: "I am a part of the sagebrush rebellion," said Watt.

91. James M. Josoff, "Friends Present Argument against Panetta Bill," *BSGZ* 3, no. 10 (Oct. 1980), 21.

92. Statement of the Vote, Monterey County: Sur, Gorda, and Palo Colorado precincts, 4 Nov. 1980 election. Sur precinct: 107 for Reagan, 110 for Carter (out of 289 voters); Palo Colorado precinct: 39 for Reagan, 42 for Carter (out of 96 voters); Gorda precinct: 31 for Reagan, 36 for Carter (out of 96 voters). Monterey County Elections Office, Salinas, California.

93. Duddleson, "Protecting the Big Sur," 36.

CHAPTER 7. DEFINING THE VALUE OF
CALIFORNIA'S COASTLINE

The epigraph to this chapter: Michael L. Fischer, executive director, California Coastal Commission, to Congressman Leon Panetta, representing California's 16th District, regarding assessment of county and state's ability to effectively control land use in Big Sur, 21 Apr. 1980. CA Arch._CCC.

1. Interview by Janet Bridges of Earth Alert! with Peter Douglas, Jan. 2006, Adelphia public-access studios, Eagle Rock, California: Earth Alert! *Heroes of the Coast,* interviews recorded 2004–12 (DVD).

2. Michael L. Fischer, oral history interviews conducted 1992 and 1993 by Ann Lage, Regional Oral History Office, University of California, Berkeley, for the California State Archives, State Government Oral History Program, 118.

3. James J. Rawls and Walton Bean, *California: An Interpretive History.* 8th ed. (Boston: McGraw Hill, 2003), 482–84.

4. William Poole, "Conservation and Patriotism: A Conversation with William Cronon," *Land & People Magazine* 18, no. 2 (Fall 2006): 46–50. Richard Brewer, *Conservancy: The Land Trust Movement in America* (Lebanon, NH: University Press of New England, 2003), 9.

5. Membership in the Sierra Club jumped from 150,000 members in 1980 to 650,000 in 1991. The Wilderness Society saw its membership rise from 50,000 to 350,000 in the same period: ibid., 37.

6. Rasa Gustaitis, "An Interview with Peter Douglas: State of the Coast," *CA C&O* 12, no. 4 (Winter 1996–97): 17. Earth Alert! interview with Peter Douglas, 2006: Earth Alert! *Heroes of the Coast,* interviews recorded 2004–12 (DVD).

7. The following ballot initiatives all passed: Proposition 1, Parklands Acquisition and Development Program, 4 Nov. 1980; Proposition 4, Lake Tahoe Acquisitions Bond Act, 2 Nov. 1982; Proposition 18, California Park and Recreational Facilities Act of 1984, and Proposition 19, Fish and Wildlife Habitat Enhancement Act of 1984, 5 June 1984; Proposition 43, Community Parklands Act of 1986, 3 June 1986; Proposition 70, Wildlife, Coastal, and Park Land Conservation Bond Act, 7 June 1988.

8. *BSRU,* Oct. 1979, 8. Big Sur Lib.

9. "Transfer of Density Credits System for Big Sur Outlined by Supervisor," *MPH,* 19 Jan. 1982, 17. Monterey Public Library.

10. Robert Miskimon, "Land Trust, Property Owners' Group Draw Battle Lines over Big Sur Plan," *CPC,* 12 Aug. 1982, A-8.

11. "County Planners Approve Sur Coast LCP with Tight Limits on Future Development," *MPH,* 12 Feb. 1981, 25. Monterey Public Library.

12. "Big Sur LCP Adopted by County Planners," *BSGZ* 4, no. 3 (Mar. 1981), 10. Naomi Schwartz, who was involved with the Coastal Act, explained that each of the brown signs that say COASTAL ACCESS along the Pacific Coast Highway from Santa Barbara to Santa Monica represents a battleground; blood was spilled to get public access. Janet Bridges of Earth Alert! interview with Naomi Schwartz, Apr. 2006, Santa Monica: Earth Alert! *Heroes of the Coast,* interviews recorded 2004–12 (DVD).

13. Big Sur Coast Local Coastal Program (LCP). Certified by the California Coastal Commission, 1986. Monterey County Planning Department. 102 The LCP named areas under private ownership with existing public use, explaining that the "legality of such use is not always clear."

14. "Supervisors Break Big Sur LCP Deadlock; Approval Expected," *MPH,* 1 Apr. 1981, 19. Monterey Public Library.

15. LCP, 85.

16. "Supervisors Adopt Big Sur LCP, Completing Five-Year-Long Effort," *MPH*, 7 Apr. 1981, 19. Monterey Public Library.

17. Judith I. de Neufville, ed., *The Land Use Policy Debate in the United States* (New York: Plenum Press, 1981), 2.

18. Fischer to Panetta. CA Arch._CCC.

19. "Fewer Big Sur Homes, Ban on Mining Urged," *MPH*, 28 Aug. 1981, 25. Ken Peterson, "State Commission Refuses to Certify Big Sur Coast Plan," *MPH*, 3 Sept. 1981, 1. Both Monterey Public Library.

20. Ric Davidge, "Federal Land Acquisition," *BSGZ* 4, no. 3 (Mar. 1981), 16. Joseph Mastroianni, "The Environmental Protection Hustle," *BSGZ* 2, no. 8 (Aug.–Sept. 1979), 13.

21. Statement by the Friends of the Big Sur Coast at the Monterey County Board of Supervisors Hearing on the Big Sur Land Use Plan, 4 Jan. 1982. Letter from John Harlan, president, Coast Property Owners Association (CPOA), to the Monterey County Board of Supervisors, 12 Jan. 1982. CA HistRm_Coastal Reg.

22. The California Coastal Council, an organization active in the early years after the Coastal Act and consisting of landowners and representatives of construction, industry, agriculture, and real-estate groups, regularly challenged the state's right to regulate private property in the interest of the public. The council used the courts to determine whether the Coastal Commission could attach such conditions as open-space dedication or public-access trails to its land-use plan policies. The Pacific Legal Foundation (PLF) was formed in Sacramento in 1973 and continues to this day. It uses the courts to argue for limited government, property rights, and free enterprise. The PLF has regularly opposed the Coastal Commission, most prominently in the 1987 U.S. Supreme Court case *Nollan v. California Coastal Commission*.

23. *Nollan v. California Coastal Commission*, 483 U.S. 825 (1987).

24. Carol M. Rose, "Property Rights, Regulatory Regimes and the New Takings Jurisprudence—An Evolutionary Approach" (1990), 578–81. Faculty Scholarship Series, paper 1821. http://digitalcommons.law.yale.edu/fss_papers/1821 (accessed 3 Sept. 2016).

25. "Citizen Group Offers to Help Supervisors Define 'Viewshed' in Big Sur LCP," *CPC*, 24 Feb. 1983, A-4.

26. Harlan, letter to Monterey County Board of Supervisors.

27. "Supervisors Approve Big Sur LCP," *MPH*, 11 Apr. 1984, 1. Monterey Public Library.

28. LCP, 73.

29. It was generally acknowledged that the price for development along the California coast increased after the Coastal Act. Thomas W. Hazlett, *The California Coastal Commission and the Economics of Environmentalism* (Ottawa, IL: Green Hill Publishers, Inc., 1980), 21.

30. CPOA written testimony to Monterey County Board of Supervisors, 9 Sept. 1985. CA HistRm_Coastal Reg.

31. Lea Brooks, "Monterey County Protects a National Treasure: Local Control Prevails in Big Sur," *California County*, July–Aug. 1990, 9.

32. Big Sur Coast Land Use Plan, Proposed Changes to Big Sur Land Use Plan, Coast Property Owners Association, Apr. 1984, 93. LCP, 96–97.

33. The CPOA presented to the Monterey County Board of Supervisors a petition signed by 847 residents, roughly 75% of the Big Sur population, saying they had concerns about the process used to create the land-use plan, prompting a suit filed in county court that was dismissed on procedural grounds. "Big Sur LCP Suit Thrown Out," *MPH*, 26 Apr. 1985, 5. Monterey Public Library.

34. Undated, untitled notes by Michael Fischer, 5. CA Arch._CCC.

35. Big Sur Coast Highway Management Plan, "A History of Road Closures along Highway 1, Big Sur, Monterey and San Luis Obispo Counties, California, Prepared for Caltrans District 5; Prepared by JRP Historical Consulting Services, Nov. 2001," 3–5–3–8. http://www.dot.ca.gov/dist05/projects/bigsur/inventory_reports/history_road_closures.pdf (accessed 15 Jan. 2016).

36. Alisa Fineman, "Where Extremes Meet: Local Perspectives on Preservation for Big Sur" (Senior thesis, Environmental Studies, University of California, Santa Cruz, 1984), 33.

37. "The Big Sur Slide," *Monterey Life* 5, no. 3 (Mar. 1984). Highway repair required the excavation of some three million cubic yards of mountainside: Jeff Norman and the Big Sur Historical Society, *Images of America: Big Sur* (Charleston, SC: Arcadia Publishing, 2004), 104.

38. Jeffrey S. Hudson, "Coast Road Is a Marvel, but May Not Be Worth Keeping," *LAT*, 4 Apr. 1983. CA Hist. Room_Hwy 1.

39. LCP, 29, 46.

40. Steven W. Hackel, *Children of Coyote, Missionaries of Saint Francis: Indian-Spanish Relations in Colonial California, 1769–1850* (Chapel Hill: University of North Carolina Press, 2005), 15. Gary Breschini and Trudy Haversat, *The Esselen Indians of the Big Sur Country: The Land and the People* (Salinas, CA: Coyote Press, 2004), 205. Donald Howard, *Big Sur's Lost Tribe: The Esselen* (Carmel: Antiquities Research Publications, 1979), 27.

41. Ansel Adams to Michael Fischer, 15 Mar. 1983. CA Arch._CCC.

42. Ken Peterson, "Coast Panel Testimony Piles Up for Big Sur, Carmel Area LCPs," *MPH*, 9 July 1981. CA HistRm_Coastal Reg.

43. Rawls and Bean, *California*, 482–84.

44. Elizabeth Drew, "A Reporter at Large: Secretary Watt," *The New Yorker*, 4 May 1981, 120.

45. California Coastal Commission to Interior Secretary James Watt, 26 Mar. 1982. CA Arch._CCC.

46. *California Coastal Commission et al., Appellants, v. Granite Rock Company*, 480 U.S. 572 (1987).

47. "U.S. Justices Back State on Mining Curbs at Big Sur," *LAT*, 24 Mar. 1987. http://articles.latimes.com/1987–03–24/news/mn-324_1_land-use-planning (accessed 15 Jan. 2016).

48. Suzanne Riess, "Margaret Wentworth Owings: Artist, and Wildlife and Environmental Defender," interviews, 1986–88, 154.

49. "A War of Wills to 'Save' Big Sur Coast," *Salinas Californian,* 7 July 1980. Nathaniel Owings argued that in the wake of the legislative debate, the two sides needed to "forget about winning and losing" and work to heal the divisions caused by the fight. "Owings Warns against Bill's Defeat: End to Big Sur Animosity Urged," *MPH,* 23 Sept. 1980. Both citations CA HistRm_Big Sur.

50. Monterey Peninsula Board of Realtors: median sale prices in Monterey County in 1978–79: Big Sur $228,000; Carmel: $135,000; and Pebble Beach: $150,000. Monterey County Planning Department, Big Sur Area Housing Draft Data Analysis Report, Aug. 1980. Monterey County Planning Department, Salinas, California.

51. U.S. Population Census, 1980 and 1990, California, Tract 115. In 1980, of the 513 occupied houses in Big Sur, 255 were rentals, and 258 were owned by the occupants. In 1990, of the 623 occupied houses, 399 were rentals, and 224 were owned by the occupants. California Median Income 1989: $35,798, from https://www.census.gov/hhes/www/income/data/historical/state/state1.html (accessed 20 Jan. 2016).

52. Anne Lage, oral history interviews with Michael L. Fischer, 156.

53. Ibid., 158.

54. Ibid., 159.

55. "Coastal Bureaucracy," guest editorial, *MPH,* reprinted in *BSGZ* 2, no. 4 (Apr. 1979), 4.

56. During the first five years of the Coastal Act, the commission had facilitated the construction of 2,500 affordable units in the state's coastal zone. Anne Lage, oral history interviews with Michael L. Fischer, 161. Peter Schrag, *California: America's High-Stakes Experiment* (Berkeley and Los Angeles: University of California Press, 2008), 122–29. 2006 Earth Alert! interview with Peter Douglas, 2006: Earth Alert! *Heroes of the Coast,* interviews recorded 2004–12 (DVD).

57. "Transfer of Density Credits System for Big Sur Outlined by Supervisor," *MPH,* 19 Jan. 1982, 17. Monterey Public Library.

58. William H. Chafe, *The Unfinished Journey: America since World War II,* 6th ed. (Oxford: Oxford University Press, 2007), 429, 467–77. Godfrey Hodgson, *The World Turned Right Side Up: A History of the Conservative Ascendancy in America* (Boston: Houghton Mifflin Company, 1996), 193.

59. In 1968 the Molera family sold 2,200 acres of the Cooper land grant to The Nature Conservancy, which later sold the property to California State Parks to become Andrew Molera State Park, with the provision that the state treat the land as Mrs. Molera had wished—as an open, undeveloped recreational area. When California State Parks did create considerable development plans for the property, The Nature Conservancy threatened to revoke the sale, and California State Parks backed down: Wendy Grissam Brokaw, "Homegrown Preservation: The Big Sur Land Trust," *Monterey Life,* Apr. 1982, 66. In 1978 The Nature Conservancy also helped facilitate the transfer of the 3,548-acre Landels-Hill Big Creek Reserve to the University of California Natural Reserve System. The Coastal Conservancy directed nearly one-quarter of its funds to land trusts operating along the state's coast at the close of the century: Janet Diehl, "A Home-Based Force for Conservation," *CA C&O* 13, no. 3 (Fall 1997): 7.

60. Ibid., 9.

61. Benjamin R. Emory, "Saving Land Close to Home," *California Waterfront Age* 3, no. 4 (1987): 13.

62. Brokaw, "Homegrown Preservation," 66.

63. John Walton, "The Land of Big Sur: Conservation on the California Coast," *California History* 85, no. 1 (2007): 60–61. Ken Peterson, "Supervisors Approve Big Sur LCP," *MPH,* 11 Apr. 1984, 1. Monterey Public Library.

64. Walton, "The Land of Big Sur," 61–62.

65. The passage of Proposition 70 in 1988 created funding that eventually led to the purchase of Hill's development rights for 3,550 viewshed acres.

66. LCP, 100–101.

67. Brooks, "Monterey County Protects a National Treasure," 7.

68. Ibid., 8.

69. LCP, 11, 101.

70. Brooks, "Monterey County Protects a National Treasure," 8. Allan Parachini, "Big Sur Development: Who's in Charge Here? Sen. Wilson's Bill, U.S. Supreme Court May Upset State Panel's Land-Use Plan," *LAT,* 20 Apr. 1986. http://articles.latimes.com/1986–04–20/news/vw-824_1_big-sur-coast/4 (accessed 1 Oct. 2015).

71. LCP, 11. The LCP required commercial-development permits to explain how the new project would limit disturbance to neighboring residents' peace and tranquility.

72. Alfred Runte, *Yosemite: The Embattled Wilderness* (Lincoln: University of Nebraska Press, 1990), 215.

73. LCP, 90.

74. Ibid., 84, 92, 86.

75. Ibid., 86.

76. Ibid., 37.

77. Ibid., 126.

78. Ibid., 9.

79. Ibid., 85. Allowable building densities: to the east of the highway, on the flat or gently sloping land (under 15% incline) only one dwelling per 40 acres could be built; on a slope between 18% and 30% only one dwelling per 80 acres; and for a slope greater than 30% only one dwelling per 320 acres. A 40-acre minimum per single dwelling guided development to the west of the highway.

80. Martha V. Diehl, "Land Use in Big Sur: In Search of Sustainable Balance between Community Needs and Resource Protection" (M.A. thesis, California State University, Monterey Bay, 2006), 9.

81. Brooks, "Monterey County Protects a National Treasure," 7.

82. William Duddleson, "Protecting the Big Sur," *American Land Forum* 7, no. 2 (Mar.–Apr. 1987): 29.

83. Victoria and David Sheff, "Ansel Adams: A Candid Conversation with America's 'Photographer Laureate' and Environmentalist about Art, Natural Beauty, and the Unnatural Acts of Interior Secretary James Watt," *Playboy Magazine* 30, no. 5 (May 1983): 86, 222. "Watt Bucks Tradition, Visiting Ex-Senator Says," *MPH,* 20 Sept. 1981. CA HistRm_Coastal Reg.

84. Big Sur Scenic Area Fact Sheet, "Key Features of Wilson Legislation." CA Arch._CCC.

85. Mac McDonald, "Unlikely Coalition Joins to Fight Wilson bill," *CPC,* 12 June 1986, 11. Harrison Memorial Library, Local History Department, Carmel, California.

86. Parachini, "Big Sur Development," *LAT.*

87. Ibid.

88. BSMAAC meeting minutes, 27 Aug. 1986. Panetta Inst. Arch. *BSRU,* July 1986. Big Sur Lib.

89. David Leland, "Los Padres Forest Plan Received High Marks," *CPC,* 21 Apr. 1988; idem, "Does County Have 'Teeth' to Protect Big Sur?" *CPC,* 30 Mar. 1989. Both Harrison Memorial Library, Local History Department, Carmel, California.

90. Leon Panetta, telegram to California Senator Ken Maddy, 18 June 1986, Leon and Sylvia Panetta Institute Archive. Proposition 70 received 65% of the vote in 1988, creating The Wildlife, Coastal, and Park Land Conservation Bond Act. This act authorized a $776-million general-obligation bond to provide funds for the "acquisition, development, rehabilitation, protection, or restoration of park, wildlife, coastal, and natural lands in California including lands supporting unique or endangered plants or animals." Twenty-five million dollars of this authorization was earmarked for Big Sur, to support the viewshed policy: Daniel Press, *Saving Open Space: The Politics of Local Preservation in California* (Berkeley and Los Angeles: University of California Press, 2002), 57.

91. Walton, "The Land of Big Sur," 62.

92. Brooks, "Monterey County Protects a National Treasure," 8.

93. The founding members included Leon Panetta and two Monterey County supervisors, the Monterey Peninsula Regional Parks District, the Big Sur Land Trust, the Big Sur Chamber of Commerce, Friends of the Big Sur Coast, the Coast Property Owners Association, five seats for Big Sur residents, and three seats for Monterey Peninsula residents. Representatives from the California Department of State Parks and Los Padres National Forest regularly attended BSMAAC meetings to coordinate the implementation of land-use regulations.

94. Michael L. Fischer, "Ahead: A More Crowded Coast," *CA C&O* 12, no. 4 (Winter 1996–97): 20.

95. Walton, "The Land of Big Sur," 62. Martha V. Diehl, "Land Use in Big Sur," 9.

EPILOGUE. MILLIONAIRES AND BEACHES

The epigraph to this chapter: Rasa Gustaitis, "An Interview with Peter Douglas: State of the Coast," *CA C&O* 12, no. 4 (Winter 1996–97): 11.

1. The Nacimiento-Fergusson Road is the only east-west road connecting Highway 1 through Big Sur to the inland Highway 101.

2. California population, 1915: 2,377,549, from https://www.census.gov /dmd/www/resapport/states/california.pdf; California population, 2015: 37,253,956, from http://quickfacts.census.gov/qfd/states/06000.html (both accessed 2 Feb. 2016). Estimates place Big Sur's population at 1,100 at the turn of the twentieth century, and fewer than 1,800 residents in 2000. Martha V. Diehl, "Land Use in Big Sur: In Search of Sustainable Balance between Community Needs and Resource Protection" (M.A. thesis, California State University, Monterey Bay, 2006), 45.

3. California Coastal Commission, Periodic Review of the Monterey County Local Coastal Program, 2003, 29.

4. Gustaitis, "An Interview with Peter Douglas," *CA C&O* 12, no. 4 (Winter 1996–97): 11.

5. The 2002 Big Sur Wilderness Conservation Act was the first California wilderness bill in eight years. It added more than seventeen thousand acres to the Silver Peak Wilderness area, first designated in 1992 by Los Padres Condor Range and River Protection Act.

6. Interview with Peter Douglas, 2011: Earth Alert! *Heroes of the Coast,* interviews recorded 2004–12 (DVD).

7. Interview with Peter Douglas, 2006: Earth Alert! *Heroes of the Coast,* interviews recorded 2004–12 (DVD).

8. *CA C&O* 12, no. 4 (1996–97), 10–20; and *CA C&O* 19, no. 4 (2003–4), 2–21.

9. Elaine Woo, "Peter M. Douglas Dies at 69; California Coastal Commission Chief," *LAT,* 4 Apr. 2012, http://articles.latimes.com/2012/apr/04/local/la-me-peter-douglas-20120404/2 (accessed 17 Jan. 2016). Dennis Hevesi, "Peter Douglas, Sentry of California's Coast, Dies at 69," *NYT,* 8 Apr. 2012, http://www.nytimes.com/2012/04/09/ us/peter-douglas-defender-of-california-coast-dies-at-69.html (accessed 17 Jan. 2016).

10. Interview with Peter Douglas, 2006, Earth Alert!

11. Michael L. Fischer, oral history interviews conducted 1992 and 1993 by Ann Lage, Regional Oral History Office, University of California, Berkeley, for the California State Archives, State Government Oral History Program, 207.

12. Interview with Peter Douglas, 2006, Earth Alert! Coastal Commissioners are appointed as follows: four appointments each by the governor, speaker of the assembly, and leader of the senate.

13. Daniel Press, *Saving Open Space: The Politics of Local Preservation in California* (Berkeley and Los Angeles: University of California Press, 2002), 6.

14. Tony Barboza, "Blocking Californians' Beach Access Will Soon Carry a Hefty Fine," *LAT,* 30 June 2014. http://www.latimes.com/science/la-me-coastal-penalties-20140630-story.html (accessed 10 Jan. 2016).

15. City of Malibu Local Coastal Program, adopted 2002, 5–9: "Access to many beaches throughout the City, however, is restricted due to blockage by development including gated communities or private compounds, unopened accessways, and lack of parking." A general objective of the city's LCP includes: "Maximize public access to and along the coast and maximize public recreational opportunities in the coastal zone consistent with sound resources conservation principles and constitutionally protected rights of private property owners."

16. David Geffen resisted providing access from 1983 until 2007; Norm and Lisette Ackerberg from 1984 to 2015: Mireya Navarro, "In Malibu, the Water's Fine (So Don't Come In!)," *NYT*, 5 June 2005. http://www.nytimes.com/2005/06/05 /fashion/sundaystyles/in-malibu-the-waters-fine-so-dont-come-in.html?r=0 (accessed 10 Jan. 2016). Ann O'Neill, "Billionaire's Beach Just Got a Lot Less Exclusive," *CNN*, 17 July 2015. http://www.cnn.com/2015/07/17/us/billionaires-beach-malibu-public-access/ (accessed 9 Jan. 2015).

17. Author interview with Coastal Commissioner Mary Shallenberger, 14 July 2015.

18. Interview with Peter Douglas, 2006, Earth Alert!

19. Professor Jonathan Zasloff's assessment was based on the "high values of its [the Coastal Commission's] jurisdiction and its high environmental assets." Jennifer Steinhauer, "In California, Coastal Commission Wields Vast Power," *NYT*, 23 Feb. 2008. http://www.nytimes.com/2008/02/23/us/23clemente.html (accessed 13 Jan. 2016). Report by the California Coastal Commission, 2014 Year in Review: http:// documents.coastal.ca.gov/assets/press-releases/2014-in-review/CA_Coastal_ Commission_2014_In_Review.pdf (accessed 2 Feb. 2016).

20. Interview with Peter Douglas, 2011, Earth Alert! And see any one of the Coastal Conservancy's *CA C&O* issues for a sense of what preservation work the agency hoped to accomplish. The periodical ran from winter 1985 to autumn 2009. For the first five years it was entitled *California Waterfront Age*.

21. Gustaitis, "An Interview with Peter Douglas," *CA C&O* 12, no. 4 (Winter 1996–97): 11.

22. Mark Baldassare, PPIC Statewide Survey, Nov. 2003, "Special Survey on Californians and the Environment," 22.

23. Mark Baldassare, PPIC Statewide Survey, Feb. 2006, "Californians and the Environment," 22.

24. Ibid.

25. The following nine ballot propositions passed: Proposition 1, Parklands Acquisition and Development Program, and Proposition 8, Water Resources Development and Protection, 4 Nov. 1980; Proposition 4, Lake Tahoe Acquisitions Bond Act, 2 Nov. 1982; Proposition 18, California Park and Recreational Facilities Act of 1984, and Proposition 19, Fish and Wildlife Habitat Enhancement Act of 1984, 5 June 1984; Proposition 43, Community Parklands Act of 1986, and Proposition 44, Water Conservation and Water Quality Bond Law of 1986, 3 June 1986; Proposition 70, Wildlife, Coastal, and Park Land Conservation Bond Act, Initiative Statute, 7 June 1988; Proposition 83, Clean Water and Water Reclamation Bond Act of 1988, 8 Nov. 1988. The following three ballot propositions failed: Proposition 1, Parklands and Renewable Resources Investment Program, 3 June 1980; Proposition 2, Lake Tahoe Acquisitions Bond Act of 1980, 4 Nov. 1980; Proposition 13, Water Resources, 2 Nov. 1982.

26. Two ballot propositions passed: Proposition 117, Wildlife Protection, 5 June 1990; and Proposition 132, Marine Resources, 6 Nov. 1990. The following seven ballot propositions all failed: Proposition 128, Environment, Public Health, Bonds; Proposition 130, Forest Acquisition, Timber Harvesting Practices; Proposition 138, Forestry Programs, Timber Harvesting Practices; Proposition 148, Water Resources

Bond Act of 1990; Proposition 149, California Park, Recreation, and Wildlife Enhancement Act of 1990 (all 6 Nov. 1990); Proposition 180, Park Lands, Historic Sites, Wildlife and Forest Conservation Bond Act, 7 June 1994; Proposition 197, Amendment of the California Wildlife Protection Act of 1990, 26 Mar. 1996.

27. Peter Grenell, "From the Executive Office," *CA C&O* 6, no. 3 (1990): 2.

28. Rasa Gustaitis, "Is California Starving the Goose That Laid the Golden Egg?" *CA C&O* 12, no. 3 (1996): 16.

29. Richard Brewer, *Conservancy: The Land Trust Movement in America* (Lebanon, NH: University Press of New England, 2003), 11.

30. John Woodbury, "The Next Million Acres: San Francisco Bay Area Groups Drive toward Ambitious 25-Year Goal," *CA C&O* 19, no. 4 (2003–4): 15.

31. Transfer development credits, though an important part of the negotiations that determined Big Sur's Local Coastal Program, have had limited application along the Big Sur coast: http://smartpreservation.net/monterey-county-california/ and http://www.montereycountyweekly.com/news/local_news/in-a-flipped-script-coastal-conservancy-sells-rights-to-build/article_91d67220-f714-11e3-9c46-0017a43b2370.html (both accessed 25 May 2017).

32. Mark Baldassare, PPIC Statewide Survey, July 2003, "Special Survey on Californians and the Environment," 23. Sixty-five percent of Californians agreed that "protection of the environment should be given priority, even at the risk of curbing economic growth."

33. Mark Baldassare, PPIC Statewide Survey November 2003, "Special Survey on Californians and the Environment," 22. Sixty-one percent said that the condition of the coast was important to the state's economy.

34. San Francisco Bay Conservation and Development Commission, 2014 Annual Report: http://www.bcdc.ca.gov/cm/2015/2014Annual-Report.pdf (accessed 25 May 2017).

35. Joan Cardellino and Rasa Gustaitis, "Coastal Access," *CA C&O* 11, no. 2 (1995): 7.

36. Mark Baldassare, PPIC Statewide Survey, June 2000, "Special Survey on Californians and the Environment," v, vi, 33. Sixty-nine percent of Americans preferenced property rights above regulations for the common good, and only 54% of Californians felt the same. Fifty-seven percent of Californians liked the idea of using public funds to buy undeveloped land in order to shield it from development, compared with 44% nationwide.

37. Mark Baldassare, PPIC Statewide Survey November 2003, "Special Survey on Californians and the Environment," 22. Sixty-nine percent said that the condition of the oceans and beaches was important to the quality of life in California; 26% said that it was somewhat important.

38. Mark Baldassare, PPIC Statewide Survey, June 2000 "Special Survey on Californians and the Environment," 2. Democrats 60%, Republicans 59%, and independent voters 58%.

39. "We realized that the coastal act's requirement of keeping the agricultural areas and the Big Sur areas, keeping large areas of the coastal zone out of the supply

of developable land would simply drive up the cost of the remaining land": Michael L. Fischer, oral history interviews, 156.

40. Mark Baldassare, PPIC Statewide Survey, June 2000 "Special Survey on Californians and the Environment," vi. Fifty-two percent would vote against a local bond measure to purchase open space, even though 57% had earlier supported the principle of using public funds for this same purpose: *CA C&O* 24, no. 4 (2008–9): 4. Said Sam Schuchat, executive officer of the California State Coastal Conservancy: "In this state the desire for public services outstrips the willingness to pay."

41. Peter Schrag, *California: America's High-Stakes Experiment* (Berkeley and Los Angeles: University of California Press, 2008), 123. Legislative Analyst's Office Report, "Common Claims about Proposition 13," 19 Sept. 2016. http://lao.ca.gov /Publications/Report/3497 (accessed 23 Sept. 2016).

42. Thomas W. Hazlett, *The California Coastal Commission and the Economics of Environmentalism* (Ottawa, IL: Green Hill Publishers, Inc., 1980). 11–15.

43. Mark Baldassare, PPIC Statewide Survey, Dec. 2015, "Californians and Their Government," 9. Sixty-seven percent of Californians surveyed said the state was divided into "haves and have-nots," even with 40% of those surveyed reporting themselves as among the "haves."

44. Gustaitis, "An Interview with Peter Douglas," *CA C&O* 12, no. 4 (Winter 1996–97): 16.

45. Woo, "Peter M. Douglas"

46. The total amount of land in Big Sur in public ownership increased from about 60% in 1988 (the year of the Big Sur LCP's certification) to about 70% by 2005: Diehl, "Land Use in Big Sur," 10–33.

47. Real-estate prices reflect the high demand for a rare piece of Big Sur property and are driven by such celebrities as Ted Turner, Rosanna Arquette, and Steve Martin. "Hollywood Jet Setters Choose Solitude, Views of Once-Bohemian Big Sur," *San Jose Mercury News,* 13 June 1992, 1D.

48. The 2000 census indicates that residents' median age in 2000 was 45.2, compared with 36.2 nationally, and 32.3 in Monterey County overall. In 1999 the average house price in Big Sur was $1,064,967; less than a decade later the average had jumped to $2,639,438. Diehl, "Land Use in Big Sur," 11–14.

49. Big Sur Multi-Agency Advisory Council Meeting Minutes, 15 Apr. 2016, http:// www.co.monterey.ca.us/home/showdocument?id=12525 (accessed 16 Sept. 2016). Chris Counts, "Should Highway 1 Be a Toll Road?" *CPC,* 22–28 Apr. 2016, 1A, 12A.

50. "The World's Greatest Destinations," *National Geographic Traveler* 16, no. 7 (July 1999): 176–78.

51. "Living Edens: Big Sur—California's Wild Coast," *NATURE* film, 2001. Elaine Woo, "Billy Post Dies at 88; Big Sur's Resident Authority," *LAT,* 2 Aug. 2009. http://www.latimes.com/local/obituaries/la-me-billy-post2-2009aug02-story.html (accessed 1 Oct. 2015).

52. Ibid.

53. Jeff Norman and the Big Sur Historical Society, *Images of America: Big Sur* (Charleston, SC: Arcadia Publishing, 2004), 79.

54. Post Ranch Inn website: http://www.postranchinn.com/about-us/our-story/ (accessed 23 Dec. 2015).

55. Philip Burchett, "Last of the Big Sur Men," *Westways,* Dec. 1952, 8–9.

56. Woo, "Billy Post."

57. Ibid. and Post Ranch Inn website.

58. "Adventure Awaits: Escape through the Skies." http://www.postranchinn.com/fly-to-big-sur/ (accessed 27 May 2017).

59. Woo, "Billy Post."

60. Interview with Peter Douglas, 2011, Earth Alert! Author interview with Mary Shallenberger.

61. In 2006 Proposition 87, Alternative Energy Oil Tax, was rejected by voters. In 2008, both Proposition 7, Renewable Energy, and Proposition 10, Alternative Fuels Initiative, were defeated. In 2010, Proposition 21, Vehicle License Fee for Parks, was defeated. In 2010 voters did defeat Proposition 23, which would have suspended California's Global Warming Act of 2006 until the unemployment rate dropped. In 2012, voters approved Proposition 39, which increased income taxes for multistate businesses with dedicated revenue going to creating energy efficiency and clean-energy jobs. In 2016 voters approved Proposition 67, the California Plastic Bag Ban Veto Referendum, to uphold earlier legislation to ban certain plastic bags. In the same election, voters rejected Proposition 65, which would have assigned revenue from the sale of disposable carryout bags to the Wildlife Conservation Fund.

62. Letter from Charles Lester, executive director, to California Coastal Commission and Interested Parties, 4 Feb. 2016, regarding W-8: Background Information and a Path Forward, 2, and Attachment 1, 4. http://documents.coastal.ca.gov/reports/2016/2/w8–2–2016.pdf, (accessed 22 Apr. 2016).

63. Adam Nagourney, "Firing Leads to Questions on California Coast's Future," *NYT,* 11 Feb. 2016. http://www.nytimes.com/2016/02/12/us/california-coastal-commission-votes-to-fire-executive-director.html?r=0 (accessed 22 Apr. 2016).

64. http://www.actcoastal.org/wiki/2015_Annual_Coastal_Commission_Vote_Chart:_A_Summary (accessed 28 Apr. 2016).

65. Tony Barboza, "Fired California Coastal Commission Director Speaks Out,' *LAT,* 11 Feb. 2016. http://www.latimes.com/local/politics/la-me-lester-interview-20160212-story.html (accessed 28 Apr. 2016).

66. Toni Atkins tweeted this remark on 10 Feb. 2016. https://twitter.com/toniatkins/status/697643818569437184 (accessed 23 Sept. 2016).

67. http://www.actcoastal.org/wiki/2015_Annual_Coastal_Commission_Vote_Chart:_A_Summary (accessed 28 Apr. 2016). http://www.actcoastal.org/wiki/images/a/a5/ActCoastal_Report_Card_2016_FINAL.pdf (accessed 25 May 2017). The average conservation score for the Coastal Commission in 2015 was 47 percent, and in 2016 it rose to 65 percent. Both years were below the 2014 average of 71 percent.

68. Lester argued that the current commission "seems to be more interested in and receptive to the concerns of the development community as a general rule": Barboza, "Fired California Coastal Commission Director," *LAT.*

69. Coastal Commissioner Mary Shallenberger, a strong supporter of Douglas's work, believes the state's North Coast would benefit from implementing a preservation model similar to Big Sur's. She acknowledges that some may say of Big Sur residents that they have been busy keeping the coast beautiful for themselves, but because they are willing to share that beauty with the public, she approves of the methods taken in Big Sur: Author interview with Mary Shallenberger.

70. *KQED Forum,* "Lawsuit Contends Cattle Ranching Harms Point Reyes National Seashore," host Mina Kim, 18 Mar. 2016. https://ww2.kqed.org/forum/2016/03/18/lawsuit-contends-cattle-ranching-harms-point-reyes-national-seashore/ (accessed 22 Apr. 2016).

71. Laura A. Watt, "The Continuously Managed Wild: Tule Elk at Point Reyes National Seashore," *Journal of International Wildlife Law & Policy* 18 (2015): 302–5.

72. Neither the 21st-Century Monterey County General Plan update nor the most recent (2003) Monterey County LCP Periodic Review identifies ranching as an environmental issue for Big Sur. Quite the opposite, as agriculture is considered a priority land use per the Coastal Act. The Coastal Act requires that "the maximum amount of agricultural land shall be maintained in agricultural production and conflicts shall be minimized between urban and agricultural land uses. The long-term viability of soils must also be protected and conversions of agricultural land to other uses are strictly limited" (Sections 30241, 30241.5, 30242, and 30243). http://www.coastal.ca.gov/recap/mco-lcp-review.html (accessed 5 May 2016).

73. Robinson Jeffers and Ansel Adams, *Not Man Apart: Lines from Robinson Jeffers, Photographs of the Big Sur Coast,* ed. David Brower (San Francisco: Sierra Club Books, 1965), 20.

74. Walter Truett Anderson, *The Upstart Spring: Esalen and the American Awakening* (Reading, MA: Addison-Wesley, 1983), 311.

SELECT BIBLIOGRAPHY

This bibliography is divided into three sections: (1) archival and manuscript collections, (2) titles of newspapers and periodicals cited throughout the book, and (3) all other sources (government documents, oral histories, primary and secondary sources). Journal, magazine, and newspaper articles cited only once in the notes are omitted from the bibliography, as are references to daily periodicals; the full citations of such sources appear in the notes.

ARCHIVAL AND MANUSCRIPT COLLECTIONS

Big Sur Historical Society. Big Sur, California.

Big Sur Library. Local History Collection. Monterey County Free Libraries. Big Sur, California.

California History Room. Big Sur File; Highway 1 Clipping File; Coastal Regulation File. Monterey Public Library. Monterey, California.

California State Archives. California Coastal Commission Records; Public Works, Highway Division, District 5. Sacramento, California.

California State Parks, Monterey District, District Headquarters Archive. Monterey, California.

Central Coast California Coastal Commission Office. Santa Cruz, California.

Harrison Memorial Library. Local History Department. Carmel, California.

Henry Miller Memorial Library Archives. Big Sur, California.

John Steinbeck Library. Local History Collection. Salinas, California.

King City Library. Local History Collection. Monterey County Free Libraries, King City, California.

Leon and Sylvia Panetta Institute Archive. California State University, Monterey Bay.

Mayo Hayes O'Donnell Library. Local History Collection. Monterey, California.

Monterey County Administrative Offices. Clerk of the Board Office; Planning
  Department. Salinas, California.
Monterey County Historical Society. Salinas, California.
National Archives and Records Administration. Pacific Region. Record Group 95.
  Laguna Niguel, California.
Shields Library. Special Collections. University of California, Davis.

NEWSPAPERS AND PERIODICALS

The Atlantic Monthly
The Big Sur Gazette
Big Sur Guide
Big Sur Round-up
California Highways and Public Works
California Transportation Journal
California Waterfront Age/California Coast & Ocean
Carmel Pacific Spectator Journal
The Carmel Pine Cone
Christian Science Monitor
Circle of Enchantment
Double Cone Quarterly/The Double Cone Register
Game and Gossip
The Grove at High Tide
King City Rustler
LIFE Magazine
The Living Wilderness
LOOK Magazine
Los Angeles Times
The Monterey New Era
Monterey Peninsula Herald
National Geographic Traveler
New York Times
The New Yorker
Noticias del Puerto de Monterey
Salinas Californian
San Francisco Chronicle
Saturday Evening Post
Smithsonian Magazine
TIME Magazine
Touring Topics/Westways

GOVERNMENT DOCUMENTS, CASES, AND REPORTS; ORAL HISTORIES AND REMARKS; PRIMARY AND SECONDARY SOURCES

Abbott, Carl. *How Cities Won the West: Four Centuries of Urban Change in Western North America*. Albuquerque: University of New Mexico Press, 2008.

———. *The Metropolitan Frontier: Cities in the Modern American West*. Tucson: University of Arizona Press, 1993.

Adams, Ansel, and Nancy Newhall. *This Is the American Earth*. San Francisco: Sierra Club, 1960.

Alinder, Mary Street, and Andrea Gray Stillman, eds. *Ansel Adams: Letters, 1916–1984*. Boston: Little, Brown and Company, 1988.

Anderson, Dewey. "Tahoe: Then and Now." *National Parks Magazine* 44, no. 271 (Apr. 1970): 4–11.

———. "Where the Forest Meets the Sea." *National Parks Magazine* 43, no. 265 (Oct. 1969): 4–12.

Anderson, Walter Truett. *The Upstart Spring: Esalen and the American Awakening*. Reading, MA: Addison-Wesley, 1983.

Babcock, Richard. *The Zoning Game: Municipal Practices and Policies*. Madison: University of Wisconsin Press, 1966.

Baden, John, and Donald Snow. *The Next West: Public Lands, Community, and Economy in the American West*. Washington, D.C.: Island Press, 1997.

Baldassare, Mark. Public Policy Institute of California [PPIC]. Statewide Surveys, 2000–2017.

Bard, Albert S. "Highway Zoning Sustained by California Court: Design in Community Planning Upheld for Monterey County." *National Civic Review*, 26 Dec. 1938, 619.

Barr, Scott. "American Agrarianism and the Back-to-the-Land Movement." M.A. thesis, Ohio State University, 1975.

Belasco, Warren. *Americans on the Road: From Autocamp to Motel, 1910–1945*. Cambridge, MA: MIT Press, 1979.

Bell, Jonathan. *California Crucible: The Forging of Modern American Liberalism*. Philadelphia: University of Pennsylvania Press, 2012.

Bennett, David. *The Party of Fear: From Nativist Movements to the New Right in American History*. Chapel Hill: University of North Carolina Press, 1988.

Berry, Wendell. *A Continuous Harmony*. New York: Harcourt Brace Jovanovich, 1970.

———. *The Gift of Good Land: Further Essays, Cultural and Agricultural*. San Francisco: North Point Press, 1981.

Big Sur Coast Local Coastal Program. Certified by the California Coastal Commission, 1986. Monterey County Planning Department.

Big Sur Coast Recreation and Visitor-Serving Facilities Background Report. Prepared by the Monterey County Planning Department, Jan. 1980. Monterey County Planning Department.

Big Sur Coastal Planning Unit. Draft Environmental Statement, Los Padres National Forest, 1976. California Room, Monterey Public Library.

Bjork, Gordon. *Life, Liberty and Property: The Economics and Politics of Land-Use Planning and Environmental Controls.* Lexington, MA: Lexington Books, 1980.

Blow, Ben. *California Highways: A Descriptive Record of Road Development by the State and by Such Counties as Have Paved Highways.* San Francisco: H. S. Crocker Co., 1920.

Bohlen, James. *The New Pioneers Handbook: Getting Back to the Land in an Energy-Scarce World.* New York: Schocken Books, 1975.

Bolin, Rolf L. "Reappearance of the Southern Sea Otter along the California Coast." *Journal of Mammalogy* 19, no. 3 (1938): 301–3.

Borth, Christy. *Mankind on the Move: The Story of Highways.* Washington, D.C.: Automotive Safety Foundation, 1969.

Boyarsky, Bill. *The Rise of Ronald Reagan.* New York: Random House, 1968.

Brady, Mildred Edie. "The New Cult of Sex and Anarchy." *Harper's Magazine* 194, no. 4 (Apr. 1947): 312–21.

Breschini, Gary, and Trudy Haversat. *The Esselen Indians of the Big Sur Country: The Land and the People.* Salinas, CA: Coyote Press, 2004.

Brewer, Richard. *Conservancy: The Land Trust Movement in America.* Lebanon, NH: University Press of New England, 2003.

Brokaw, Wendy Grissam. "Homegrown Preservation: The Big Sur Land Trust." *Monterey Life,* Apr. 1982.

Brooks, Lea. "Monterey County Protects a National Treasure: Local Control Prevails in Big Sur." *California County,* July–Aug. 1990: 6–9.

Brophy, Robert, ed. *The Robinson Jeffers Newsletter, A Jubilee Gathering, 1962–1988.* Los Angeles: Occidental College, 1988.

Brown, William. *The History of Los Padres National Forest, 1898–1945.* San Francisco, 1945.

Burby, Raymond J., and Peter J. May. *Making Governments Plan: State Experiments in Managing Land Use.* Baltimore: The Johns Hopkins University Press, 1997.

Burke, Flannery. *From Greenwich Village to Taos: Primitivism and Place at Mabel Dodge Luhan's.* Lawrence: University of Kansas Press, 2008.

Butler, Tom. *Wild Earth: Wild Ideas for a World out of Balance.* Minneapolis: Milkweed Editions, 2002.

California Coastal Act. https://www.coastal.ca.gov/coastact.pdf.

California Coastal Commission. Periodic Review of Monterey County Local Coastal Program, 2003. https://www.coastal.ca.gov/recap/mco-lcp-review.html.

California Taxpayer's Association. "Financial History of California State Highways, 1909–1934." Shields Special Collections. University of California, Davis.

Callicott, J. Baird, and Michael P. Nelson. *The Great New Wilderness Debate.* Athens: University of Georgia Press, 1998.

———. *The Wilderness Debate Rages On: Continuing the Great New Wilderness Debate.* Athens: University of Georgia Press, 2008.

Cannon, Lou. *Governor Reagan: His Rise to Power.* New York: Public Affairs, 2003.

Carson, Rachel. *The Sea around Us.* Oxford: Oxford University Press, 1951.

Cawley, R. McGreggor. *Federal Land, Western Anger: The Sagebrush Rebellion and Environmental Politics.* Lawrence: University of Kansas Press, 1993.

Chafe, William H. *The Unfinished Journey: America since World War II.* 6th ed. Oxford: Oxford University Press, 2007.

Chiang, Connie. *Shaping the Shoreline: Fisheries and Tourism on the Monterey Coast.* Seattle: University of Washington Press, 2008.

Clark, Donald Thomas. *Monterey County Place Names: A Geographical Dictionary.* Carmel Valley, CA: Kestrel Press, 1991.

Clarke, Thurston. *California Fault: Searching for the Spirit of State along the San Andreas.* New York: Ballantine Books, 1996.

Coffman, Taylor. *Building for Hearst and Morgan: Voices from the George Loorz Papers.* Berkeley, CA: Berkeley Hills Books, 2003.

Cronon, William. "The Trouble with Wilderness; or, Getting Back to the Wrong Nature." In *Uncommon Ground: Rethinking the Human Place in Nature,* ed. William Cronon, 69–90. New York: W. W. Norton & Co., 1996.

Culver, Lawrence. *The Frontier of Leisure: Southern California and the Shaping of Modern America.* Oxford: Oxford University Press, 2010.

Dana, Samuel T., and Myron E. Krueger, *California Lands: Ownership, Use, and Management.* Narberth, PA: Livingston Publishing Co., 1958.

Dasmann, Ray. *The Destruction of California.* New York: Macmillan, 1965.

Davis, Kathleen. "Cultural Resource Inventory of Pfeiffer Big Sur State Park." Preliminary Draft. Cultural Resource Inventory Unit, Resource Protection Division, California Department of Parks and Recreation. 9 Feb. 1990.

Davis, Mike. *City of Quartz: Excavating the Future in Los Angeles.* New York: Verso, 2006.

Dearborn, Mary V. *The Happiest Man Alive: A Biography of Henry Miller.* New York: Simon & Schuster, 1991.

Demars, Stanford E. *The Tourist in Yosemite, 1855–1985.* Salt Lake City: University of Utah Press, 1991.

Didion, Joan. "Notes from a Native Daughter." In *Slouching Towards Bethlehem,* 171–86. New York: Farrar, Straus, and Giroux, 1968.

———. *Where I Was From.* New York: Alfred A. Knopf, 2003.

Diehl, Janet. "A Home-Based Force for Conservation." *CA C&O* 13, no. 3 (Fall 1997): 3–11.

Diehl, Martha V. "Land Use in Big Sur: In Search of Sustainable Balance between Community Needs and Resource Protection." M.A. thesis, California State University, Monterey Bay, 2006.

Ducsik, Dennis. *Shoreline for the Public.* Cambridge, MA: MIT Press, 1974.

Duddleson, William. "Protecting the Big Sur." *American Land Forum* 7, no. 2 (Mar.–Apr. 1987): 28–36, 45.

Dunlap, Thomas. "Communing With Nature." *History Today* 52, no. 3 (Mar. 2002): 31–37.

————. *Faith in Nature: Environmentalism as Religious Quest.* Seattle: University of Washington Press, 2004.

Earth Alert! *Heroes of the Coast.* Interviews recorded 2004–12. [DVD collection.]

Edsall, Thomas, and Mary Edsall. *Chain Reaction: The Impact of Race, Rights, and Taxes on American Politics.* New York: W. W. Norton & Company, 1991.

Euclid v. Ambler Realty. 272 U.S. 365 (1926). https://www.law.cornell.edu /supremecourt/text/272/365.

Fairfax, Sally. *Buying Nature: The Limits of Land Acquisition as a Conservation Strategy, 1780–2004.* Cambridge, MA: MIT Press, 2005.

"Federal Drive to Acquire Private Lands Should Be Reassessed." Washington, D.C.: U.S. Government Accounting Office, CED-80-14. 14 Dec. 1979.

Fiege, Mark. "The Atomic Scientists, the Sense of Wonder, and the Bomb." *Environmental History* 12, no. 3 (2007): 578–613.

Fineman, Alisa. "Where Extremes Meet: Local Perspectives on Preservation for Big Sur." Senior thesis. University of California, Santa Cruz, 1984.

Fingal, Sara. "Designing Conservation at The Sea Ranch," *Environmental History* 18 (Jan. 2013): 185–90.

Flippen, J. Brooks. *Nixon and the Environment.* Albuquerque: University of New Mexico Press, 2000.

Foster, Edward Halsey. *Understanding the Beats.* Columbia, S.C.: University of South Carolina Press, 1992.

Freyfogle, Eric T., ed. *The New Agrarianism: Land, Culture, and the Community of Life.* Washington, D.C.: Island Press, 2001.

Friedan, Bernard. *The Environmental Protection Hustle.* Cambridge, MA: MIT Press, 1979.

Godfrey, Anthony. *The Ever-Changing View: A History of the National Forests in California, 1891–1987.* Vallejo, CA: USDA Forest Service, 2005.

Goldman, Marion S. *The American Soul Rush: Esalen and the Rise of Spiritual Privilege.* New York: New York University Press, 2012.

Gould, Rebecca Kneale. *At Home in Nature: Modern Homesteading and Spiritual Practice in America.* Berkeley and Los Angeles: University of California Press, 2005.

Gudis, Catherine. *Buyways: Billboards, Automobiles, and the American Landscape.* New York: Routledge, 2004.

Gustaitis, Rasa. "An Interview with Peter Douglas: State of the Coast," *CA C&O* 12, no. 4 (Winter 1996–97).

Hackel, Steven W. *Children of Coyote, Missionaries of Saint Francis: Indian-Spanish Relations in Colonial California, 1769–1850.* Chapel Hill: University of North Carolina Press, 2005.

Harvey, Mark. *Wilderness Forever: Howard Zahniser and the Path to the Wilderness Act.* Seattle: University of Washington Press, 2005.

Hays, Samuel P., and Joel A. Tarr. *Explorations in Environmental History.* Pittsburgh: University of Pittsburgh Press, 1998.

Hazlett, Thomas W. *The California Coastal Commission and the Economics of Environmentalism.* Ottawa, IL: Green Hill Publishers, Inc., 1980.

Healy, Robert G. *Protecting the Golden Shore: Lessons from the California Coastal Commissions.* Washington, D.C.: Conservation Foundation, 1978.

Helvarg, David. *The Golden Shore: Californians' Love Affair with the Sea.* New York: Thomas Dunne Books, 2013.

———. *The War against the Greens: The "Wise-Use" Movement, the New Right, and Anti-Environmental Violence.* San Francisco: Sierra Club Books, 1994.

Henson, Paul, and Donald J. Usner. *Natural History of Big Sur.* Berkeley and Los Angeles: University of California Press, 1993.

Hirt, Paul. *A Conspiracy of Optimism: Management of the National Forests since World War Two.* Lincoln: University of Nebraska Press, 1994.

Hobsbawm, Eric. *Fractured Times: Culture and Society in the Twentieth Century.* New York: The New Press, 2013.

Hodgson, Godfrey. *The World Turned Right Side Up: A History of the Conservative Ascendancy in America.* Boston: Houghton Mifflin Co., 1996.

Hofstadter, Richard. *The Paranoid Style in American Politics.* Cambridge, MA: Harvard University Press, 1965.

Howard, Donald. *Big Sur's Lost Tribe: The Esselen.* Carmel, CA: Antiquities Research Publications, 1979.

Hughey, Richard, and Boon Hughey. *Jeffers Country Revisited: Beauty without Price.* Shields Library. Special Collections. University of California, Davis.

Hunt, Tim. "A Voice in Nature: Jeffers' Tamar and Other Poems.' *American Literature* 61, no. 2 (1989): 230–44.

Igler, David. *Industrial Cowboys: Miller & Lux and the Transformation of the Far West, 1850–1920.* Berkeley and Los Angeles: University of California Press, 2001.

Isenberg, Andrew C. *Mining California: An Ecological History.* New York: Hill and Wang, 2005.

Jakle, John. *The Tourist: Travel in Twentieth-Century North America.* Lincoln: University of Nebraska Press, 1985.

Jeffers, Robinson. *The Alpine Christ and Other Poems.* Cayucos, CA: Cayucos Books, 1973.

———. *The Collected Poetry of Robinson Jeffers.* ed. Tim Hunt. 5 vols. Stanford, CA: Stanford University Press, 1988–2001.

———. *The Double Axe and Other Poems, Including Eleven Suppressed Poems.* New York: Liveright, 1977.

———. *Stones of the Sur: Poetry by Robinson Jeffers; Photographs by Morley Baer; Selected and Introduced by James Karman.* Stanford, CA: Stanford University Press, 2001.

———. *Such Counsels You Gave to Me.* New York: Random House, 1937.

Jeffers, Robinson, and Ansel Adams. *Not Man Apart: Lines from Robinson Jeffers, Photographs of the Big Sur Coast.* Ed. David Brower. San Francisco: Sierra Club Books, 1965.

Kahrl, Andrew. *The Land Was Ours: African American Beaches from Jim Crow to the Sunbelt South.* Cambridge, MA: Harvard University Press, 2012.

Kains, M. G. *Five Acres and Independence.* Scarborough: New American Library, 1948.

———. *Five Acres and Independence: A Handbook for Small Farm Management.* New York: Dover Publications, 1973.

Karman, James, ed. *The Collected Letters of Robinson Jeffers: With Selected Letters of Una Jeffers.* 3 vols. Stanford, CA: Stanford University Press, 2009–15.

Kazin, Michael. *The Populist Persuasion: An American History.* New York: Basic Books, 1995.

Kennedy, David M. *Freedom from Fear: The American People in Depression and War, 1929–1945.* Oxford: Oxford University Press, 1999.

Kerouac, Jack. *Big Sur.* New York: Penguin Books, 1962.

Kripal, Jeffrey, and Glenn W. Shuck, eds. *On the Edge of the Future: Esalen and the Evolution of American Culture.* Bloomington: Indiana University Press, 2005.

Kuttner, Robert. *Revolt of the Haves: Tax Rebellions and Hard Times.* New York: Simon and Schuster, 1980.

Lage, Ann. Interviews with Wallace Stegner and Ansel Adams, 1982; (and Suzanne B. Riess [q.v.]) with Margaret Wentworth Owings, 1986–88; with Frederick S. Farr, 1987; with Michael L. Fischer, 1992–93. Bancroft Library of the University of California, Berkeley, and California State Archives. State Government Oral History Program.

Larson, Shawn E., ed. *Sea Otter Conservation.* San Diego: Elsevier/Academic Press, 2015.

Lienesch, Michael. *Redeeming America: Piety and Politics in the New Christian Right.* Chapel Hill: University of North Carolina Press, 1993.

Limerick, Patricia. "Seeing and Being Seen." In *Seeing and Being Seen: Tourism in the American West,* ed. David M. Wrobel and Patrick T. Long, 39–58. Lawrence: University of Kansas Press, 2001.

Louter, David. *Windshield Wilderness: Cars, Roads, and Nature in Washington's National Parks.* Seattle: University of Washington Press, 2006.

Lutrin, Carl, and Allen Settle, "The Public and Ecology: The Role of Initiatives in California's Environmental Politics." *The Western Political Quarterly* 28, no. 2 (1975): 352–71.

Lyndon, Donlyn, and Jim Alinder. *The Sea Ranch.* Hudson, NY: Princeton Architectural Press, 2004.

Lyon, Horace. *Jeffers Country: The Seed Plots of Robinson Jeffers' Poetry.* San Francisco: Scrimshaw Press, 1971.

MacCannell, Dean. *The Tourist.* New York: Schocken Books, 1976.

Maher, Neil. *Nature's New Deal: The Civilian Conservation Corps and the Roots of the American Environmental Movement.* Oxford: Oxford University Press, 2008.

Makley, Michael J. *Saving Lake Tahoe: An Environmental History of a National Treasure.* Reno: University of Nevada Press, 2014.

May, Elaine Tyler. *Homeward Bound: American Families in the Cold War Era.* New York: Basic Books, 1988.

McGirr, Lisa. *Suburban Warriors: The Origins of the New American Right.* Princeton: Princeton University Press, 2001.

McKenzie, Matthew. "Iconic Fishermen and the Fates of New England Fisheries Regulations, 1883–1912." *Environmental History* 17 (Jan. 2012): 3–28.

Merchant, Carolyn. *Green versus Gold: Sources in California's Environmental History.* Washington, D.C.: Island Press, 1988.

Merrill, Karen. *Public Lands and Political Meaning: Ranchers, the Government and the Property between Them.* Berkeley and Los Angeles: University of California Press, 2002.

Meyer, Amy, with Randolph Delehanty. *New Guardians for the Golden Gate: How America Got a Great National Park.* Berkeley and Los Angeles: University of California Press, 2006.

Miller, Henry. *The Air-Conditioned Nightmare.* New York: New Directions, 1945.

———. *Big Sur and the Oranges of Hieronymus Bosch.* New York: New Directions, 1957.

Miller, Norman. *Environmental Politics: Interest Groups, the Media, and the Making of Policy.* Boca Raton, FL: Lewis Publishers, 2002.

Mogulof, Melvin B. *Saving the Coast.* Washington, D.C.: Lexington Books, 1975.

Monterey Coast Master Plan. County of Monterey. Skidmore, Owings, Merrill, Planning Consultants. Oct. 1960. California History Room, Monterey Public Library.

Monterey County. Statement of the Vote. Sur, Gorda, and Palo Colorado precincts. Monterey County Election Office. Salinas, California.

Monterey County. Tax Assessor Rolls, 1850–1957. Monterey County Free Libraries. Seaside Branch Library.

Myrsiades, Kostas, ed. *The Beat Generation: Critical Essays.* New York: Peter Lang, 2002.

Nash, Roderick. *Wilderness and the American Mind.* 3rd ed. New Haven: Yale University Press, 1982.

Nearing, Helen, and Scott Nearing. *Living the Good Life: How to Live Sanely and Simply in a Troubled World.* New York: Schocken Books, 1954. [Reprint: 1970.]

de Neufville, Judith, ed. *The Land Use Policy Debate in the United States.* New York: Plenum Press, 1981.

Nin, Anais. *Diary of Anais Nin.* Volumes 3 and 4. New York: Harcourt, Brace & World, Inc., 1969, 1971.

Nollan v. California Coastal Commission. 483 U.S. 825 (1987).

Norman, Jeff, and the Big Sur Historical Society. *Images of America: Big Sur.* Charleston, SC: Arcadia Publishing, 2004.

Norris, Hundley, Jr. *The Great Thirst: Californians and Water: A History.* Rev. ed. Berkeley and Los Angeles: University of California Press, 2001.

Norris, Richard Patrick. "Back to the Land: The Post-Industrial Agrarianism of Ralph Borsodi and Austin Tappan Wright." Ph.D. dissertation, University of Minnesota, 1977.

Norris, Scott, ed. *Discovered Country: Tourism and Survival in the American West.* Albuquerque: Stone Ladder Press, 1994.

Oelschlaeger, Max. *The Idea of Wilderness: From Prehistory to the Age of Ecology.* New Haven: Yale University Press, 1991.

Olmstead, Alan L., and Paul W. Rhode. *Creating Abundance: Biological Innovation and American Agricultural Development.* New York: Cambridge University Press, 2008.

Orsi, Jared. "Restoring the Common to the Goose: Citizen Activism and the Protection of the California Coastline, 1969–1972." *Southern California Quarterly* 78, no. 3 (1996): 257–84.

Orsi, Richard J., Alfred Runte, and Marlene Smith-Baranzini. *Yosemite and Sequoia: A Century of California National Parks.* Berkeley and Los Angeles: University of California Press, 1993.

Orvell, Miles. *The Real Thing: Imitation and Authenticity in American Culture, 1880–1940.* Chapel Hill: University of North Carolina Press, 1989.

Ostrum, Elinor. "Self-Governance and Forest Resources." Center for International Forestry Research, Feb. 1999. http://www.cifor.org/publications/pdf_files/OccPapers/OP-20.pdf.

Owings, Margaret Wentworth. *Voice from the Sea and Other Reflections on Wildlife & Wilderness.* Monterey, CA: Monterey Bay Aquarium Press, 1998.

Owings, Nathaniel. *The American Aesthetic.* New York: Harper & Row, 1969.

———. *The Spaces in Between: An Architect's Journey.* Boston: Houghton Mifflin Company, 1973.

Patrons of Husbandry. *California State Grange: Journal of Proceedings.* 1945.

Paxson, Frederic. "The Highway Movement: 1916–1935." *American Historical Review* 51, no. 2 (1946): 236–53.

People of the State of California, Plaintiff, v. Lawrence Ferlinghetti, Defendant. Hon. Clayton W. Horn presiding. 1958. http://mason.gmu.edu/~kthomps4/363-s02/horn-howl.htm.

Pincetl, Stephanie Sabine. *Transforming California: A Political History of Land Use and Development.* Baltimore: The Johns Hopkins University Press, 1999.

Piteaithley, Dwight T. "A Dignified Exploitation: The Growth of Tourism in the National Parks." In *Seeing and Being Seen: Tourism in the American West,* ed. David M. Wrobel and Patrick T. Long, 299–312. Lawrence: University of Kansas Press, 2001.

Pomeroy, Earl. *In Search of the Golden West: The Tourist in Western America.* New York: Knopf, 1957.

Poole, William. "Conservation and Patriotism: A Conversation with William Cronon." *Land & People Magazine* 18, no. 2 (Fall 2006): 46–50.

Popper, Frank. *The Politics of Land-Use Reform.* Madison: University of Wisconsin Press, 1981.

Press, Daniel. *Saving Open Space: The Politics of Local Preservation in California.* Berkeley and Los Angeles: University of California Press, 2002.

Rawls, James J., and Walton Bean. *California: An Interpretive History.* 8th ed. Boston: McGraw Hill, 2003.

Reagan, Ronald. "A Time for Choosing," Presidential campaign speech in support of Senator Barry Goldwater (R-Ariz.) delivered 27 Oct. 1964 via television program *Rendezvous with Destiny*. [Also known as simply "The Speech."]

Ridgeway, Ann N., ed. *The Selected Letters of Robinson Jeffers*. Baltimore: The Johns Hopkins University Press, 1968.

Riess, Suzanne B., and Ann Lage. *Margaret Wentworth Owings: Artist, and Wildlife and Environmental Defender*. Interviews 1986–88. Published by the Regents of the University of California. Berkeley, CA: Regional Oral History Office, Bancroft Library, University of California, 1991.

Rogers, David. "A Brief Land Status History of the Monterey Ranger District, Los Padres National Forest, Monterey County, California." *Double Cone Quarterly* 5, no. 3 (2002). https://www.ventanawild.org/news/feo2/mrdmaps.html.

Rome, Adam. *The Bulldozer in the Countryside: Suburban Sprawl and the Rise of American Environmentalism*. Cambridge: Cambridge University Press, 2001.

Rose, Carol M. "Property Rights, Regulatory Regimes and the New Takings Jurisprudence—An Evolutionary Approach" (1990). Faculty Scholarship Series. Paper 1821. http://digitalcommons.law.yale.edu/fss_papers/1821.

Rose, Vivien Ellen. "Homesteading as Social Protest: Gender and Continuity in the Back-to-the-Land Movement in the United States, 1890–1980." Ph.D. dissertation, Binghamton University, 1997.

Ross, Lillian Bos. *The Stranger: A Novel of the Big Sur*. New York: W. Morrow and Company, 1942.

Roszak, Theodore. *The Making of the Counter Culture: Reflections on the Technocratic Society and Its Youthful Opposition*. Garden City, NY: Doubleday & Company, Inc., 1969.

Roth, Matthew William. "Concrete Utopia: The Development of Roads and Freeways in Los Angeles, 1910–1950." Ph.D. dissertation, University of Southern California, 2007.

Rothman, Hal K. *Devil's Bargains: Tourism in the Twentieth-Century American West*. Lawrence: University of Kansas Press, 1998.

———. *Saving the Planet: The American Response to the Environment in the Twentieth Century*. Chicago: Ivan R. Dee, 2000.

Runte, Alfred. *Yosemite: The Embattled Wilderness*. Lincoln: University of Nebraska Press, 1990.

Schama, Simon. *Landscape and Memory*. New York: Alfred A. Knopf, 1995.

Schrag, Peter. *California: America's High-Stakes Experiment*. Berkeley and Los Angeles: University of California Press, 2008.

———. *Paradise Lost: California's Experience, America's Future*. New York: The New Press, 1998.

Schulman, Bruce J. *Lyndon B. Johnson and American Liberalism: A Brief Biography with Documents*. Boston: Bedford Books of St. Martin's Press, 1995.

Scott, Mel. *American City Planning since 1890: A History Commemorating the Fiftieth Anniversary of the American Institute of Planners*. Berkeley and Los Angeles: University of California Press, 1969.

Shaffer, Marguerite S. *See America First: Tourism and National Identity*. Washington, D.C.: Smithsonian Institution Press, 2001.

Shebl, James M. *In this Wild Water: The Suppressed Poems of Robinson Jeffers*. Pasadena: Ward Ritchie Press, 1976.

Sheff, Victoria, and David Sheff. "Ansel Adams: A Candid Conversation with America's 'Photographer Laureate' and Environmentalist about Art, Natural Beauty, and the Unnatural Acts of Interior Secretary James Watt." *Playboy Magazine* 30, no. 5 (May 1983): 5–6, 67–73, 76, 81–82, 84, 86, 87, 222, 224, 226.

Shi, David. *The Simple Life: Plain Living and High Thinking in American Culture*. Oxford: Oxford University Press, 1985.

Short, C. Brant. *Ronald Reagan and the Public Lands: America's Conservation Debate, 1979–1984*. College Station, TX: Texas A&M University Press, 1989.

Smith, Daniel A. "Howard Jarvis, Populist Entrepreneur: Reevaluating the Causes of Proposition 13." *Social Science History* 23, no. 2 (Summer 1999): 173–208.

Solnit, Rebecca. *Savage Dreams: A Journey into the Landscape Wars of the American West*. New York: Vintage Books, 1994.

———. *Storming the Gates of Paradise: Landscapes for Politics*. Berkeley and Los Angeles: University of California Press, 2008.

Spaulding, Jonathan. *Ansel Adams and the American Landscape: A Biography*. Berkeley and Los Angeles: University of California Press, 1995.

Spence, Mark David. *Dispossessing the Wilderness: Indian Removal and the Making of the National Parks*. Oxford: Oxford University Press, 1999.

Starr, Kevin. *Golden Dreams: California in an Age of Abundance, 1950–1963*. Oxford: Oxford University Press, 2009.

Stegner, Wallace. *The Geography of Hope: A Tribute to Wallace Stegner*. eds. Page Stegner and Mary Stegner. San Francisco: Sierra Club Books, 1996.

Stevens, Jennifer Audrey. "Feminizing the Urban West: Green Cities and Open Space in the Postwar Era, 1950–2000." Ph.D. dissertation, University of California, Davis, 2008.

Strong, Douglas Hillman. *Tahoe: An Environmental History*. Lincoln: University of Nebraska Press, 1984.

Sugihara, Neil G., et al. [Sugihara, Neil G., Jan W. van Wagtendonk, Kevin E. Shaffer, JoAnn Fites-Kaufman, and Andrea E. Thode.] *Fire in California's Ecosystems*. Berkeley and Los Angeles: University of California Press, 2006.

Sutter, Paul. *Driven Wild: How the Fight against Automobiles Launched the Modern Wilderness Movement*. Seattle: University of Washington Press, 2002.

Switzer, Jacqueline Vaughn. *Green Backlash: The History and Politics of Environmental Opposition in the U.S.* Boulder, CO: Lynne Rienner Publishers, 1997.

Sze, Julie. *Noxious New York: The Racial Politics of Urban Health and Environmental History*. Cambridge, MA: MIT Press, 2007.

Thompson, Hunter S. "Big Sur: The Tropic of Henry Miller." *Rogue Magazine* 6, no. 10 (1961): 33–36, 50.

Turner, James Morton. *The Promise of Wilderness: American Environmental Politics since 1964*. Seattle: University of Washington Press, 2012.

———. "'The Specter of Environmentalism': Wilderness, Environmental Politics, and the Evolution of the New Right." *The Journal of American History* 96, no. 1 (2009): 123–49.

Udall, Stewart. *The Quiet Crisis.* New York: Holt, Rinehart and Winston, 1963.

U.S. Bureau of the Census. *U.S. Population and Housing Census, 1880–2010.* California, Tract 115 [from 1960 forward]. Monterey Township.

U.S. Congress. Senate. *Congressional Record.* Proceedings and Debates of the 87th Cong., 1st sess., 7 Feb. 1961. Volume 107, part 2, no. 24: 1870–81.

U.S. Congress. Senate. Committee on Energy and Natural Resources. Subcommittee on Parks, Recreation, and Renewable Resources. *A Bill to Establish the Big Sur Coast National Scenic Area in the State of California: Hearing on S.2551 before the Committee on Energy and Natural Resources, Subcommittee on Parks, Recreation, and Renewable Resources,* 96th Cong., 2nd sess., 24 Apr. 1980. Publication no. 96–125.

U.S. Congress. Senate. Committee on Interior and Insular Affairs. *A Bill for the Establishment of a National Outdoor Recreation Resources Review Commission: Hearing on S.846 before the Committee on Interior and Insular Affairs,* 85th Cong., 1st sess., 15 May 1957.

———. Subcommittee on Public Lands. *A Bill to Establish the Point Reyes National Seashore: Hearings on S.476 before the Committee on Interior and Insular Affairs, Subcommittee on Public Lands,* 87th Cong., 1st sess., Mar. 1961: 28–31.

Vogt, Evon Z. *Modern Homesteaders: The Life of a Twentieth-Century Frontier Community.* Cambridge, MA: Belknap Press of Harvard University Press, 1955.

Walker, Richard A. *The Country in the City: The Greening of the San Francisco Bay Area.* Seattle: University of Washington Press, 2007.

Wall, Rosalind Sharpe. Memoir. Monterey County Historical Society. Salinas, California.

———. *A Wild Coast and Lonely: Big Sur Pioneers.* San Carlos, CA: Wide World Pub./Tetra, 1989.

Walton, John. "The Land of Big Sur: Conservation on the California Coast." *California History* 85, no. 1 (2007): 44–64.

———. "The Poet as Ethnographer: Robinson Jeffers in Big Sur." *California History* 87, no. 2 (2010): 22–41, 66–67.

Warren, Louis, ed. *American Environmental History.* Malden, MA: Blackwell Publishing, 2003.

Watt, Laura A. "The Continuously Managed Wild: Tule Elk at Point Reyes National Seashore." *Journal of International Wildlife Law & Policy* 18, no. 4 (2015): 289–308.

———. *The Paradox of Preservation: Wilderness and Working Landscapes at Point Reyes National Seashore.* Oakland, CA: University of California Press, 2017.

Wayburn, Edgar, M.D., with Allison Alsup. *Your Land and Mine: Evolution of a Conservationist.* San Francisco: Sierra Club Books, 2004.

Wernick, Robert. "Big Sur." *Smithsonian Magazine* 30, no. 8 (Nov. 1999): 98–110.

Western Center for Community Education and Development. California State Office of Planning. *Open Space in California: Issues and Options.* Los Angeles: The Center, 1965.

White, Richard. *"It's Your Misfortune and None of My Own": A New History of the American West.* Norman: University of Oklahoma Press, 1991.

Whyte, William. "Open Space Action." Report to the Outdoor Recreation Resources Review Commission, no. 15. Washington, D.C.: U.S. Government Printing Office, 1962.

Wickes, George. "Henry Miller, The Art of Fiction No. 28." Interview with Henry Miller. *The Paris Review* 28 (1962). http://www.theparisreview.org/interviews/4597/the-art-of-fiction-no-28-henry-miller.

Wilderness Act. Public Law 88–577 (16 *U.S.C.* 1131–36). 88th Cong., 2nd sess., 3 Sept. 1964. http://www.wilderness.net/index.cfm?fuse=NWPS&sec=legisAct.

Wilkinson, Charles F., and H. Michael Anderson, *Land and Resource Planning in the National Forests.* Washington, D.C.: Island Press, 1987.

Wills, John. "'Welcome to the Atomic Park': American Nuclear Landscapes and the 'Unnaturally Natural.'" *Environment and History* 7, no. 4 (2001): 449–72.

Wilson, Alexander. "The View from the Road: Recreation and Tourism." In *Discovered Country: Tourism and Survival in the American West,* ed. Scott Norris, 5–20. Albuquerque: Stone Ladder Press, 1994.

Wood, Linda Sargent. "Contact, Encounter, and Exchange at Esalen: A Window onto Late Twentieth-Century American Spirituality." *Pacific Historical Review* 77, no. 3 (2008): 453–87.

Woodhouse, Keith M. "The Politics of Ecology: Environmentalism and Liberalism in the 1960s." *Journal for the Study of Radicalism* 2, no. 2 (2008): 53–84.

Woolfenden, John. *Big Sur: A Battle for the Wilderness, 1869–1981.* Pacific Grove, CA: Boxwood Press, 1981.

Works Progress Administration. "A Guide to the Monterey Peninsula, Tour 3: Big Sur." Berkeley, CA: Press of the Courier, 1941.

Wright, John B. *Rocky Mountain Divide: Selling and Saving the West.* Austin: University of Texas Press, 1993.

Wrobel, David M., and Patrick T. Long, eds. *Seeing and Being Seen: Tourism in the American West.* Lawrence: University of Kansas Press, 2001.

Yonay, Ehud. "Big Sur: The Politics of Preservation." *New West,* 22 Dec. 1980.

———. "Big Sur Revisited: Notes from the Fire." *New West,* 29 Aug. 1977.

Zaller, Robert. *Robinson Jeffers and the American Sublime.* Stanford, CA: Stanford University Press, 2012.

INDEX

Adams, Ansel, 1, 228n67, 135*fig.*; in Carmel
  Highlands, 74; and the Coastal Initiative, 124; and Esalen, 75; and federal
  proposals, 6, 13, 131–41, 143–45, 147,
  149–52; and Jeffers, Robinson , 145–46;
  and Monterey County Coast Master
  Plan, 94–95; and national parks,
  226n31; photography, 118, 146, 228n66;
  and Pico Blanco, 165–66; and Watt,
  James , 175–76
American frontier, 27–28, 44, 51–52, 55, 84,
  130, 142
American Institute of Architects,
  81–83
Andrew Molera State Park, xiv*map*, 110,
  111*fig.*, 233n59

back-to-the-landers, 112–16
Bay Conservation and Development Commission (BCDC). *See* San Francisco Bay
  Conservation and Development
  Commission
beatniks, 62–64, 79
Big Sur Coast Local Coastal Program
  (LCP), 178, 195; and BSMAAC, 177–
  78; and California Coastal Commission, 155, 157, 160, 171, 175–76, 180;
  and community involvement, 127,
  161–63; and federal proposals, 147–48,
  150; logistics of, 125, 157–60, 172–75;
  and real estate, 160–61, 168–70.
  See also Big Sur Citizens Advisory
  Committee

Big Sur Citizens Advisory Committee
  (CAC), 125–27, 129, 142, 157, 222n80
Big Sur Foundation, 149, 164, 166, 176,
  222n79
Big Sur Grange: formation, 65–68; and
  hippies, 108, 112; and incorporation, 129,
  187, 210n32, 222n79, 223n85
Big Sur Gazette, 128, 142, 148
Big Sur Guide, 61, 70
Big Sur Land Trust, 128–29, 164, 170–71,
  176–77
Big Sur Multi Agency Advisory Council
  (BSMAAC), 177–78, 235n93
Big Sur softball league, 127, 187–88, 189*fig.*
Bixby Bridge, 29, 29*fig.*, 38, 144
Brown, Edmund Gerald "Pat," Sr., 72–73,
  120
Brown, Edmund Gerald "Jerry," Jr., 154–55
Burton, Phil, 142, 150–51

California Coastal Commission: and Big
  Sur Coast Local Coastal Program,
  158–67, 171–72, 174–75, 180, 195; and
  federal proposals, 138, 150–51; formation
  and early involvement in Big Sur, 123–
  27, 154; and low-income housing, 169;
  and politics, 155–56, 169, 180–86, 192–
  94; and voting record, 240N67. *See also*
  Coastal Act; Douglas, Peter
*California Coastal Commission v. Granite
  Rock,* 165–68
California Coastal Council, 141–42,
  231n22

Author and son in Andrew Molera State Park. (Photo: author.)